THE CUBAN FAMILY

To the memory of Surendar S. Yadava,
friend and colleague

THE CUBAN FAMILY

Custom and Change in an Era of Hardship

by Rosemarie Skaine

McFarland & Company, Inc., Publishers
Jefferson, North Carolina, and London

ALSO BY ROSEMARIE SKAINE
AND FROM MCFARLAND

Paternity and American Law (2003)

The Women of Afghanistan Under the Taliban (2002)

Women College Basketball Coaches (2001)

Women at War:
Gender Issues of Americans in Combat (1999)

Power and Gender:
Issues in Sexual Dominance and Harassment (1996)

LIBRARY OF CONGRESS CATALOGUING-IN-PUBLICATION DATA

Skaine, Rosemarie.
    The Cuban family : custom and change in an era of hardship /
by Rosemarie Skaine.
        p.   cm.
    Includes bibliographical references and index.

    ISBN 0-7864-1677-7 (softcover : 50# alkaline paper) ∞

    1. Family — Cuba.   2. Cuban American families.   I. Title.
HQ580.S58   2004
306.85'097291 — dc22   2003020300

British Library cataloguing data are available

Cover photograph ©2003 Index Stock

Manufactured in the United States of America

McFarland & Company, Inc., Publishers
  Box 611, Jefferson, North Carolina 28640
  www.mcfarlandpub.com

Acknowledgments

For his pivotal first interview, I thank Dr. Delvis Fernández Levy, president, Cuban-American Alliance Education Fund, Inc., and member of the board of directors of Americans for Humanitarian Trade with Cuba, the U.S.–Cuba Sister Cities Association, and the U.S.–Cuba Business Association.

I thank Lisa Valanti, president, U.S.–Cuba Sister Cities Association, Inc., Pittsburgh, Pennsylvania, for her guidance in the beginning of the research for this book.

I thank the following people for their interviews: Robert A. Pastor, vice president of International Affairs and professor of International Relations, American University, Washington, D.C.; Alex, teacher, Havana, Cuba; Dr. Luis Enrique Vidal Palmer, professor and vice director, Psychiatric Hospital, Havana, Cuba; Alejandro Concepcion, Waterloo, Iowa; Leonardo M. Marmol, Ph.D., ABPP, professor and chair, Department of Graduate Psychology, Seattle Pacific University, Seattle, Washington; Pedro Ferreira, Ph.D., M.B.A., licensed psychologist, PA, DE, Wilmington, Delaware; Betsy Campisi, anthropologist, State University of New York at Albany; Ron Howell, reporter, *Newsday*; Geri Díaz, Miami, Florida; Adelfa Fernández, Miami, Florida; and Asley L. Marmol, Miami, Florida.

I thank Dr. Alberto N. Jones, DVM — EH, Caribbean American Children Foundation, for granting permission to use his article, "A Cuba in Diaz-Balart's Image or That of Today's Miami."

I thank Walter Teague, LICSW, LCSW-C, Adelphi, Maryland, for help, guidance and educational research material.

I am deeply grateful to the XII International Congress on Family Law, Havana, Cuba, September 22–27, 2002, for the numerous presentations on "Family Law in Front of the Challenges of the New Millennium." The conveners of the conference are appreciated: Olga Mesa Castillo, President, the School of Law of Havana University, the National Union of Cuban Jurists, namely its Cuban Society for Civil and Family Law, the Federation of

Cuban Women and the Law Development and Research Institute (IDID). I also appreciated that the Congress was an excellent host. They provided the delegates freedom to move about in Cuba, thus enabling us to combine the knowledge presented from scholarly papers with firsthand experiences of visits in the Cuban society.

Special thanks to Harold A. Mayerson, Esq., Mayerson Stutman, LLP, Association of the Bar of the City of New York, for his tireless efforts in making travel in Cuba educationally beneficial.

I am especially grateful to Cubans in Cuba and in the U.S. My husband and I enjoyed their spirit of acceptance, warmth and sophistication.

I thank Mercedes Ayala, Grand Island, Nebraska, for her skillful and professional translations of scholarly papers needed for this book. I also thank Marco Poblete, Spanish teaching assistant, Department of Modern Languages, University of Northern Iowa, Cedar Falls, Iowa, for his excellent translation of scholarly work.

I thank Sue Ravn, Cedar Falls, Iowa, for her assistance in transcribing tape recordings.

I thank Tonya Evenson, Cedar Falls, Iowa; John R. Brownell, attorney with Lauritsen, Brownell, Brostrom, Stehlik, Thayer and Myers, Grand Island, Nebraska, and Dr. Robert R. Krueger and Mark S. Welty, Department of Modern Languages, University of Northern Iowa, Cedar Falls, Iowa, for their assistance.

I am grateful to the H-Caribbean Network of H-Net at Michigan State University for scholarly support and information.

I thank Fred Schuster, regional director of the U.S. Department of Health and Human Services, Kansas City, Missouri, for his assistance.

I thank James C. Skaine, professor emeritus, Communication Studies, University of Northern Iowa, for his editing skills and his research and translation assistance. I also thank him for his coauthoring. I extend a special note of gratitude to him for sharing his intellect and his willingness to collaborate on all aspects of this book. His full support, freely given, brought this book to fruition.

I thank family members for their love and support: Richard L. and Nancy L. Craft Kuehner and William V. and Carolyn E. Guenther Kuehner.

I thank Robert Kramer, professor emeritus, Center for Social and Behavioral Research and Department of Sociology, Anthropology, and Criminology, University of Northern Iowa, for his expertise in technology.

I thank longtime friends Jerod and Twyla Moschel for helping out in special ways that made this book possible.

I thank Cass Paley, my friend of yesteryear, who came and gave without taking. His gifts are lifelong.

Contents

Preface

Heart that takes defeat
The faithful anchor of the home,
Goes like a lost boat,
That does not know where it goes...
— José Martí, *Simple Verses*[1]

Events shape society. The events of the past five decades have shaped the Cuban family. The Fidel Castro–led revolution in Cuba and the subsequent United States embargo have produced three different Cuban families. The family in Cuba, the Cuban family in the United States, and the family with members in both countries. The Cuban family cannot be understood properly without examining all three elements.

In September 2002, my husband James and I were fortunate to travel to Cuba as delegates to the XII International Congress on Family Law. The United States delegation was sponsored by the Association of the Bar of the City of New York. In cooperation with the Congress, the bar association made it possible for us to freely move in Cuban society. Our positive thoughts about Cuba are reflected in the words of Martin Guggenheim:

> As is well known it is a rare privilege for United States citizens to visit this wonderful country and we feel truly privileged to spend this time among you. I can report how especially wonderful it has been to roam freely throughout the country and to feel the warmth of the Cuban citizens despite the unfortunate political chill between our governments.[2]

In our travels in Cuba, we moved freely throughout Havana and the southwest provinces. We visited Pinar del Río, where we toured a factory that made the world-famous Cuban cigars, and Viñales, where we observed the crops and livestock grown there. We took in the great beauty of the countryside, mountains and caves. We saw the people as they went about their daily lives. It was a real education.

The Congress on Family Law was also educational. We heard presentations on "the challenges facing the family as a result of the accelerated unfolding of science and its impact on the human being, the advance
of the globalization process and the influence of communication technology on the family, the increasing environmental degradation, the
expansion of the pandemic AIDS, the augmentation of poverty and intra-
family violence, among others, [and how they] affect both today's family
and its ruling law and therefore become a reason for concern and exchange
by family law scholars and professionals from other related sciences."[3]

A universal understanding of the family may not exist, but everyone
has ideas about how relationships of blood, marriage, sex, and residence
should relate and articulate with processes of social reproduction. We cannot deny the impact of social organization on a society. There is an interaction between domestic arrangements, the material aspects of making a
living and the cultural value attached to the family.[4] The Cuban family
uniquely underscores these interactions. When we discuss the Cuban family, we need to focus on the family in Cuba, the family in the United States
and family that is divided, having some members living in Cuba and some
in the United States.

Chapter 1, "Historical Perspectives on the Cuban Family," examines
the family in Cuba from the time of its colonial relationship with Spain
to the revolutionary period. Families are viewed by ethnicity and race. The
early 20th century family laid the basis for family forms of today. Consensual unions and orphaned and abandoned children are not new characteristics in the Cuban society. The Republican Period brought some
change to family form. The early revolutionary period under Fidel Castro was marked by a successful socialist society that sought to treat all citizens equally. The revolutionary period introduced equality for women,
which posed new challenges for the family.

Chapter 2, "Influences on Today's Cuban Family," examines Cuba's
confrontation with the end of economic support from the former Soviet
Union and increased U.S. economic and political sanctions. The overview
of the country's government shows how it is able to impact the family. A
transition is occurring in Cuba.[5] Cuba has struggled with the long-term
effects of the United States' embargo and has worked to transform its economy into a dual economy. The transformed economy affects family relationships. Cuba continues to try to provide equal services for all people
in the areas of health and education, but budget constraints hamper the
ongoing efforts. How the family is responding to improvements in the
economy, health care and education is creating a revolution within the
family.

Chapter 3, "The Impact of Society on the Cuban Family," analyzes the effects on the family in Cuba's "special period in time of peace" of the 1990s. Specific effects include the housing shortage, emigration, the role of women, the extended family and kinds of families.

Chapter 4, "Cuban Family Rights and Forms," coauthored by Rosemarie Skaine and James C. Skaine, introduces two major bodies of law that govern the family, The Constitution of the Republic of Cuba of 1976 and The Family Code of 1975. Marriage, dissolution of marriage, parent-child relations and paternity-maternity issues are specifically addressed in the context of equality of all people. Special discussions include consensual unions, one-parent families, the homeless, domestic violence, protection of minors, and adoption. In addition to internal adoption, one Cuban jurist shares a view on international adoption.

Chapter 5, "Politics, Emigration and Families," provides insight into United States policy relative to immigrating Cubans and the tremendous impact on the Cuban family. The laws and migration agreements are outlined within the significant societal events, including the Elián González case, which gave impetus to the policy. Although the 107th Congress worked to change the United States' policy towards normalization of relations with Cuba, the executive branch is steadfast in its resolve to continue the status quo. Cuban government perspectives toward U.S. policy are presented. Citizenship issues are examined, as are the views of some Cuban émigrés.

Chapter 6, "Emigration to the United States," coauthored by Rosemarie Skaine and James C. Skaine, examines the numbers and various waves of emigration. From 1959 to 1962, regular commercial air traffic moved between the United States and Cuba. This period included the Peter Pan or Pedro Pan Project. From 1965 to 1973, freedom flights were permitted. In 1980, the Mariel Boatlift occurred. In the 1990s, attention focused on the rafters or *balseros*. Indirect third country flights have spanned several of the emigration waves that have occurred during the revolutionary Period.

Chapter 7, "Cuban American Families," addresses Cuban families in the United States. Family types and characteristics are examined to determine the causes that enable Cubans to lead successful lives in the United States. The balancing of cultural traditions with the process of assimilation leads Cuban American families to adapt successfully to new ideas of home. The marriage patterns, family, parenting and educational levels of Cuban Americans lend insight into their acculturation patterns.

Chapter 8, "Family Narratives of Life in Cuba," focuses on narratives of childhood memories from pre-revolutionary Cuba to the late 20th century. They talk about the good times and the bad.

Chapter 9, "Family Narratives of Life in the United States," focuses on the experiences of Cubans living in the United States from pre-revolutionary times through the early 21st century. Universally, they express their abiding love for Cuba.

Chapter 10, "Looking Forward," centers on Cuba as an integral part of the global community. The visits of Pope John Paul II and former President Jimmy Carter led the way for change both in Cuba and in the global community. The policies of the United States and Cuba are deeply affecting families. Some Cuban Americans believe that families will heal emotionally when freedoms are restored in Cuba. Others believe that the Cuban government does not need to change but that the healing will occur when the United States' sanctions and embargo are lifted. Meanwhile, Cuban families find strength in simple truths, such as celebrating the continuity of their struggle to have full and happy lives.

Historical Perspectives on the Cuban Family

We will grieve not, rather find
Strength in what remains behind;
— William Wordsworth[1]

When we look at the history of the Cuban family, we see that its present forms and traditions were shaped by ethnic heritage, social justice and religious influence. If family members emigrate to the United States, those traditions may give way, in whole or in part, to new customs acquired during the process of assimilation. Cuban family ties have been diverse and strong since the colonial period. These ties remain strong today, whether the entire family remains in Cuba or emigrates to the United States, or whether some family members are in Cuba and others have emigrated to the United States.

The Colonial Period Under Spain

The contemporary Cuban family must be viewed from the perspective of their country's relation to Spain and its colonial rule. Cuban laws originated in the Roman and Germanic periods, and were influenced by the Spanish Civil Code that prevailed in Cuba for almost a century, by the French Civil Codes of 1804 and by the Italian codes of 1865.[2]

NAMES

In the Cuban culture, traditionally, surnames were precisely determined. It was illegal to change one's surname. It took an act of the Cuban legislature to change a surname. Therefore, Cubans did not change their surnames often. Surnames are modeled after the Spanish, including "both the father's surname and the mother's surname in that order, sometimes separated by the word 'y' ('and')."[3] Dr. Delvis Fernández, president, Cuban American Alliance Education Fund, Inc., says, "It's kind of nice. It gives recognition to both sides. In the long run, the father's name tends to linger on.... In the United States, I go by just Fernández, but, in Cuba, I am Fernández Levy. The last name is my mother's name."[4] The maternal surname is usually dropped in everyday use to avoid confusion, or if both surnames are retained, they are hyphenated. An example of how both surnames are preserved is:

> José López marries María Famosa. Their son is named Juan López Famosa. Juan, in turn marries Isabel Fernández García. The son of Juan and Isabel could be named Pedro López Fernández, Pedro López y Fernández, Pedro López Famosa y Fernández, or Pedro López Famosa y Fernández García — the last two forms preserving the "Famosa" surname for future generations.[5]

Wives keep their maiden names when they marry. If they wish, they may legally add their husband's surname(s) after their own. The husband's name is preceded by the word "de" ("of," implying "spouse of"). If the spouse has died, the words "viuda de" (widow of), abbreviated "vda. de."[6]

This regulation and the requirement that births, deaths, marriages and confirmations be recorded in local parishes began before the Council of Trent that was held in Italy between 1545 and 1563. Parish register books have been found in some parts of Spain. The registries are dated approximately a century previous to the council. In many parishes of Castille, books still exist that date from the late 1400s. Cardinal Cisneros issued the requirement.[7]

FEUDAL TRADITIONS

During Cuba's relationship with Spain, certain feudal traditions were transplanted into "the very fabric of society."[8] The ideals of chivalry dictated conduct, piety, honor, valor, courtesy, chastity and loyalty. Love was platonic. Another man's wife was worthy of a man's attention because it demonstrated pure or true love and bravery. Attention to a virgin indicated obsession with virginity and became merged with the "Cult of the Virgin Mary."[9] Women, because they were delicate, were to be respected and protected.

The Catholic Church valued virginity and decency. Machismo upheld the double standard and the sexual reification of women. Cuba reflects these religious and gender values, but departs from this image in its matriarchal traditions. Cuba merged the customs of chivalry or placing noble Spanish women on a pedestal and the experience of the woman and mother in New World slavery. The Spanish Civil Code of 1888 formed the basis of Cuban law and of matters affecting male and female relationships, family life and parental responsibilities. The law "assigned undisputed authority to men."[10] Thus, since the church, the family and the law upheld this position for men and women, these hierarchies became Cuba's culture. Traces of these sentiments survived down through the 1980s.[11]

AFRO CUBAN FAMILIES AND FAMILIES OF COLOR

In the 16th century, mixed family households existed. Aboriginal towns were assimilated into urban areas and by the mixed marriages between Spaniards and indigenous people. In turn, some from these groups migrated to the mountains mixed with slaves. From a religious, moral and legal point of view, the presence of these Spanish people for four centuries represented a contradictory family model. The model consisted of a mother's and father's name being passed on to the offspring, but in practice, a husband might practice polygamy — have more than one wife. Not all wives were aware they were sharing a husband. Because of financial dependence, wives, if they knew, accepted the situation. The Catholic Church blessed the practice of heterosexual coupling. An elder male led a number of families. This patriarchal family organization placed women in a subordinate position.[12]

The Africans present in colonial times were subjected to slavery. They also tended to form mixed marriages and males tended to practice polygamy. The language learned and place of residence were factors in social status. Legal discrimination existed, but many were able to form a family based on religious background and bloodlines.[13]

Two conflicting views of Cuba's society prevailed in the 19th century — hierarchical (slaves and free, blacks and white) and egalitarian (all people were equal before God).[14] In the hierarchical view, family origin was an important status determinant. A relationship existed between social class and honor. Social class was based in the economic system whereby an unequal distribution of resources "preserved by an emphasis on heredity, with regard both to property as well as to status, coupled with a class endogamous marriage pattern."[15] Thus, women of the lowest class, the women of color, had the least honor.[16]

Filiation was bilateral; a child was recognized by two parents. Choice of a marriage partner maintained the system. Thus, control over the choice was done through child marriage, for example.[17]

Family type was determined by mating forms which in turn was determined by the relative social position of the partners. Verena Martinez-Alier's work examines social placing of the free people of color in the Cuban slave society as determined by the needs of a slave regime. A hierarchical society determined the sexual marginalization of woman of color. This placement affected her forms of mating. She was more likely to select a consensual union that was mother-centered and usually lacking the presence of a father. This type of society also determined the low status of the males of color. He had no economic wherewithal, thus no status. He could not advance socially and had to compete with the selection of consensual unions by the female of color, thus was rejected from the beginning in the mating process. In spite of this situation, Martinez-Alier found that both marriage and consensual unions were regarded as alternatives in the mating selection process. The preference was for marriage, and consensual unions "stretched their values."[18]

The egalitarian view, all people were equal before God, partially prevailed. Intermarriage was accepted even though it didn't occur often. People of color made efforts to advance socially — if not for themselves, then for their children — by marriage and free unions. Social mobility demonstrated that the dominant sector of society partially accepted free unions and marriage even though an agreement of legitimacy was not evident. Since the prevailing norm was like-married-like, marrying into the dominant sector meant equality. In these cases, the unions entailed no loss of status for the white male.[19]

In 1967, Martinez-Alier went to Cuba to study its families. She stayed two months "in a small, predominantly coloured coffee-growing village in the Sierra Maestra."[20] She concluded that consensual unions prevailed in the villagers' family organization. She also believed that the revolution had begun to affect family values. Residents asked her whether she had been sent by the government in association with the "collective marriage" campaign. The purpose of the campaign was to provide couples living in consensual unions the opportunity to legally marry.[21] Marriage palaces were established so that young couples could marry in the luxury afforded the upper classes. Martinez-Alier wrote that the palaces gave the lower classes a sense of equality, but did not get at the basis of the problems. She concluded that traditional values would remain. Women's participation in the work force reflected the Cuban males' desire to sexually control their partners. Virginity remained valued. The conflict contributed to a rise in the divorce rate.[22]

The origins of the Cuban society, the legal basis of the independent republic and the traditional forms of society at the beginning of the 20th century have shaped the characteristics of family diversity in Cuba in the 21st century.[23]

Ethnic composition is an important component in understanding the Cuban family. Delvis Fernández Levy believes that ethnic origin is missed by so many of the people doing research on Cuba. He explains,

> You will see that Cubans tend to be from very light skin to very dark skin. The basic ethnic components of Cubans are Spanish and African. Also in there are Chinese, French and all the other people who stopped in Cuba on their way to Europe, from Dutch to British to the whatever you can name in Europe. But, the main components are Spanish and African. You will find that, if you go to Miami, you will look around and most Cubans you see are white. There are only about two percent Afro-Cubans in Miami. Yet, if you go to Cuba, the ratio is inverted. You will find that, when you look at a crowd, the vast majority seem to be of African origin, which is missed by so many of the people doing research on Cuba because they tend to go only to sources in Miami or in the Cuban-American community and then extrapolate from that and say this is what Cubans are like.[24]

Dr. Jesús Guanche Pérez, Cuba, agrees that Cuban ethnicity has roots reaching to Europe, Latin America, Africa and Asia. Further, the diverse current-day family in Cuba is a living reflection of this mixture that began in the colonial period.[25]

When identified with a social cultural quality and with equality of human beings that makes individuals a part of a group until they have consciousness of differences compared with other groups, ethnicity provides the concept of family. The family gives us a learning environment. The diversity of family structure throughout history has been directly related to the establishment of very different cultural groups. These groups led to the impact of Spanish presence with a different chronology and different indigenous structures.[26]

CHINESE CUBANS

From 1847 to 1874, about 50,000 Chinese males lived in worse conditions than the African slaves. These males formed families with females born in Cuba and of low social status. Maternal cultural traditions prevailed in this mixed family. An additional 5,000 Chinese males were able to bring or send for wives, and thus contributed their own cultural traditions to Cuba. From 1880 to 1913, immigrants came to eastern Cuba from the French and English of the Caribbean Islands. Cuba also received Europeans, Asians, Hebrews, Arabians, Mexicans and Venezuelans during this time.[27]

At the end of the 19th century and the beginning of the 20th century, the majority of the population of Cuba comprised those people who were Cuban-born. Cuba became a nation at this time with reproduction from its own people combined with the diverse ethnic groups of the past. The customs and prejudices were passed down from generation to generation. In the 21st century, Cuba recognizes marriages acknowledged by the church and common law marriages.[28]

Early 20th Century Laws Affecting Women and Families

In 1917 a law concerning the rights of parents was passed. In 1918, the right to divorce was granted and women were enfranchised in 1934. The 1940 constitution (abolished under Batista) acknowledged the equality of all citizens regardless of race, class or sex. It also acknowledged the rights of married women to administer their own property, and freely engage in trade, industry, a profession or the arts. As well, they gained the right to make use of all profits derived from their work without the need for spousal license or consent. The 1940 constitution regulated the maternity rights for working women.[29]

CONSENSUAL UNIONS

The consensual union between a man and a woman is a reality and a product of a natural impulse. Historically, these unions are as old as marriage originating in old Rome, but have lacked legal character. In Roman times, the unions were not punished by law or censured by social conscience. Germanic law also accepted unions legally and socially. Down through time, descendants of these unions were discriminated against until social values produced laws that recognize them as legitimate. The taboos that remain and the controversy that surrounds consensual unions led Cuban author Lic. Xóchitl Aguirre Tamayo to analyze consensual unions in Cuba, historically to the present time.[30]

Under old Spanish law unions took the name concubinage. Laws began to call it a mortal sin and declared a concubine must be single. The Spaniards wished to protect the Catholic religious marriage. Cuba moved forward in recognizing unions with the Constitution of 1940. The

Constitution recognized unions through a married comparison, but it was limited by old social morality, classist principles and in part, the Spanish law.[31]

The laws of the new socialist regime after the revolution established the equality of children and ended the discrimination toward women. Free unions are legal but are not totally accepted.[32]

THE ORPHANED AND ABANDONED CHILD

Marquetti Pérez and Sosa write that care of abandoned orphans in Cuba goes back to 1687 when the "House of Abandoned" was founded. The House was neglected, but in 1705 new management named it "Foundling House." This House also fell into disrepair. Other facilities were also built early in Cuba's history. Before the revolution the children were taken care of in the famous "House of Charity." Here, also, protection was not guaranteed and conditions were not good. The revolution brought the beginning of new laws and norms to protect children and youth. In 1959, the Ministry of Social Welfare was created wherein such houses became property and obligation of the state to provide for minors in need.[33]

Republican Period

The Republican period changed Cuba's traditional family form. Most upper-class families remained in the traditional colonial period form. They lived with extended family in an urban area and the father remained dominant. The sheltered mother's position had little to do. Children attended private schools.[34]

The middle class family was comfortable. They may have had a maid, but not a car or a chauffeur. Correspondingly, the mother had more responsibilities in the home and may have worked outside the home.[35]

Common law marriages and illegitimacy were more common among the lower class, urban dwelling family. The family pattern that evolved consisted of single parent families, headed by females that lived in *solares*, or "one-room squalid barracks." The *solares* were found in some sections of well-to-do neighborhoods. Living conditions were not good and the families served as cheap labor for the more wealthy.[36] Anton L. Allahar describes the *solar* as

> a world unto itself. Vice, violence and corruption were typical situations where otherwise decent people were reduced to living in human scrap

heaps. One survey of 50 Havana *solares* in 1945 found 1,434 rooms, each inhabited by at least one family. In one case twelve adults and four children occupied a room approximately 10 × 16 feet.[37]

Allahar describes another solar, "187 persons shared two toilets and paid an average rent of $12 per month per room at a time when the minimum wage was $45 per month."[38]

These social factors, among others, sowed some of the seeds for the Castro-led revolution.

Role of the Cuban Family in the Socialist Period (1959–present)

In October 1960, the United States imposed an embargo on trade with Cuba. As the years passed, the embargo expanded to include normally exempt items such as medical supplies, food and emergency aid, disaster relief and all diplomatic and cultural links. The revolution sought to muster support of women by giving women equality. Evidence of progress for women occurred in education, employment, civil rights and human rights. Some customs lingered. Mothers, for example, would show favor to sons and sons-in-law over their daughters.[39]

State policy plays an important role in shaping the increase of women in employment. Class equality is more important than gender. In 1955, women represented 13.0 percent of Cuba's labor force.[40] Agricultural work was the chief employment and involved heavy manual labor for men on sugar plantations. As the revolution progressed, even though the law provided for equality in education, a woman working outside the home signified that a man could not support her. Women lacked material reason to work in the early part of the revolution.

For twenty years after the revolution, these social problems remained due to a population explosion from six to ten million. The government's inability to keep pace and the scarcity of building materials resulted in a housing shortage. Allahar found that opinions vary among scholars as to what form the family took. Some believe that the nuclear family never was and is not the basic family structure of Cuba. Others say that the nuclear family dominated the modern era. Others think the Cuban family has elements of both, with 20 percent of the households consisting of extended family members.[41]

Another reason for Cuba's social problems was that women worked at home, worked outside of the home, served in a volunteer brigade and studied part time. The opportunities made women more mobile and the laws made divorce easier and more financially feasible, and education more attainable. One in three marriages ended in divorce.[42] The housing shortage decreased marital privacy. Couples, married or unmarried, who lacked privacy to make love could go to a *posades* or rooming house. They rented a room by the hour and no questions were asked.[43]

After the revolution, the government sought to make marriage affordable. Common law unions and acceptance of illegitimate births contributed to the number of marriages doubling from 1960 to 1970. High divorce rates, early marriage and teen pregnancy led to most single parents being single mothers. Allahar demonstrates that the adolescent children of the revolution held very different values from the older generation. He lists as causes "the widespread promotion of sex education and contraception, the availability of abortion on demand, the revolution's emphasis on equality between the sexes, the major transformation of family values and relations, and the erosion of the cult of virginity...."[44]

On the plus side, the Maternity Law safeguarded the working woman. The law allows up to 18 weeks paid leave, job protection, excused time for doctor's visits or family care needs and up to a year of unpaid leave. Day care centers are free or inexpensive.[45] Writing at the time of the demise of the USSR, Allahar concludes that family life under the revolution was enriched. He stresses that home and family relations are far from traditional. Children are protected through the Code on Children and Youth of June 1978.[46] After the Code of 1978, Cuba signed the United Nations Convention on the Rights of Children. Currently, the Cuban Constitution and Family Code defines parent-child relationships and responsibilities.[47]

Children are educated in highly politicized school systems. The teachings often are at odds with the values of older generations. So Cuba's changes are not independent of changes in the family. Allahar says the family is viewed as a basic or elemental cell of the society, transmitting culture and values and setting the tone for continuing revolution. This is the reason the government promotes and protects the family.[48]

Although Dr. Ediltrudis Panadero de la Cruz's study was comparative and did not specifically include Cuba, Cruz noted that socialist countries consider the transmission of domestic goods an integral part of the personal property. The right to inherit personal property is the right of a resident in a socialist country. The new Cuban Civil Code is historically based in Cuba.[49]

The revolution sought to eliminate discrimination of all kinds, including racial. Black people realized considerable improvement in their standard of living. Gisela Arandia Covarrubia writes that evidence that the problems of the Afro-Cuban have not disappeared can be seen in the migratory process. During the Mariel Boatlift of 1980, for the first time in 20 years more blacks than whites migrated. Arandia Covarrubia views the problems as sociocultural rather than economic. The *El Nuevo Herald*, Nov. 11, 1990, reported that once in the United States,

> The Black Cuban is invisible in Miami. He makes himself invisible in order not to attract attention. Here there is racism on the part of the white Cuban, the same racism that had existed in Cuba. The AfroCuban lives a double life here, because he is afraid that the white Cubans will retaliate against him. The white Cubans think they are superior to everyone....[50]

Arandia Covarrubia writes that discrimination does not disappear just because it is illegal. It remains because of its universality and the mistaken belief that it would disappear as whites and Blacks worked toward the ideals of the revolution. blacks and whites had different starting points. Prejudice of five centuries is difficult to erase, because attitudes are handed down from one generation to the next, Arandia Covarrubia concludes.[51]

As in the United States, Cuba's efforts through a quota system is not without pitfalls for both races. Arandia Covarrubia believes that the biggest mistake in the "treatment of Blacks in Cuba has been the denial of the existence of a problem."[52] Arandia Covarrubia is hopeful the discrimination can be solved within Cuba as blacks and whites work together and consider the social, economic and cultural aspects.

LA PATRIA POTESTAD, MOTHER COUNTRY POWER

Mother country power had its origins in "la pater potestas" of Roman law. When parents do not or cannot fulfill their duties, their power ceases and the state becomes the trustee of the minors. Colonial Cuban law inherited the Spanish Feudal Law and like Roman law, gave the absolute power to fathers.[53]

Belkis Caridad Núñez Travieso writes that mother country power "is understood like the set of rights and duties that the parents have with respect to their children, content that appears [in a] statement in Article 85" of the Cuban Family Code.[54] Unlike Roman Law and early Cuban law, modern law in the Family Code gives total equality to both ancestors to exert mother country power. The mother country power is not altered by divorce. When the ancestors decide who will exercise the mother country power, it continues as long as they allow it. In some cases, when parents do not live together, the court decides which parent will be more beneficial to the minor. If both parents are considered injured parties, generally, the court will prefer the mother. The Code states that minors must be provided for by parents: housing, food, healthcare, recreation, protection, guarding of good conduct, education, and direction in social life; the parents take care of their goods in the interests of minors and represent them in legal matters. In turn children are to respect, help and obey their parents during the period of mother country power.[55]

Mother country power ceases upon the death of the parents, the minor becomes of age, marriage of the minor who is not of age or the adoption of the minor. Mother country power can be suspended in incapacity or absence of parents. Parents are considered so if they seriously do not fulfill their duties, induce the minor to commit a criminal act, leave the national territory or commit a crime against the minor. In these cases, the state becomes the trustee of the minors.[56]

Conclusions

After Cuba gained its independence from Spain, some of the Spanish traditions continued; most significantly, the tradition of language. From its proud heritage, Cuba continues to evolve as it strives for equality for all of its citizens. Measures of the government affect family life. As we turn to examine family life in a socialist country faced with globalization, the control of the government over the family impacts the material aspects of making a living and the cultural value attached to the family.

2

Influences on Today's Cuban Family

It is beautiful that people hold a full and absolute concept of their dignity and honor.

— José Martí[1]

The Cuban government is a fusion of the political, military and economic. In this one-party system of communism, certain political committees and organizations perform specific functions to maintain the government. This system of government has been in place since 1959. The 1976 Constitution denotes communism as the only directing political power. The Communist Party is composed of a first secretary general of the Central Committee, a second secretary general of the Central Committee and members of the Central Committee, which includes, for example, secretaries and presidents of the political organizations.[2]

The Government and Families

Organizations oversee that communism is taught and carried out. In each community the Young Communists Union has as its members those youth over 14 years of age. Children under 14 years old are grouped in the Organization of José Martí Pioneers. The Committees for the Defense of the Revolution (CDR) operates on every block to monitor the activities of citizens. The Labor Centers, the Federation of Cuban Women, the National Association of Rural Agriculture Workers and the Institute of Friendships Among Towns each monitor their area for the advancement of the system. The Fast Response Brigade is a civilian group designated to handle protests or dissenting activity.[3] All of these committees and organizations legitimized by Cuba's Constitution and other codes interact with family life.

One provision governing the family is found in the Constitution of the Republic of Cuba: "The parents have the right to provide nourishment to their children and the right to assist them in the defense of legitimate interests and in the realization of their inspirations. The parents also have the right in the active contribution of their children's education and integral shape as good citizens and to shape them for a Socialist society."[4] The Committees for the Defense of the Revolution exerts one form of social control over the family.

COMMITTEES FOR THE DEFENSE OF THE REVOLUTION

The United States State Department explains, "The mass organizations' ostensible purpose is to improve the citizenry, but in fact their goal is to discover and discourage nonconformity."[5] Further, the State Department believes that citizen participation in mass organizations has decreased. Reasons for the decline are based in Cuba's economic crisis, which has lessened its government's ability to provide material incentives for participation. Thus, the lack of material incentives has forced many to engage in black market activities, which the mass organizations are supposed to report to the authorities.[6]

In 2000, the Reuters news agency reported the 40th anniversary of the CDR: "'In every neighborhood, Revolution!' reads the CDR slogan on walls and banners in every neighborhood across the island of Cuba."[7] The neighborhood revolution was created January 1, 1959, and formally established by Castro on September 28, 1960, to bind neighbors together in vigilance against possible counterrevolution. Humberto Carrillo, who is in charge of ideology for the CDRs' national committee, told Reuters, "The CDRs know exactly who lives in each block, who they are, what they do, if they work or not ... and keep a registry in coordination with the Interior Ministry."[8] Reuters explains, "The CDRs keep a detailed register of each neighborhood's inhabitants, not only listing each occupant by house but also recording such information as academic or work history, spending habits, any potentially suspicious behavior, contact with foreigners and attendance at pro-government meetings."[9]

These committees have purposes other than watching to protect the revolution. These committees do vital community work such as collecting blood for hospitals, organizing graduation parties and acting as response teams in emergencies and natural disasters.[10]

But whatever the function of the committees, the U.S. Department of State views the organizations as arbitrary interference with privacy, family, home, or correspondence, using "a wide range of social controls."[11]

Some Cubans are members of the CDR because they fervently back the revolution, while others belong to avoid problems.[12] Others do not approve and choose to emigrate.

Some Cuban-Americans interviewed said they disliked the Cuban government's arbitrary interference with personal affairs. Their position is in step with reports from the U.S. Department of State, which explains,

> Although the [Cuban] Constitution provides for the inviolability of a citizen's home and correspondence, official surveillance of private and family affairs by government-controlled mass organizations, such as the CDR's, remained one of the most pervasive and repressive features of daily life. The State has assumed the right to interfere in the lives of citizens, even those who do not oppose the Government and its practices actively.[13]

INDIVIDUAL RIGHTS

The Constitution makes clear that speech and press are controlled by the government and Article 54 states that rights of assembly and association are exercised through the organizations.[14] Other freedoms are also curtailed, which led to dissidents and a movement in Cuba known as the Varela Project. Treatment of those speak who against the revolution is reportedly harsh. According to Rafael Contrera, Cuba Free Press, in January 2001, "Political prisoner, Ramon Suarez Díaz, remains persecuted in the Provincial Prison of Pinar del Río by authorities of the Ministry of the Interior."[15] Arrested in October 2000, public visitations by family members are no longer permitted and must occur in a prison office with an official present.

Citizens expressing opposition are sometimes detained and warned. The Center of Information on Democracy in Cuba reports an incident in which a mother who breast fed her baby was detained and, she could not feed her child. Once citizens are released, surveillance continues.[16] The Inside Cuba website continues to report unrest. The homes of political dissidents are ransacked. Citizens suffer blackouts due to a lack of petroleum. The government addresses the crisis by moving truckloads of people from one city to another. Workers are striking to protest the closing of an El Salvador sugar mill. Since striking is illegal, the government is seeking the leader. The workers say they "acted under mutual agreement, so that they would all be responsible."[17]

Haroldo Dilla and Philip Oxhorn's report says that opposition groups "seeking legal recognition are numerous but very small." As long as their activities remain private, the Cuban government allows them. The groups emphasize human rights, but have no systematic proposals. They do not have much influence in Cuba and their sympathies are compatible with U.S. policy toward Cuba.[18]

Varela Project

The U.S. State Department reported that the Varela Project, a movement in Cuba calling for increased personal and political freedoms, sponsored by the Christian Liberation Movement and led by Oswaldo Paya Sardinas, had 10,000 supporters in 2001. Their petition requested a popular referendum, as provided for by the Constitution of 1976, on the need for political and economic changes. The State Department explained, "Project Varela proposes five areas where laws should be changed based on existing constitutional rights, including the right to free expression, the right to free association, amnesty for those jailed for 'political motives,' the right to set up businesses, and a new electoral law allowing citizens to vote for multiple candidates as a better form of 'participatory democracy.'"[19]

In May of 2002, former President Jimmy Carter made an historic trip to Cuba. Robert A. Pastor, vice president of International Affairs and Professor of International Relations at American University in Washington, D.C., accompanied President Carter to Cuba. Pastor was asked, since the Cuban government allows such a petition, whether that government is more open than some believe it to be. He replied,

> Yes, certainly. If the Cuban government did allow a free vote on the Varela Project that would reflect a very important step towards openness on the part of the Cuban government that very few people believe. I hope they'll do that, but there hasn't been any sign as of yet. Is that openness limited in that it must be expressed in specified ways for organizations? Certainly it is limited right now. Most non-governmental organizations are not permitted to be registered and therefore, technically, are not legal. Even though they may be human rights organizations or independent lawyers or independent economists, these are not really legal because the government views them as outside what is permissible and has not registered them as legal.[20]

Pastor explains that "Technically, what the Varela Project is all about is utilizing the Constitution for the purpose of making modest changes in the government."[21] The Cuban government proposed an amendment to the Constitution which would make it unchangeable. The National Assembly's unanimous approval of that amendment would mean that there is no legal or peaceful way to change the Constitution. Pastor says, "That would be very unfortunate for Cuba and the Cuban people."[22]

On June 26, 2002, the Varela Project was defeated. *The New York*

Times reported, "Vowing never to return to capitalism, the National Assembly has voted unanimously that the country's socialist system is 'irrevocable.'"[23]

ELECTORAL SYSTEM

Cuba has a national system of elections. Citizens do not vote in private and voters are those persons who are endorsed as devoted Communists and adhere fully to Fidel Castro.[24] Pastor says that the lack of free elections makes it impossible to determine whether Castro is popular in Cuba. Yet, few leaders in the world have exercised more important personal power in a country than Castro has. He achieves his power, Pastor maintains, "through coercion, inducement and charisma; it's a combination of all three."[25] He concludes,

> There's no question that Castro is unequivocally the strongest leader in Cuba and has been since he took office in 1959. Whether he is very popular is impossible to judge because there has never been a free election that gives people a chance to choose. So the normal way in which one can assess whether a leader is popular is not available in the case of Cuba. I don't think it's enough that just because he can bring a million people into the streets on behalf of one of his initiatives that that reflects a high degree of popularity, when, in fact, most of these people work for the government and their jobs do depend on their coming into the streets. They may be also very rabidly supportive of Fidel Castro. Indeed, he may have a lot of popular support in the country. It's just that no one can tell you that for sure because there is no good way to measure that.[26]

In October 2002, millions of Cubans participated in local one-party elections to vote for representatives in municipal assemblies. President Fidel Castro said more than 80 percent of Cuba's 8.2 million registered voters had turned out.[27]

Economy

Since 1959 when Fidel Castro led a rebel army to victory in Cuba, his rule has held the country together. Cuba's communist revolution, with Soviet support, was exported throughout Latin America and Africa during the 1960s, '70s, and '80s. The year 2002 found Cuba slowly recovering from the severe economic recession of the early 1990s when the former Soviet Union withdrew annual subsidies worth $4 billion to $6 billion.[28]

Over 80 percent of Cuba's trade had been with the USSR.[29] According to the United States Central Intelligence Agency, Havana depicts its problems as the result of the United States' embargo established in 1961.

Illegal immigration to the United States is an ongoing problem. In 2000, the United States Coast Guard interdicted only about 35 percent of approximately 3,000 Cubans migrating to Florida.[30]

In the 1950s under Batista, Cuba was likened to "a colonial appendage of its great neighbor. Beaches, gambling, and a heady nightlife made the island's capital, Havana, a choice destination for America's famous and fortunate."[31] Andrew Yurkovsky said this vacation paradise contrasted with Cubans living in "grinding poverty" that included makeshift housing and seasonal employment. In the 1960s, the United States imposed economic sanctions. The Eastern bloc provided fuel and technology.

In 1991, the breakup of the Soviet Union halted aid to Cuba and began a period of economic descent.[32] Blackouts resulted because Havana had to operate with only 15 percent of the oil that it had before the Soviet Union's withdrawal.[33] Thousands left for Florida in small boats and rafts. Castro released prisoners, sending them in like fashion to Florida. The United States ceased to welcome Cubans, and the magnitude of the exodus dropped.[34]

The crisis years of 1993–1994 gave impetus to the acceptance of the U.S. dollar and the encouragement of more foreign investment.[35] As a result of Cuba's debt doubling in the late 1980s, along with the collapse of the Soviet bloc, Cuba's imports fell 70 percent from 1989 to 1993 and the gross domestic product fell by about 50 percent. These developments impacted living standards. Douglas Hamilton writes that the industrial production fell to 15 percent of capacity, factories closed, the sugar harvest produced half as much, public transportation and agriculture ceased, electrical plants operated on and off, and the fresh water supply was disrupted.[36] The economy touched bottom in 1994. Agriculture produced 55 percent of what it had in 1990. By 2000, the country's situation improved, but imports were still 40 percent lower than in 1989.[37]

Complicating the crisis was the U.S. tightening of the embargo with the passage of the Cuban Democracy Act of 1992. U.S. subsidiaries in Third World countries could not trade with Cuba. Ships that delivered items to Cuba could not dock in U.S. ports for six months. Cuba's shipping costs increased by about 40 percent. In 1996, the Helms-Burton Act passed with a controversial provision, Title Three. The provision sanctions foreign companies making investments in Cuban properties expropriated from citizens of the United States. Although U.S. presidents have waived Title Three every six months, Dr. Miren Uriarte, University of

Massachusetts, writes that it "hangs like the Sword of Damocles over Cuba, its foreign investors, and U.S.-Cuba relations."[38]

As an adjustment, Cuba declared a "Special Period in Time of Peace" in 1990. A Food Plan was implemented to create self-sufficiency by breaking up large state farms into smaller units of production. These units were self-managed and financially independent, but the output was directed by the Ministry of Agriculture. Foreign investment was allowed, mainly in tourism, and the U.S. dollar was made legal.[39]

The economic crisis of the early 1990s produced social classes. The black market and illegal activities brought about a newly rich class who benefited from the crisis. With them were the new self-employed, private farmers and employees of the dollar economy. On the other hand, in 2002, the marginalized masses consisted of one-third of the population and were public service and state employees. About one-half of the work force were poorly paid in industry and rural cooperatives. Unemployment rose to about 30 percent.

In addition, racial stereotyping and prejudices still exist in Cuban society. Having low levels of migration, black Cubans are also limited in number in the political structure, prestigious positions and in the dollar sector.[40] According to Professor Lourdes Pérez of the University of Havana, "[Socioeconomic] disparities were further exacerbated by historical factors and social inequalities that linger in society despite long-term efforts to achieve equality and general social well-being."[41]

Migration to Havana has disrupted the good relations between urban and rural. Living in the city is becoming more appealing. Since 1990 and in 1995, the number of internal migrants exceeded the pre-revolutionary exodus, because the rural subsidize the food supply of urban dwellers without being able to improve their own standards of living. The supply of food by the government is better in urban areas. Hans-Jürgen Burchardt writes, "The concentration of provisions in urban farmers' markets is estimated at 80 percent, with Havana alone accounting for 50 percent."[42]

Basic Cuban social policy remained intact throughout the Special Period. All services are free of charge. Some minimal fees are in place, such as for adult education and for lunches in high schools. Universal accessibility also continues in that Cuba has not excluded any part of its population from basic benefits and services. Social benefits in health, education, social security and social assistance to the poor have remained. The government remains the main actor.[43]

Cuban life is not at the high level that it was before the crisis, but levels are improving. The money that Cuban-Americans provide has become the largest source of foreign exchange, exceeding sugar. Tourism has boomed. About 60 percent of the Cubans have access to dollar incomes and 85 percent live in family owned homes. The economy started to recover in 1994.[44]

Allowing dollars challenges the social justice goals of the revolution. A disparity exists between those who have no access to dollars and Cubans who can get them from their friends and relatives in the U.S. or from tourists.[45] The positive result is that the dollar has created employment opportunities for some, and "a high markup in dollar stores funds food and other social programs for the less well-off."[46] Uriarte reports that about 35 percent of Cuban workers receive some pay in dollars and that Cubans receive from Cubans living in the U.S. between $400 million and $800 million a year. Cubans who do not have access to dollars may not be able to purchase food and goods beyond that which is allowed by the state ration card.[47]

Uriarte believes the Cuban government's initial responses brought positive change to daily lives. These changes included allowing foreign investment, allowing Cubans to work privately, and legalizing the use of the dollar. The dual economy of pesos and dollars brought two different pay scales and working conditions.[48] Burchardt summarizes the new Cuban social dynamics also at work. The income and its sources are producing an appearance of social inequalities shown in strengthened sources linked to private property, the weakening value of state sector wages, the arrival of new social classes, a disparity between the enriched and impoverished, and the existence of groups with high incomes not resulting from their own labor.[49]

Uriarte writes that Cuba's Special Period has made life difficult for many families. Not only is there a lack of income, but family members often have to work at more than one job. The deteriorated transportation system people use to get to work takes still more time away from the family. These factors leave less time for family life, including looking after children. Secondly, within the family, different forms of participation in the economy exist. Uriarte explains, "A teenager can earn more money in one afternoon showing a tourist around Old Havana than his father earns in a month working in his government job."[50] Families feel a lot of pressure to raise their children under new circumstances. Parents do not have funds to buy goods at the dollar stores that their children prefer. Critics of the dollar economy contend that it has a negative effect.

In 2001, Paul Cullen wrote that the "dollar rape" eats away at Cubans' self-belief. He maintained that the ever-present economic distortion is dealt with through tourism:

Why be a doctor when there's more money in driving a taxi? Why go with a local boy when "escorting" visitors is so much more rewarding?

In Havana, we stayed in a room rented out by a young couple, both lawyers. She earns US$12 a month, and he earned US$16 until he realized it made more sense to stay at home and make the bed that earns this family US$25 a night. The state's take on this form of basic capitalism is a US$100 a month tax.[51]

Some Cubans we spoke with when we were in Cuba in 2002 were employed in the dollar economy. Several were trained professionals. Others shunned the financial benefits and were continuing to work in their professional occupations.

Stress from the new economy is indicated in three distinct ways. The divorce rate increased from 3.5 percent in 1990 to six percent in 1993. In 1998 the rate returned to the 1990 level. Secondly, more children were begging from tourists or working as unofficial tourist guides. Most children working the streets were boys between 5 and 11. In 1996, there were over 2,200 children doing these activities. Thirdly, social problems of illicit street life, primarily prostitution and petty crime, have returned.[52]

Uriarte writes that there is a growing tendency toward collaboration in the delivery of services. She offers three areas where collaboration has been successful, but not without some resistance: reducing low-weight births, helping mothers raise children and working together for clean communities. The Ministry of Public Health and local governments collaborated since the early 1990s to address the nutritional needs of at-risk pregnant women. Once they were identified in every neighborhood, the women were connected with a workers' lunchroom to receive at least one free meal each day. By 1995 low birth weights had been reduced to 7.9 percent, down from 9 percent in 1993.[53]

In 1997, lack of fuel caused irregular garbage pickup in Pogolotti. Uriarte explains that at first, families hung the waste from trees and posts in small plastic bags to permit traffic in the streets. But later garbage filled sidewalks, streets and empty lots. Fifty residents, at a community meeting with the Popular Council, the Metropolitan Park of Havana, the Taller de Transformación Integral de Pogolotti, and the Martin Luther King Center, advocated the importance of eliminating the dumping sites and the need to reforest the areas to develop recreational areas for children. The project was funded in part by the Canadian International Development Agency. The program affected 150 families.[54]

Fidel Castro's government has accomplished good health and education programs, but because of United States's sanctions and the loss of the Soviet Union as a trading partner, it has not achieved economic well-being.[55]

In spite of near total literacy, "there's nothing to read," but there is clean drinking water and excellent health services. Yet, Cubans still flee. Those citizens who remain are met with economic hardship.[56] Figures are not available for population below the poverty line, household income or consumption by percentage share. In 2000, the estimated labor force stood at 4.3 million. Seventy-five percent worked in the state sector, with 25 percent in the non-state sector. In 1998, agriculture represented 25 percent of the labor force, with industry representing 24 percent and services, 51 percent.[57]

Cubans pay for services and supplies that are subsidized by the state in the national currency that also pays their salaries. When supply and demand prevails, the internal market sets prices. Pork or lamb at the farmer's market for example, costs 25 pesos. The average monthly salary is 198 pesos, making those products unattainable for some citizens.[58] In 2001, Aldo Mariátegui described the Cubans' economic situation as "desperate:"

> Salaries average US$15 per month (except for the police, who earn US$40), and the rations card given to each family provides one chicken, 3.3 pounds of rice and beans, about the same amount of sugar, about 2 pints of cooking oil, and a few other tidbits to make you feel fuller — all of it less than enough to last a few days.[59]

Some free enterprise exists through street markets or *cuenta propistas*, even though it is against the law without a special license. Even with a license the government's share is sizeable and the fee for a space is about $2 per day. Vendors sell books, art and handicrafts, mostly to tourists, to make ends meet. Selling books to promote the revolution is tolerated and has been done over a longer period of time. Selling crafts started around 1994 to promote tourism. Although some vendors are licensed, others sell products for the craftsmen illegally.[60]

The government is concerned, but reports are mixed as to whether street markets in Havana provide enough earnings for Cubans. On the one hand, one 32-year-old had earned about 520 pesos per month (around $25) as a doctor. She stopped practicing for a job selling hammocks. She earns enough to get by, which is more than she made when she was practicing medicine. On the other hand, some say income is limited. One vendor reported earning about $3 per day. Yet, artists can earn $15 to $25 for excellent work. Successful artists pay $159 per month in taxes, regardless of earnings.[61]

The government may fine violators to such an extent that penalties could be months of earnings, back tax payments or jail. Vendors believe the laws are unreasonable because they can't make and sell products fast enough to meet the government's demands. Thus, vendors set up illegal street markets.[62]

We asked Alex, a young Cuban, how a Cuban person may earn a certain amount of money. "Do you have to give any of that back to the government? Or is the money yours?"

He answered,

> For example, a doctor can make around 400 pesos a month. That money is his own. He has earned his money, so he can use it. People who work in other places, for example, I work in tourism and the money I make, I donate a month or two, according to where you have worked, for the health system, which is a very good thing. You have to take into account that some people need your help, because they have suffered from cancer or something like this and they need money to buy the medicines. This money is used for that, which is a very good thing.[63]

We asked Alex, "Is this something like a tax?" He replied:

> It's not exactly like a tax. That depends. In the slower season, you don't have to pay that much. It is according to the time you have been working and the amount is not significant. When they get many people who have made money on this money, it is used to buy medication for people who are suffering from cancer and to buy toys for the kids who are suffering from cancer and some other diseases. That's a very good thing.[64]

Education

Cuba's Constitution guarantees the right to an education free to children regardless of family economic position. Adults are also guaranteed this right.[65] (See Appendix 1.)

EDUCATION OF CHILDREN

The 1959 revolution changed conditions for children in Cuba. New formal opportunities and protections honored equality regarding class, color and gender. Before 1959, 22.3 percent of those aged 10 to 49 were illiterate. About 46 percent of primary-age and 8.7 percent of secondary-age children were enrolled in school in 1952-53.[66] The 1940 Constitution had an article devoted to children, but family law was rooted in the Spanish civil code that was in effect from 1868 to 1950. The 1940 Constitution made a distinction between illegitimate and legitimate children. Provisions enabled poverty, unequal access to health and education, street labor, racism and patriarchal families. In 1961, education was nationalized, private schools were eliminated, and a literacy campaign was aimed at the entire population of Cuba. The combination of work and study and adult education became distinctive parts of the education.[67]

In 1961, preschool education was included in the system. In 1961, there were 37 daycare centers enrolling 108,729 children; in 1970, there were 606, and in 1990-1991, there were 1,116. In 1958, one special education program existed. In 1960-1961 there were 964 students enrolled in special education; in 1970-1971, 7,880 in 129 centers; and by 1990-1991, 512 centers with 59,035 students.[68] The focus of special education has changed from one of repression to one of prevention and reeducation. The year 1839 saw the first asylum established in Cuba. At the beginning of the 20th century, asylums became reform schools. Girls received religious instruction. Orphaned and abandoned boys were placed with boys who had committed crimes.[69]

In 1961 the system emphasized education and was governed by the Commission for Social Prevention of Juvenile Delinquency. The commission included the Ministries of Interior, Education, and Health, the National Institute of Sports and Recreation, the National Council of Culture, the attorney general and representatives of the mass organizations. Schools for children with conduct problems emphasized smaller care centers.

In 1982, the current system was established. It recognizes multiple levels of conduct. In 1984, 90 to 100 percent of all delinquents were boys ranging in age from 10 to 16. Enrollment in these schools varied little: in 1986-1987, 0.4 percent for ages 9–16; in 1990-1991, 0.3 percent; and in 1995 only severe cases were institutionalized or 0.04 percent of those children age 9–16 years.[70] Street children and child labor were not cited as causes of delinquency problems, but rather children could not take advantage of what the system offered.

A high dropout rate indicated problems afoot before the economic crisis of the 1990s. In 1988, 4.1 percent of junior high students dropped out, 7.0 percent left universities and 8.7 percent quit technical and professional schools. In 1989-1990, 0.7 percent of children 6-11 years, 5.7 percent of ages 12-14, 18 percent of age 15 and 33 percent of age 16 were not enrolled.[71] On a more positive note, giving girls an equal opportunity to be educated has made them a force to be reckoned with in society.

Roslyn Arlin Mickelson summarizes the statistical picture of the crisis of the 1990s, which contributed to the reemergence of street children and put stress on the family units.

Ministry figures for 1994-1995 show a dropout rate of 0.8 percent at the primary level and 3.3 percent at the junior high level; 98.2 percent continued their studies after graduating 6th grade, while 92.8 percent continued after 9th grade (*Cuba: Organization of Education* 1996). In 1996-1997, the percentage of dropouts in primary was 0.6, in basic secondary 1.5, and in preuniversity 5.6; in 1997-1998, 2.7 percent of 9th-grade graduates did not continue their studies (down from 7.2 percent in 1995-1996).... In Havana retention improved in 1995-1996, with a[n] overall rate of 98.3 percent (0.7 percent higher than 1994-1995), and 92.3 and 90.6 percent in polytechnical and trade schools, respectively. There were 2,380 minors *desvinculados* (neither studying or working) at the end of the 1995-1996 term, 1,669 of whom were "relinked" to the institutional network.[72]

Mickelson explains the crisis meant less material goods within the family. In the street, the mercantile system of expanding tourism brought with it a rise in illicit prostitution.

According to Uriarte, enrollments and dropout rates were most affected by the crisis of the Special Period. Postsecondary school enrollments decreased slightly while higher education's decreased more sharply. In 1990 and 1991, 94.5 percent of the ninth grade graduates from secondary schools continued their education, compared to 86.4 percent in 1994 and 1995. In addition, most 1990 students continued in pre-university high schools, while in 1995 most went on to technical schools. Tighter enrollments at the university level are due to the reduced number of positions available in the economy. Higher education enrollments decreased from 21 percent in 1990 to 12 percent in 1996. High school dropout rates increased due to the hardships of living in the countryside, food scarcity and transportation problems. Teachers found it difficult to get to the schools. Teachers began entering private-sector employment.[73]

In 2002, Uriarte reported, "There are no children in Cuba who live in the streets."[74] Further, she wrote that a large percentage of students finish high school, drug use among children and young people is almost nonexistent, and little violence exists by or toward youth in cities. Daycare is not yet available for all children, but primary schools located in neighborhoods are clean and schoolbooks are free. Only about four percent drop from middle school. From 7th through 9th grade, children spend three weeks working in the countryside. Students compete for the elite preuniversity schools and technical and art schools. About eight percent drop out of universities and technical schools. Most children are in school until their late teens. Since no child labor is allowed in Cuba, children cannot work until they are 17.[75]

EDUCATION OF YOUTH AND PROFESSIONALS

The crisis of the 1990s translated into the philosophy that education could no longer assure employment for professionals. University enrollments declined by over 50 percent between 1987 and 1997. Secondary schools were redirected to serve the economy. Funds were scarce to repair school structures, provide supplies or pay teachers. When medical supplies became less plentiful, contagious illnesses increased.[76]

Cuba's major socio-economic problems dictated new approaches. New social work education and training programs were among many improvements. The field of social work had no identity of its own in the postrevolutionary government. Problems were addressed by other professionals, local political leaders and representatives of Cuba's mass organizations such as the Federation of Cuban Women and Committees for the Defense of the revolution.[77]

Because of the socioeconomic hardships of the "Special Period," Cuba educated more advanced social workers at the university level. It also organized schools of social work for Cuban youth. These training programs are more quickly completed and the youths return to their communities as social workers. In September 2000, the Cuban government opened its first school of social work on the outskirts of Havana for young people age 16 to 22. Three additional schools now exist with 2,000 students attending each. Graduates are expected to stay on the job ten years and receive a salary of 300 pesos a month. They also may study for a license, but most do not.[78]

David Strug and Walter Teague say it is unknown how long Cuba's social work program will remain in effect, but it is an excellent "model for quick training of large numbers of young social workers to participate in local and nationwide public health and educational campaigns."[79]

Health Care

A glance at Cuba's population statistics tells us that health is good and life expectancy is good. With a birth rate of 12.08 for 1,000 population, an infant mortality rate of 7.27 and about a 0.03 percent adult prevalence rate of HIV/AIDS, the death rate is 7.35 per 1,000 with a total life expectancy of 79.15 years. The literacy rate is high, 95.7 percent.[80] (See Table 2.1.)

THE RIGHT TO HEALTH CARE

The Cuban Constitution guarantees the right to health protection and care. Medical, dental and hospital care is free and provided through

TABLE 2.1
THE CUBAN PEOPLE AT A GLANCE

Characteristic	Jan. 2002 (estimate)	
	Number	Percent of Total Population
Population (July 2002 est.)	11,224,321	
0–14 years		20.6
male	1,188,125	
female	1,125,743	
15–64 years		69.3
male	3,902,162	
female	3,880,531	
65 years and over (2001 est.)		10.1
male	520,849	
female (2002 est.)	606,911	
Life expectancy in years		
population	76.60	
male	74.02	
female (2001 est.)	79.15	
Population growth rate (2002 est.)		0.35
Birth rate/1,000 (2002 est.)	12.08	
Death rate/1,000 (2002 est.)	7.35	
Net migration rate/1,000 population (2002 est.)	-1.21	
Infant mortality rate/1,000 live births (2002 est.)	7.27	
Total fertility rate/children born/woman (2002 est.)	1.6	
HIV/AIDS (1999 est.)		
adult prevalence rate		0.03
people living with HIV/AIDS (2001 est.)	2,800	
deaths (1999 est.)	120	
Literacy rate(percent aged 15 and over who can read and write)		95.7
male		96.2
female (1995 est.)		95.3
Sex ratio (2002 est.)	1 male/female	
Ethnic groups		
mulatto		51.0
white		37.0

Characteristic	Jan. 2002 (estimate)	
	Number	*Percent of Total Population*
black		11.0
Chinese		1.0
Religion nominally 85% Roman Catholic prior to CASTRO assuming power; Protestants, Jehovah's Witnesses, Jews, and Santeria are also represented		

Note: Illegal emigration is a continuing problem; Cubans attempt to depart the island and enter the U.S. using homemade rafts, alien smugglers, direct flights, or falsified visas; some 3,000 Cubans took to the Straits of Florida in 2001; the U.S. Coast Guard interdicted about 25% of these migrants. Cubans also use non-maritime routes to enter the U.S.; some 2,400 Cubans arrived overland via the southwest border and direct flights to Miami in 2000.

Source: CIA, "The World Factbook 2001—Cuba," Jan. 1, 2002. Jan. 5, 2003, http://www.cia.gov/cia/publications/factbook/geos/cu.html#People.

a network of medical services. The population participates in health education and preventive medicine.

Before the breakup of the Soviet Union, the government made public health care and free medical care a priority. Polio, malaria, tetanus, diphtheria and human rabies were eliminated. Preventive care through the Family Doctor Program included one physician and one nurse for each 100 to 200 neighborhood families.[81]

Cuba's health care system has long been a model with an emphasis on preventive medicine. Dr. Michèle Barry writes that in 1997 and 1998, "Cuba has twice as many physicians per capita as the United States, and the infant mortality rate is 10 per 1,000 births."[82]

Family medicine has achieved in low technology and high technology areas. Low technology includes the neighborhood based primary care, regional hospital services, professional training, public health reforms, disease surveillance and universal access. High medical technology includes new pharmacology and biotechnology, surgical procedures, and care of patients infected by HIV.[83]

HEALTH PROFESSIONALS

The health professionals in Cuba provide a wide range of services for citizens. The vice director of the Psychiatric Hospital of Habana-Cuba,

Professor Dr. Luis Enrique Vidal Palmer, says he is privileged to work in the hospital located in Province Ciudad Habana. When asked why he became a doctor in a psychiatric hospital, he answered,

> It isn't always easy to explain motivations, they have an unconscious element that for those of us in the field of psychiatry is not simple to recognize when we must do it about ourselves; nonetheless, to find out the manner and the reasons others have affections, behaviors, feelings and different thoughts is always a challenge; to help others not to feel sick; to have the ability to listen and to put oneself in the other's place and to understand the physiology of the human brain has been something very important in my life and I think that this, tied to a personal history not very plentiful in great accomplishments, guided me to become a psychiatrist.[84]

On September 24, 2002, we had the opportunity to visit the Hospital Psiquiátrico de la Habana-Cuba (the Havana Psychiactric Hospital) and saw firsthand Dr. Vidal Palmer's compassion toward patients. A woman patient began to cry when our group entered one patient work area. Dr. Vidal Palmer immediately went to her and guided her from the group talking with her, and thus calmed her. She returned to her work composed. In another instance, a young man approached James, my husband, speaking in Spanish. Not understanding Spanish very well, James listened. Dr. Vidal Palmer playfully encircled his arm around the young man's shoulders. Then the doctor caringly massaged the man's head with his forearm, then sent him happily on his way.[85]

MENTAL HEALTH SERVICES

Families are physically affected by a shortage of medical supplies, but they are also affected when one of their members requires mental health services. During our visit to the Hospital Psiquiátrico de la Habana-Cuba, we learned of the hospital's advances in treatment of patients. We toured the hospital with Dr. Vidal Palmer and later interviewed him by email. He explains that, in spite of the many psychiatric services in Cuba, the embargo has had an effect.

> At the psychiatric hospitals, the needs are the same as those found in the rest of the hospitals around the country; these are related in the majority of cases with the economic embargo our country is subjected to and it is always the intention that the mental health patient be the least affected. In most of the facilities we don't have the most modern or sophisticated means, or the newest generation drugs; nonetheless, they receive the most highly qualified attention from the scientific and

human point, with no patient being left without food or medications nor residential treatment. All of this is of course free.[86]

Although all hospitals suffer from the economic embargo, Dr. Vidal Palmer explains there are psychiatric services available in all of the hospitals in the capital of Cuba and in all of the hospitals in the capitals of the provinces, Ciudad Habana, Pinar del Río, Villa Clara, Camagüey and Santiago de Cuba. These are also Cuba's larger cities.[87] Dr. Vidal Palmer explains that every Cuban has free access to the mental health system:

> We have community psychiatry (Community Centers for Mental Health) where the individual has the possibility of receiving care and rehabilitating himself in his own environment, surrounded by those he lives with, whenever his mental health permits it; if this would not be the case, depending on the severity of the case he would go through the following stages of attention until reaching the psychiatric institutions and specialized hospitals. I don't have the exact number of patients being cared for in all of Cuba, but I can tell you that the Psychiatric Hospital of Havana cares for close to 4,000 patients per year, with schizophrenia and depression as the most common presenting illnesses.[88]

We asked Dr. Vidal Palmer to elaborate on the kinds of psychiatric illnesses and mental health problems treated in the hospitals. He explains,

> All of the psychiatric illnesses are treated in these hospitals, including those of neurotic behavior as well as psychotic and addictions to various substances; of course they are all handled using different modes of hospitalization treatments, in close coordination with the community mental health system.[89]
>
> I think that these illnesses are in themselves a problem, in psychiatry we can't separate them, at the origin of any psychic alteration one must evaluate all of the aspects that influence the individual (the family, his living environment, the social group and of course the biological as it relates to his own organism). To explain myself better let's use an example: A 38 year old male with a history of depression (Major Depression) comes into our office with a suicidal ideation; all is motivated because his wife has left him (ended the relationship). What do we have here? With a quick look we could say we have a problem; but we aren't before a severe psychiatric condition that threatens to have the human being end his life; the origin appears simple, "a conjugal problem," but if we go beyond this we will see that this individual has weak adjusting mechanisms that favor the presence of this situation. Then it isn't so easy to separate the factors, we must see the individual as a bio-psycho-social-family-spiritual being.[90]

How long a person remains as a patient in the hospital depends "on the service being offered, the patient's evolution and the clinical severity the patient is presenting."[91] Dr. Vidal Palmer says that there are different lengths of time for different services. "There are short term stays (30 to 45 days) for patients in a severe outbreak, medium stays (45 days to 6 months) for patients with a severe outbreak and long term evolution and patients with chronic incidences will have prolonged stays (more than 6 months), until the patient can reincorporate into the community."[92]

Our tour of the hospital combined with Dr. Vidal Palmer's discussion on hospital services led us to ask what roles the family of a psychiatric patient has in the treatment and rehabilitation of the patient. He replied,

> The family is, was and will be, as was stated by a great thinker, the primary cell of society, therefore its role is basic; the family is important for the pharmacological, psychological and social treatment. The success of the cure depends on its acceptance of the illness and its participation in the therapeutic process.[93]

AIDS Program

Barry found that Cuba's aggressive quarantine approach to combating AIDS was met with human rights criticism and was hindered by the embargo affecting the availability of medication. Cuba responded with an AIDS program that constructed 13 more sanitariums.[94] Residents were closer to their homes and, in 1993, Cuba launched ambulatory HIV care. Educational programs, promotion of condom use and identification of infected persons, including mandatory tracing and testing of sexual partners, resulted in "the lowest reported prevalence of HIV in the hemisphere. As of May 1999, Cuba reported a total of 761 cases of AIDS."[95]

Cuba was at first criticized for having violated human rights with its proactive program regarding HIV. The program included screening for AIDS. Although the screening at first was for parts of the population, it soon became part of routine health care. If test results were positive, the individual was quarantined in a sanitarium in Havana. In response to criticism, Cuba's AIDS program placed a sanitarium in each province. The patients received public assistance and full wages. They also received medicine and food that was unavailable to most of the population.[96]

Pressures on Health Care

The economic crisis in Cuba has affected the health care system with serious shortages of medical supplies. Profound changes have occurred in the past 15 years. Dr. Michèle Barry believes that the economic decisions the Cuban government may have made and the progressive U.S. sanctions since the embargo of 1961 have led to the deterioration. The Cuban Democracy Act passed by the United States Congress in 1992 has one of the few sanctions worldwide that explicitly includes food and defines trading constraints that block access to medical supplies. The act prohibits foreign subsidiaries of U.S. companies from trading with Cuba. The 1996 Helms-Burton law further discouraged foreign investors by threatening non–U.S. intermediaries with lawsuits in U.S. courts.

Cuban people's caloric intake decreased between 1990 and 1994, as did available food. In the early 1990s the average loss of weight among adults was estimated at about 20 pounds. In 1990 7.6 percent of babies had a low birth rate. In 1993, the rate rose to nine percent.[97]

In 1999, upon a return visit to Cuba, Barry found a lack of food in grocery stores and a decrease in the weight of Cubans. In turn, less food intake caused outbreaks of certain diseases. At the same time, medications and vaccines were in short supply.

Agricultural Economy

The countryside in Cuba is beautiful. We asked Alex, a teacher: "We saw a lot of the farm country. What are the different kinds of farmers that Cuba has?"

> In Cuba, some people have private land that raise products for the state. Some people work with the state, for example, we have 4 million people that grow tobacco. Of the people who grow tobacco, some of them work for the government and some of them have private land. When they work for the government, they make money because of that. Some grow sugar cane and others are part of the production. The other part of the production is sales. They can sell it in farmers markets and the benefits are for themselves. Some people work in cooperatives. For example, if you have some land and you want to be integrated into a cooperative, so you work there and see the amount of money they make, also you receive part of the food for the year. Those people who live in cooperatives are given a house. Together they have good products and it is a way for people to improve production.[98]
>
> If you go to the regions in the western part of the country you have tobacco as the main production, but in the whole country, we have sugar cane. It is the second most important product in Cuba after tourism. We have also oranges in the Matanzas Province, near Batabano. Three hundred square kilometers [are] dedicated to oranges production which [is] for orange juice. We have pineapple in the eastern part of the country, in Granma Province. Bananas also are raised in Granma Province

and in the south part of Havana Province. Minor crops are all over the country.[99]

Loss of assistance from the Soviet Union and increasing sanctions from the United States have left Cuba without resources to maintain previous production and consumption levels. A crisis in consumption is the basis of Cuba's transition. For Cubans this crisis translates into a reduction in the availability of food, lack of consumer durables, shortages of personal toiletries and medical supplies, power cuts in urban areas, a lack of transportation, lack of supplies in schools and hospitals and a reduction in programs considered nonessential such as house building and engineering.[100]

Agricultural reform includes decentralizing units. Industry has significantly downsized. Labor displacement has led to more self-employed since the early 1990s. Farmers' markets or *mercados agropecuarios* have increased. The government has allowed self-employment under certain conditions to provide income.[101]

In 2002, Uriarte found that families struggle to make ends meet, but the government provides a basic set of benefits. The ration card provides food for two weeks each month. The family supplements that with pork, chicken, rice, beans and vegetables purchased in the black market, farmers' markets or dollar food stores. By law parents pay only ten percent of their salaries for rent. Most own their homes. Utilities are subsidized. She concludes, "But, in most cases, children live in households where the essential things are taken care of, but there is not a lot left for luxuries."[102]

For the Cuban household, alternative ways to earn income became necessary to maintain subsistence. A growing difference exists "between the officially managed economy and the mechanisms and activities by which most Cubans acquire goods and services for consumption."[103]

Transportation

Although Cuba does not have many new cars, it has a large supply of old American cars. There are between 50,000 and 100,000 pre–1960 United States cars in Cuba. These cars are well maintained. Cuba is in the process of making its own bicycles. Approximately 1.2 million bikes have been purchased from China. Bikes are provided by the government to citizens for $6.[104] During our travel in Cuba in 2002, we saw a number of American made 1950s cars. Some cars were Russian made in the 1970s and 1980s. We also saw newer buses and newer cabs that resulted from the dollar economy. The taxis owned by the Cuban people were older. Some people rode bicycles.

We also saw a number of Cubans, both in the city and on the national highway in the rural areas, standing on the side of the road. We asked our taxi driver why. He said they were waiting for a ride. Later, we asked our bus tour guide the same question. We were told that any government owned vehicle is required to pick up any Cuban who needs transportation.

Religion

In 1991, the Fourth Congress of the Communist Party adopted a more flexible position about religion that was reflected in the 1992 constitution. The 1998 visit of Pope John Paul II also gave impetus to the increase of people publicly identifying with religion and observing the rituals of their church.[105]

Most practicing Cubans follow Afro-Cuban cults. Although the cults have no national or territorial centers, their informal networks are very effective within the communities. The more organized and positioned Protestant and Catholic churches have held the political spectrum. Although Protestants are in the minority, their numbers are increasing. The Catholic Church remains "elitist and hostile to the revolutionary project."[106] Only after the Cuban president's meeting with the Pope in the Vatican and the Pope's later visit to Cuba have the tensions begun to relax.[107]

Decreasing Influence of Catholic Church

Ron Howell, a reporter for *Newsday*, was last in Cuba for a month in March 2001 and before that for a month in December 2000. Between 1987 and 1994, he had made half a dozen other trips there. He believes that family and the church clearly have much to do with each other. He said that it was very striking to see the Christmas trees in homes and on the streets.

> It was not something one expected in a nation that is by its own definition communist. But the fact is that Cuba is a country with very Western traditions and one that is eminently Catholic in its background and history. I think you see that very clearly not only around Christmastime but also during the feasts of San Lazaro and other spiritual icons. It was impressive to see the thousands of people walking and crawling up the

streets to get to the Catholic church in the town of El Rincon, at the time
of the feast of San Lazaro. It reminded me of being in Mexico City, 15
years before, for the feast Our Lady of Guadalupe. Both events are
notable, to me, for the way they represent Catholicism as it was in the
old days, from the Middle Ages all the way to the 1960s, when Vatican
II opened the church up to modernism in its thinking and its practices.[108]

Howell says it's true that there isn't the same strong hostility now
between Cuba and the Catholic Church that one found in the 1960s and
prior. He elaborates,

> Especially after the visit of Pope John Paul in the late '90s, Cuba promised
> to open up a bit and allow people to celebrate Christmas in the ways
> they once did. But it would be a mistake to conclude that the wider
> acceptance of Christmas signifies a true rapprochement between Cas-
> tro's Cuba and the Catholic Church. What's more, I did not notice a
> really significant presence of the Catholic Church in the lives of most
> Cubans. If anything, it is the Protestant Evangelicals who are making
> inroads among Cubans searching for ways to express their spirituality.
> I think it's possible also that the Protestants are much [more] aggressive
> in their willingness to challenge the State on issues like their right to
> travel outside the island, for instance. The Catholics, I think, have dam-
> aged themselves greatly in the eyes of many Cubans. First, because they
> were so identified with the upper classes, and second because they were
> so aggressively anti–Castro back in the 1960s, when they opposed the
> regime at the very time it was doing things to benefit poor masses of peo-
> ple, like improving health care and increasing the opportunities for edu-
> cation. Needless to say, the more recent sex scandal can only have made
> prospects worse for the Catholic Church in Cuba.[109]

Santeria is a religious practice gaining members at an increasing rate.
With the rising numbers of Santeria and other religions, Latin American
religious expression is changing.[110] Santeria originated with the West
African Yoruban people who were taken to Cuba as slaves during the 16th
through the 19th centuries. The slaves were forced to hide their religious
traditions, so the santeros masked their faith in Roman Catholic imagery.
For example, the god of thunder and lightning, Chango, was worshiped
in the image of Saint Barbara. The fusion of images became known as
Santeria, the worship of the saints. According to Keith Aoki, santeros are
often found lining the pews of a Roman Catholic Church. Often a devout
Catholic will seek a Santeria priest for advice. Unlike the slaves in the
United States, the Caribbean and Latin American slave populations were
able to keep much of their language, culture and religion.[111]

Since Cuba's constitution during 1940 to 1959 provided religious freedom, the Santeria religion experienced a period of growth. From 1959 to the mid–'70s, the Cuban Revolution viewed Santeria as folklore. Religious freedom was curtailed in the 1970s and believers began to conceal their practices once again. In the 1980s and 1990s the government allowed more religious freedom, bringing Santeria into the mainstream to attract tourists. Castro realized that Santeria offset the powerful institution of the Catholic Church. That most people practice Catholicism may be a misnomer.[112] Estimates are that 70 percent of Cubans practice Santeria in the 21st century. Santeria is based on belief in a single supreme being who created the world, "but holds that God delegated orishas, or spirits, with human characteristics to watch over it. Because worshiping orishas was heresy to Catholics, practitioners identified each with a Catholic saint."[113]

In 1997, Cuba observed Christmas for the first time since 1969. Cubans turn to the church, but many turn to Santeria, which is deeply imbedded in the culture.[114]

Laws

Many laws exist pertaining to the family. Perhaps none is as important as the Family Code. Although the Family Code was enacted in 1975, it, like other laws if not periodically revised, is recommended by various scholarly groups for revision.

FAMILY CODE

The Family Code of 1975 legislated more rights for women both within their families and within society. On the part of some, acculturation remained resistant. The code included provisions that favored the integration of women in public and private spheres. Marriage, divorce, children's rights, adoption, and marital property relations provisions supported women. One provision legalized the division of family responsibility. Equal rights for marriage partners and sharing household tasks have been incorporated into the marriage vows. Yet, certain inequalities remain for women who must be responsible for domestic work and care of children in addition to civic and employment obligations.[115]

The improvements in education, family income, and health care brought with it a revolution in the family. In education, child care facilities almost doubled, increasing the number of children enrolled from 54,382 in 1975 to 96,000 in 1981. More than 970 new schools were built.

The ability to work added to family economic stability. Through the efforts of the Federation of Cuban Women and Communist Party congresses, the percentage of women in the work force in 1989 was 38.7 percent. More families had access to home appliances. In health care, maternity hospitals care improved. Paid maternity leaves and child care became available. Women then had the right to abort on demand, free of charge, as are all medical services.[116]

The Family Code with provisions for more freedom brought a revolution within the family. A change in attitudes took place. State assistance for children and the availability of jobs for women made divorce more feasible. It was no longer necessary to stay together to protect the children, because divorce was easier to get.[117]

The revolutionary period gave Cuba an economically comfortable society until economic assistance from the USSR ended. Today, Cuba has a sputtering economy, political prisoners and is listed by the United States in its global terrorism report.

The United States Embargo

Ambassador George McGovern believes that the unilateral sanction of the U.S. embargo has contributed to periodic food shortages. In 2001, he wrote,

> It is ironic, in an era when advocacy of free trade has become almost an article of faith, that, in the face of the recent severe drought in eastern Cuba, our government still considered it a crime for Americans to send food to hungry Cuban children.[118]

In 2002, Alex, a young Cuban, told how he saw the embargo affecting the people of his country:

> The embargo is difficult for everybody. Certain products you can't bring directly to Cuba. You have to go to get it in a third country in another part of the world. It is out the way. It is very, very difficult. The government has to spend a lot of money and when the other countries know that Cuba needs those products, they charge much more money because you need it, for example, for some vaccines necessary for people. The Cuban government cannot buy it from any company in the world that has the American patent. So they have to do it anyway. So they are going to have to pay much more and that causes problems — shortages in oil consumption, electricity — because of that. The main objective of the government is to provide the services that people need and the most

important ones, for example, education. The embargo has created a problem in the population also…. For example, the raw material for houses and clothing is very hard to buy, it is very expensive because of that, because the government has to import much clothing. So they make clothing here, but it is not enough sometimes. It is very difficult because of the embargo that has created problems. Also, for example, food. Food has created problems. In 1994, food was a problem because of the crisis. So we all keyed to the government to the correct way to do that.[119]

Delvis Fernández Levy, president, Cuban American Alliance Education Fund, Inc., finds the family restrictions abhorrent. He says that he can't imagine the United States going to an international forum defending human rights, and having this type of policy imposed on Cuban people.

Every year, for the last seven or eight years, the vote [in the U.N.] has been overwhelming. Only two votes against, one is the United States and one is Israel. In the last vote, there was the third country, the Marshall Islands. There is strong condemnation about the embargo. The aspects of the embargo that affect the most human beings are the restrictions on travel and on the people-to-people type engagement, for example, to conduct research.[120]

Douglas Hamilton writes, "There is no other country in the world that has had to endure so sustained period of economic and political aggression as Cuba at the hands of the United States."[121] The embargo has great and devastating effects on Cuba's economic, political and cultural life. Health and nutrition in Cuba is affected. If the embargo were to be lifted, access to medicine, medical equipment, educational resources and consumer and capital products would be available. Cuba's people would experience a better standard of living.[122]

Robert A. Pastor believes former President Jimmy Carter's speech in Cuba was the most important legacy of his trip in May 2002.

In that speech, he laid out clearly an alternative vision, both for U.S. policy and for U.S.-Cuban relations. He talked about the necessity of lifting the embargo, of approaching Cuba with a degree of respect. He also talked about the importance of Cuba becoming democratic in order to integrate into the Western Hemisphere, which has, over the last two decades, become democratic. By "democratic," we are not referring to a U.S. definition, but rather to a universal set of values and definitions, most clearly articulated in the Inter-American Democratic Charter, approved unanimously by the thirty-four countries of the Organization of American States on September 11, 2001, in Lima, Peru.[123]

Based on my own research, I concluded Americans tend to think of democracy only in the form it takes in the United States. Pastor says this specific American concept of democracy is not correct.

> There is a clear understanding of what we mean by "democracy" that is written into the Universal Declaration of Human Rights signed by all the nations of the United Nations and by a number of documents in the Western Hemisphere as well. So we are not talking about the U.S. definition, we're talking about a global universal definition. That definition is the right of a people to choose their leaders in a secret ballot in a free environment at regular intervals. Cuba does not have that right at this time. It is virtually the only nation in the hemisphere that does not.[124]

As to lifting the U.S. trade embargo, Pastor believes that would be a very important step. He says, "When that occurs is anybody's guess. I think the Congress would like to do it, but President [G.W.] Bush made very clear in mid–May [2002] that he had no intention of approving it. So it could be a long time."[125] Pastor believes the obstacles preventing more open trade include the embargo and Cuba's economic policies themselves. He explains that Cuba not only has very high tariffs, it has not really paid any of its debts. Thus, very few nations give the country any credit.[126]

Pastor reports that the economy is just as dependent on the outside world today as it was when Castro came to power, indeed, perhaps even more so—dependent on sugar, dependent on tourism, dependent on dollar remittances. "Cuba had one of the highest per capita incomes in Latin America in 1959. Now it has one of the lowest."[127] He adds that Cuba has free education and health care which are among the best in the hemisphere. "Even though it had been as well, that is to say, it was one of the best in terms of education and health care, that system has improved significantly."[128]

In 1994 and 1995, 150 executives and representatives of 174 U.S. companies traveled to Cuba to explore business opportunities should the embargo be lifted. In 1996 more contacts developed between sectors of U.S. society and Cuba—legislative, religious, academic and business.[129]

LIFTING THE EMBARGO

Global terrorism remains a great concern to the United States. Seven nations appeared on the 2002 roster of state sponsored terrorism: Cuba, Iran, Iraq, Libya, North Korea, Sudan and Syria.[130] In 2001, the U.S. Department of State's Global Terrorism Report explained why it lists Cuba. Reasons given include that Cuba provides safe haven and is associated with some groups.[131] After forty years, the embargo remains in place and travel to Cuba is restricted. The embargo and travel restrictions hurt the Cuban economy.[132]

In 2002, the U.S. House of Representatives voted to defeat a measure that connected the removal of the Cuba travel ban to evidence the communist nation is not developing biological weapons. The defeat cleared the way for the 262-167 passage of a second spending-bill amendment to lift the travel ban without restrictions. The White House planned to veto the bill if it had passed.[133] Even though the House defeated an amendment to lift the embargo, it did agree to two other embargo-related amendments. One amendment allows private financing of food and medicine sales to Cuba. U.S. law allows Cuba to buy food and medicine if it obtains financing through international means. The second increases the dollar limit that people in the United States can send annually to people in Cuba. At present, the limit is $1,200.[134] In Fall 2003, the U.S. House and Senate voted to end the travel ban to Cuba. There is the threat of a presidential veto, according to AP Oct 23, 2003.

Pastor says that normalization of relations between Cuba and the United States will probably not happen any time soon. Normalization not only means lifting the embargo and establishing normal trade relations, but a good relationship, and he believes that's not going to happen as long as Fidel Castro is in power and that may be for another ten or fifteen years.[135]

The Cuban American Alliance Education Fund works diligently for reassessment of U.S. policy without harm to either Cuba or the U.S. Some of their activity includes humanitarian travel, relief efforts to assist natural disasters in Cuba, social work projects, U.S.-Cuba Sister-City ties to promote people-to-people engagement, cultural exchanges, forums and debates, press outreach, congressional visits and joint activity with other groups to monitor legislation. Through these projects they learn much about the family life of Cubans in Cuba and in the United States.[136] Their newsletter, "*La Alborada*" (*The Dawn*), has accounts written by Cubans.

Conclusions

Recently, the Cuban government has undertaken limited economic reforms. The priority of political control makes extensive economic reforms unlikely. "Living standards for the average Cuban, without access to dollars, remain at a depressed level compared with 1990.... As the government balances the need for economic loosening against its concern for firm political control," growth in 2001 should continue, the CIA predicted.[137]

Scholars believe that the Cuban Revolution has shown adaptability in overcoming without distorting the social justice ideals. The ideals will be preserved after an eventual normalization of relations with the United states.[138]

In socialism, the means of production belongs to the state. The capital and the whole economy are centralized under the state. Since Cuba's economy is in difficulty, perhaps some hope for the "balance of economic loosening and firm political control" lies in an emerging middle class. With the development of the entrepreneurial middle class, some American firms are investigating potential business opportunities. The Cuban middle class is ready to conduct business with its contacts in the United States. Cuba has excellent resources that are of interest to retirees, vacationers, and industries; for example, good health care, a pleasant climate, beaches, music, sports, rum and tobacco.[139]

Donald and Marjorie Bray describe life in Cuba in the early 21st century as Spartan, but not bleak and without texture. Based on our own trip to Cuba in 2002, I would agree that in spite of the evidence of modern capitalism, "human relationships seem less superficial and scant material things more appreciated. Popular culture is vibrant, and art is nourished and flourishing."[140]

Since Cuba is the cultural and political common ground for the Cuban and the Cuban American family, the role of the family living in Cuba must be viewed in relationship to the recent historical events. Cuba has braved her economic crisis of the 1990s. Cuba is rebuilding its economy and facing challenges to the socialist system. Population sectors that include the vulnerable and the aging as well as providing services damaged during the special period are critical challenges. Uriarte concludes, "Cuba faces these challenges armed with a considerable accumulation of strengths."[141] She writes that Cubans know how to take care of their own. They have improved and maintained Cuba's health status, eradicated illiteracy and have one of the most educated workforces in the hemisphere. They have not only accomplished this during the Special Period, but over the past 40 years. The values and practices of equity and responsibility that have framed the development of their social policy will continue to help Cubans face the challenges of the future.[142]

Events that have happened since the Cuban Revolution in 1959 make it necessary to examine the Cuban family in two countries, Cuba and the United States. The Cuban family lives in these two countries and some families have members in both.

3

The Impact of Society on the Cuban Family

In Marxism, the locus of social reality is to be found in the social relations of a group or society. The object can never be a single individual taken in isolation.

— Rosemarie Skaine[1]

During the 1990s, some of the Cuban people who supported the revolution may have lost faith in the system's ability to achieve an acceptable level of equity. Lack of supplies was particularly evident in the schools. Teachers and students were faced with the effects of Cuba's dwindling economy. Supplies, good food, transportation and good working conditions were not always available. People recognized that "education is no longer central to the system of incentives and rewards which has hitherto been the basis of systems of allocation of labour and scarce services and goods. By contrast, people are aware of the rewards for working in tourism."[2]

In 2002, when I attended the XII International Congress on Family Law in Havana, one of the tour guides told us that he was trained to be an engineer and another, a teacher. Both individuals said they could earn more income in tourism than in their professions.[3] This phenomenon has weakened the popular class and decreased the size of the working class. "The new class is made up of those in the traditional bureaucracy who now work with foreign investors and those who operate in world markets in state enterprises, together with commercial intermediaries, service providers and the self-employed."[4]

So, energies people previously expended on the system are now given to ensure the survival of the family and household. Portions of two interviews conducted by Ruth Pearson show,

People have stopped thinking about collective solutions; they worry for their children (Teacher, Havana, 1994).

Now we are only interested in what goes on in the house and not what goes on en la calle [in the street] (33-year-old housewife, Havana, 1994).[5]

Pearson states "that the role of the household in long-term social reproduction is now being reformulated."[6] New ways will be necessary to insure economic recovery that represent a long-term adjustment between household and the state. The needs of household members have to be met. The recovery has to be more than sitting out the crisis. Cubans are having to take back into the family and the household a more active and responsible role in reproduction.

Ron Howell, reporter for *Newsday*, said in 2001 that the family is affected by the economic difficulties Cuba endures.

Clearly, the economic straights in which Cuba finds itself cannot help Cubans as they try to sustain bonds of nuclear and extended kinships. The very worst effects of the strains imposed by poverty were seen in the mid–1990s during the era known as the "special period." The special period began after the collapse of the Soviet Union, which had been the financial mother's milk of socialist Cuba almost from its inception. With the end of the Soviet subsidies, the economy almost imploded and people in the cities survived any way they could. Prostitution increased, causing great embarrassment not only to the women and their families, but to the ideological architects of Castro's Cuba, who had long denounced prostitution as a type of oppression of the poor. There is evidence that during the special period, some Cuban men were "pimping" their own wives and lovers. One of the most interesting experiences I had was visiting Pedro Juan Gutierrez, the author of "Dirty Havana Trilogy," which was a thinly veiled autobiographical account of life in Havana during those difficult years. It ain't pretty stuff.[7]

The bright light on the horizon is that Cuba has emerged from the special period and is now trying with degrees of success to make its way within the wider capitalistic world, building hotels, exploring for fossil fuels, and developing medical products. Cuba is a great, one could also say unique, country in so many ways and its greatness must owe much to the families that are its flesh and bones.[8]

Housing Shortage and the Family

In the 1990s, the demise of the Soviet bloc and the continuing U.S. embargo put stress on marriages. A 1998 *Johns Hopkins Magazine* special report described the situation this way:

The housing shortage is severe, the daily search for jobs and food daunting. Food, in fact, is the most expensive commodity: at about 50 cents a liter on the black market, fresh milk purchased daily could cost three-quarters of a monthly salary. Because the state has assigned all houses and apartments (and laws prevent Cubans from selling property), newly married couples often live with relatives, many sharing a bedroom with their children. Since getting married young is the norm, these problems translate quickly into domestic trouble.[9]

In 2002, Miren Uriarte, Ph.D. at the University of Massachusetts, wrote that Cuban citizens participated in community based housing rehabilitation projects in the Havana municipality of Marianao. "Over half of Havana's housing is in need of repair or replacement. Self-help housing repair brigades are one of the community based responses to this challenge."[10]

The shortage and inflexibility of housing is a contributing factor to Cuba's high divorce rate and increasing number of single parent families. Generations must live together. "Minimal housing and privacy needs for married couples and families are often unmet," wrote Archibald R.M. Ritter.[11] Asley L. Marmol, Miami resident and 2001 émigré, says that when more than one family lives together, it is more difficult for a marriage to succeed. He says,

> It affects the marriage a lot. When you have the case of two marriages [living] in the same house, you are going to have a lot of issues to deal with, many issues. Even when it is the mother, the father, the daughter and the son-in-law, and the brother, which is a common case in Cuba, you are going to deal with a lot of issues in between the two nuclear families. When you are dealing with the marriages of three different brothers in the same house with the marriage of the mother, you are talking about four nuclear families in the same house. There is going to be a lot of problems there because of normal differences and because of normal needs that you cannot fulfill. That will give consequences both short and long term.[12]

Cuba's Special Period affected the availability of housing for several reasons. First, materials were not available to build housing. In 2002, Uriarte interviewed an architect working in the neighborhood of Cayo Hueso in Havana who said seven tenements were to be demolished. Families were placed within the neighborhood in special hostels. People without housing remained. The architect said that they did not know what to do with the people. They began fixing buildings to house them. He gave this example:

> We found a shelter and we adapted it for three families with a common
> bathroom ... it was not a complete solution but it was better than 14 fam-
> ilies and one bathroom.... We took the care to make sure they all got
> along. We found a solution for about 100 families in these ways. We still
> have 10 families left.[13]

The housing shortage in Cuba is due also, in part, to the absence of
normally functioning markets. People's housing needs change as they move
through their life cycles, growing up, marrying, raising families and retir-
ing. Yet, Archibald R.M. Ritter wrote in 1992, that a Cuban could not buy
or sell a house.[14]

Hurricanes also take a great toll on housing structures. Two hurricanes, Isadore and Lily, bookended our travel to Cuba in late September
2002. In Viñales Valley, we saw some evidence of Isadore's damage. One
has little difficulty understanding nature's toll. Alex, a young Cuban we
met during our visit, explained that he was planning to build his own
house but because of Cuba's housing problems, it will take time.

> I am planning to build my own house. I live with my family, so what I
> am going to do in some years— because of the shortage of materials, it
> takes time to build a house — and it is a little bit expensive so you have
> to make some money to build it. I expect to do it for this year or the com-
> ing year, I don't know. It takes time. A housing problem exists in Cuba.
> The government builds in each province from 30,000 to 40,000 houses
> every year. Then, when we had a hurricane, most of the materials are
> used for the people who lost their houses because of the social security.
> We are living in an underdeveloped country so that takes time. This year,
> we had this hurricane, two weeks ago, and we're restoring and repairing
> the houses of people who lost their houses. The people who are work-
> ing in the construction companies are hurrying up because they want to
> finish before the other came. There is a will, good will, to solve the prob-
> lem. You have to take into account that in 1959 in Cuba we had only six
> million people, now we have almost 12 million, eleven something.[15]

Cuba's growing population contributes to the housing shortage. We
asked Alex whether he believed that there is a housing shortage in Cuba.
He further explained the housing system.

> In housing, it was easy to have a house in Cuba in the '70s. We had all
> the materials for free. The cost was symbolic. Now it is very difficult
> because of the world economy. The Cuban economy went down during
> the '90s. The government had to recover part of it because you have to
> take into account that we have to use money for education, health sys-
> tem, social security, and schools for handicapped people. In a way, it is
> a little bit difficult. Sometimes, it takes time to build a house. You can

build it because the government provides you the materials when you are building a house. It takes time because sometimes there is a period in which they have to use the materials in another place. For example, you are building your house. The government is selling you the materials at good prices, at reasonable prices for Cubans. A hurricane comes and there is a problem because some people have lost their house. The government has to take care of these people because there is a whole family living in that house. The people who lost their house have to keep living in it, so the government has to hurry up to repair those houses.[16]

We then asked, "In Cuba, your parents own their house. Is that house something they can sell? How does that go?"
    Alex responded,

> My family owns their house. There's one thing about it. During the '80s, the government allowed people to sell their house. That was an amazing event. You have to take into account that the city of Havana [is] a city of three million people. So most of the people come to the city. All over the world that happens. So there is a housing problem. In the '80s, it was a mess. People had twenty to twenty-five houses because they had money. They were making money. Our workers were having a hard time to get a house in Havana Province. So, the government stopped that problem by selling the houses to the people who made it and avoided having them sell it. The government also put in rules about how many people could live in a house. If a house had two rooms and you have three kids, you have to have three rooms and your house is in good condition, you can exchange houses. That's the way you can exchange houses. You are not allowed to sell it because of those problems that took place in the 1980s. In the '90s, some people were selling houses in the black market. The government has taken care of that because the real people who need them, the workers, were not getting houses. Some people had houses for business and they didn't work. They were smugglers. In that way, the government was trying to have equality. That is why we have assistance for housing. The main objective of the system [is] to keep account of equality, although we are living in a world in which it is a little bit difficult to do that, to keep that equality.[17]

Family Members Separated by Emigration

Alex told us about those who are left behind when people leave Cuba to live in the United States and how it affects them to have their family split. He said,

> Those families who have members who go to live in the States find it is a very hard thing. In the 1960s, people left Cuba because of the system.

> In the 1970s, some people left because of the system too. In the 1990s, most people that have migrated, have left Cuba, did so because of economic reasons, to build their lives a little bit more. So that is very hard for families. Some of the families leave and feel homesick and miss their families. That's very hard. In that way, they keep that kind of relation. Younger people have kept the relationship. People who go to the States work hard to send money to their families in Cuba. They keep in touch. They have a close relation in, I think, 90 percent of those families. Most Cubans keep in mind they have to help their families because of the economic situation, because of the economic crisis that started in the 1990s.[18]

Regardless of family form, Cuban family members are still very close. So, when members leave, they still care about each other. The people that remain in Cuba feel a lot of anguish because their loved ones have gone somewhere else. They would like to be together somewhere.

The Role of Women

Katia de Llano Cuesta writes that prerevolutionary Cuba addressed freer roles for Cuban women. In 1917, the law concerning the right of parents was passed. In 1918, women were granted the right to divorce. In 1934, women were enfranchised. The 1940 constitution acknowledged the equality of all citizens regardless of race, class or sex. In addition, the 1940 constitution gave married women the rights to administer their own property, freely engage in trade, in industry, in a profession or the arts and make use of all profits derived from their work without spousal license or consent. The 1940 constitution regulated the maternity rights for working women. In 1952, the 1940 constitution was abolished when Batista took control. De Llano Cuesta writes,

> Women joined with men in the revolutionary groups of different organizations during the 1952–1958 period. A platoon of women soldiers was organized in the Sierra Maestra Mountains as part of the Rebel Army. In the cities, they participated in the 26th of July Movement and the March 13th Revolutionary Directory. They also formed their own groups. The best known of them was The Civic Front of Women."[19]

Social changes accelerated by the revolution changed and expanded women's lives and responsibilities. Access to birth control provided women with new sexual freedom. Yet, women's roles pertaining to home and family remained important. The greater mobility and use of contraception and abortion "reflected a continuing concession to male prerogative and a profound social ambivalence about women's sexual lives."[20]

The role confusion has contributed to social problems that are incompatible with the goals of the revolution. The revolution as a watchdog of Cuban morality has pursued social problems, such as prostitution, that the Catholic Church could not or did not try to eliminate. The revolution and the church have some common views of sexuality. Monogamous heterosexuality within the bounds of matrimony is favored. Reproduction is an essential part of sexuality. A hostility toward homosexuality exists. The Cuban state differs with the church in that both men and women should enjoy their sexuality. It also holds that even though male sexuality is more "sensation-oriented," men are urged to incorporate "emotion and contemplation of familial stability into their sexual life. Men should consider the sexual needs of their partner, exercise self-restraint, and forego their traditional multiple conquest prerogative."[21] Lois M. Smith concludes that it will take time to see whether this education will stabilize social society as well as shape sexual behavior.

With the overall decrease in machismo and chivalry, women gained more equality. This gain positively affected families. The government's effort to give women equality resulted in the Family Code, passed on March 8, 1975. The code saw both men and women equally responsible for household tasks and for the rearing of children.[22] The code views the family as a continuation of the socialist society. It addresses marriage, divorce, marital property relations, rights of children, adoption and sharing of domestic responsibilities.[23] Scholars dispute to what degree the Family Code has led to a division of labor and responsibility for children. The economic crisis of the 1990s reinforced traditional gender divisions of labor.[24]

The laws favored the integration of women into public and private life. Socialist family theory also supports the equality of men, women and children. However, practice has lagged behind the laws that integrated women into public and private life.[25] Pearson suggests women are overrepresented in the unemployed labor force and says women over 40 years of age are leaving their formal jobs for the informal sector. Reasons include the economy's problems, their job no longer exits, lack of transportation, or household needs dictate they remain at home.[26] The 1980s brought higher divorce rates, juvenile delinquency, double standards and gendered division of labor in the home, more single mothers and teenage pregnancy.[27]

The 1975 Family Code is generally viewed as "a station along the steady Cuban march toward women's equality." Some scholars maintain that, in reality, the Family Code also signified "a return to the notion of the family as a major arena of child socialization, which had dissipated in the first decade of the revolution." More importantly, the code attempted "to prescribe a particular concept of the family — the nuclear family — that was and is, it could be argued *not* the dominant family type in Cuba."[28]

The Extended Family

The extended family remains strong, but the reasons why have changed. The housing shortage is a significant reason extended families live together. Also in 2000, the Cultural Orientation Resource Center maintained that the nature of the extended family is changing. The "traditional family pattern in which children are almost totally cared for by parents or grandparents has been substantially replaced by a reliance on day care centers and other public institutions. The community (neighborhood, church, school and production cooperative) also serves as something of an extended family, helping to reinforce social values and emotional security."[29]

Uriarte writes that most children are born into families that have several generations living in the home. Since day care is not available for all children yet and because both parents work, grandparents are important in family life.[30]

The government provides day care to enable women to work outside the home. The state also uses it as a way to start education in socialist values early. In the beginning, two types of centers existed, alternative and mainstream. The Cultural Orientation Resource Center in Washington, D.C., describes these two types: "The alternative centers (based on the Swedish model) emphasized free play, inter-age groupings, flexibility, and exploration, and the mainstream centers focused on cleanliness, structured learning, achievement, and fixed schedules. In 1971, all programs were centralized and only the mainstream approach was continued. Centers emphasize group play, and children are overtly taught that they should be part of a group. One observer has found that day care centers try to break down sexist attitudes: Boys play with dolls or pretend to be nurses, while girls pretend to be the household providers or doctors."[31]

The Kinds of Cuban Families

Dr. Luis Enrique Vidal Palmer, professor and vice director of the Havana Psychiatric Hospital has these observations of the family in Cuba.

The typical Cuban family is not a nuclear family, it is an extended family where several generations are present. There are important generational differences that provoke conflict with the roles, problems with
cohabitation related to the houses, material and economic needs, which
produce dysfunctional families. There are few studies focused on the
family, the latest one reports that 79 percent of family relationships are
harmonious and that only 5 percent are hostile; this statistic changes in
favor of the hostile when the family has in its midst patients predominantly neurotic.[32]

The number of children in a nuclear family "varies depending on the
zone where the family lives. At present, the urban family has an average
of two children and the rural family has between three and five. These
numbers are the product of my observations."[33]

Regarding consensual unions, marriage and divorce, Dr. Vidal Palmer
notes that "it is very common to see couples that live together without
being married, and that [married] couples are formed at a very early age,
without the adequate maturity, which causes the rupture of these unions.
Housing availability provokes divisions, loss of affectionate values and in
some occasions divorce because of the conflicts with the roles."[34]

We asked, "Have you seen any changes in how your society defines
family, father, mother? If so, what have those changes been?" Dr. Vidal
Palmer replied, "The most noticeable change is related to the women's
emancipation, in the couples where both are equal, the men take part in
the household tasks such as direct care of the children, the kitchen, the
cleaning, the shopping, tasks that used to be solely for women."[35]

We also asked, "What have been the effects on men of the changes in
definitions? On women? On children?" He said,

> In a general sense, I don't think that there are great effects in the cou-
> ples where these changes occur, these happen by mutual consent and are
> the result of the love of the couple and the family, as well as being the
> leaving to one side the selfishness. Even though there are still some that
> maintain the taboos and are resistant to the change, fortunately they are
> the fewer.[36]

Because of the emigration of Cuban citizens to the United States, we
asked, "What effects do you see on the families in your country that are
separated due to emigration? How do they cope?" He replied,

> Migration during these years has an economic character and the major-
> ity of the families that are living [in] this situation have agreed to it pre-
> viously as a way to the solution to their economic needs, so from my
> point of view they gladly substitute affection for money and so they are

able to adapt in a very incredible manner to the absence of the mothers, fathers, or brothers, if these are covering in the distance their comfort and satisfy their pleasures which (for reasons not part of this interview) can't be satisfied by those that remain on this side by their own means; I would go so far as to say that for some it has become a way of life. It is undoubted that migration generates anxiety within the family; there is a significant difference between the migrations of the '60s and those of the '80s. In the first, the differences were political and in many cases it produced total rupture with the families because of ideological differences; fortunately these now are of economic nature and the differences have been overcome.[37]

Despite government policy and family stresses, Delvis Fernández Levy, president, Cuban American Alliance Education Fund, Inc., explains that the extended family is important to Cubans.

In the idealized situation, most Cubans tend to place a great importance on the extended family in which, compared to the U.S., grandparents, aunts and uncles seem to play a more active role with the children. Part of it is due to the small town or small country living. Within Cuba there is not the mobility that you find in a large country like the United States, where somebody might be from the east coast and move to the west coast, making it more difficult to have interaction with the extended family. That is one issue. Another one is the willingness to have the grandparents play a parental role where the children might live for long periods of time with grandparents. The grandparents might even assume financial responsibilities. It seems more common in Cuba than it is in the U.S. Also, there is more interaction with neighbors, especially in the provinces. Cubans tend to be more outgoing. Also, the neighbors seem to play a role in that overly extended family. Perhaps they will watch over a child that is going to school. There are more frequent visits between neighbors than you find in the United States. That might be, again I am generalizing, due to economic circumstances. People that are richer might live more in fenced houses and have more of a private family unit than you would find among people of a lower economic position.[38]

Alex speaks frankly about living together in the family unit in Cuba.

I am working in Havana so I don't live with my family. I live alone here because I'm working here, but I am from Havana Province which is 60 kilometers from Havana City. It used to be part of Havana until 1878 when the Spanish divided the country. After the division, in 1976 it was put in another province. My hometown is kind of a small town, 40,000 inhabitants. My parents live there. My parents live together with my grandmother. One of my grandmothers died. My two grandfathers both died, my mother's side and my father's side. I have a sister. She is married but she lives in another house. Our family gets along pretty well. Both of my parents are retired. They get a retirement, they get money because of that. My sister also sends money to my parents although she lives nearby. She goes there from time to time. When I make money, I send money to them because in that way they can keep their way of life. My sister who is married has a daughter and a boy. The girl is seven years old and the boy is eleven years old. Where I live, next to my home in town, I have a cousin. She lives there with her husband and a boy who is five years old. My grandmother used to live next to them, but she moved out to another part because she didn't have any house. The measurements of this other house was not enough so they had to move out to the land and they have a new house there. I have a cousin in town too. So we get along pretty well. In a family, as a rule, people get along pretty well. Some families have problems. As a rule, my family gets along pretty well.[39]

If you live with your parents and your relatives so there is a close relationship within the family ... people get along pretty well. Sometimes, problems exist all over the world that, normally, people help each other a lot. For example, if I make more money than my sister, I help her with money. So, sometimes, when you don't live with parents — I am working now and they are older — so you send them money to improve their standard of living. Especially now, we have a crisis after the collapsing of the former socialist countries. So, that's the way people help each other a lot.[40]

The extended family may be under stress, but in all of the interviews that I conducted, Cubans and Cuban Americans place a great deal of importance on it. They have a lot of affection for their extended family. In the case of Cuban Americans during the time they lived in Cuba, they were often helped by family members. Now that they are in the United States, they are being helped by another part of that same extended family.

Comments from our interviews revealed that the extended family often provided housing, love and support and child care. Asley L. Marmol speaks of his love for his extended family. He also has many fond memories of customs celebrated in Cuba and continued here in the United States. On the other hand, lack of privacy in Cuba presents issues of concern. He explains, "The economic conditions in Cuba affect the relationship within a marriage. The social and economic conditions such as the lack of space for a place to live ... make violence take place easier than in a society where you have your own space, your own possibilities, your own economy."[41]

Leonardo Marmol Ph.D., ABPP, professor and chairman of the Department of Graduate Psychology at Seattle Pacific University, lived in Cuba as a child with his extended family:

I was born in Havana and grew up in different urban areas of Havana. My parents are both teachers. My father was an elementary school teacher and he was an educator. He had a degree of pedagogy, an education degree. My mother was home economics teacher, taught the girls sewing and cooking, that kind of thing. I grew up in that kind of environment. My grandfather on my mother's side was also a teacher. My grandfather on my father's side was a bookkeeper, a general business type person. He lived in the westernmost province of Pinar del Rio with a tobacco growing company in a small town called San Luis. I used to spend summer vacations and Christmas vacation there with a large extended family. My father had three siblings. I had two uncles and one aunt and their extended children, have a zillion cousins.[42]

Conclusions

Although the "Special Period" has put stress on the family, we see the extended family remaining strong. Some extended families live in the same house due to the housing shortage. Traditionally, extended families take care of the children. Day care centers such as the church, school and production cooperative also help replace the child care role of extended families. Cubans, whether they reside on the island or in the United States, maintain strong family ties.

Cuban Family Rights and Forms

by Rosemarie Skaine and James C. Skaine

> *In Cuba, issues of social concern are prioritized within the struc-*
> *ture of the political system. This is evident in various projects*
> *directed toward different sectors of society — children, youth,*
> *women, seniors, and the disabled.*
> — The Cuban American Alliance Education, Fund[1]

The XII International Congress on Family Law of September 2002 in Havana, Cuba, had a formidable agenda. From an interdisciplinary perspective, the Congress sought to address the challenges that face the family. The family stands before an accelerated development that will impact its members. The advance of the globalization process and the communicative technologies, the challenges of AIDS, the increase in poverty, to name a few examples, influence the family of today.[2]

Cuba has many laws that address the rights of the family, the foremost being the Constitution of the Republic of Cuba of 1976 and the Family Code of 1975. These two regulations have not only been amended down through time, but appropriate legislative bodies and scholars yet today, as occurred at the XII Congress, are making recommendations for improvements.[3] The reporters for the Congress's closing session, as well as many of the authors of professional papers, recommended improvements in the existing law.

Yet, the current laws and recommendations for change have to be understood in the context of a socialist government. This concept is expressed well in the Constitution's Preamble. In part it reads,

> GUIDED
> by the ideas of José Martí and the political and social ideas of Marx,
> Engels and Lenin; ...

WE DECLARE
our will that the law of laws of the Republic be guided by the following
strong desire of José Martí, at least achieved:
> "I want the fundamental law of our republic to be the tribute of
> Cubans to the full dignity of man...."[4]

The Constitution of the Republic of Cuba

The National Assembly of People's Power in 1992 approved reforms
for the Constitution of the Republic of Cuba originally proclaimed on
February 24, 1976. The Constitution contains provisions relating to marriage, dissolution of marriage, parent-child relations, filiation, equality
of the sexes, the right to health care, and the right to education. The Family Code of Cuba also speaks to these issues.[5]

The Constitution declares, "The state protects the family, motherhood and matrimony."[6] The family is recognized as the main nucleus of
society. It is responsible for the education and formation of new generations.

MARRIAGE, DISSOLUTION OF MARRIAGE, PARENT-CHILD RELATIONS

The Constitution governs the formalization, recognition and dissolution of marriage and the rights and obligations of each partner. A legally
fit man and a woman voluntarily establish a marriage in order to live
together. It is based on full equality of rights and duties for the partners
both within the home and in support of the home. Each partner is responsible for the education of their children.[7]

FILIATION (PATERNITY AND MATERNITY)

Establishing biological paternity in Cuba is legalized under civil law,
more specifically under its constitution. Civil law lacks the mechanism to
go beyond investigating paternity if the alleged father is not willing to
provide needed biological material.[8] Cuban authors at the Institute of
Legal Medicine in Havana write that the Constitution says, "The Cuban
State guarantees to every person the right to be recognized and protected
by their progenitors and the duty of the parents to satisfy the material and
affective needs of their children."[9]

Filiation conflicts can involve establishing maternity, but do not as often as paternity. Usually maternity is proved at the time of birth. The impetus for establishing paternity includes,

- The claim of one of the parents when the other one in their moment [time], denies the paternity according to the possibility that he/she has of doing it.
- The claim of the father who originally contested the paternity before the Record of the Civil State and later he tries to recognize the son [as his], but the mother does not give her assent.
- The claim of paternity when one tries to recognize later the child and the father who already [is] recognized does not give his assent in order that the same one is effected (carried out) in the Record.
- The claim of the child when he/she is already of age and has not been recognized by his/her parents or by one of them.[10]

In Cuba, subsidiary paternal relationships are legally recognized in the articles in the Constitution on the family, in the civil Code on the specially protected inheritors, in the code of the Childhood and the Youth, in the law on adoption and foster families, in the Law of Civil, Administrative and Labor Procedure, in the Family Code, and in the Law of the Civil Record of the inscription of birth.[11]

A study by Dr. Ruth Juarez Fontanet and her colleagues found that even though in the last ten years there has been an increase in requests for the Institute's Biological Investigative Report, the judicial system's decisions are often made without considering all of the scientific evidence. That forensic evidence could solve the conflict.[12]

Other Cuban authors who are attorneys agree the civil process system could be improved and make specific recommendations to the Cuban Legislature and to the Supreme Popular Court regarding the establishment of paternity and maternity. They conclude that the civil process should allow those in contention to object to expert decisions or to challenge the expert's qualifications; that a lapse of time should be established for requests of clarification of expert decisions; that establishment of paternity and maternity through the accuracy of biological DNA makes its admissibility unquestionable proof by the courts; that the legal process should offer sanctions to a presumed parent who refuses to participate in DNA testing; that genetic testing is based in the law and approved by the judicial system and the Constitution that children's rights are placed above the individual rights of the parent; that the courts' freedom of interpretation of legal tests does not correspond to the level of certainty and reliability of DNA testing; and that in Cuba, use of DNA testing is not a judicial practice "as a preparatory act during the presentation of merits in the process for contesting paternity."[13]

PARENT-CHILD RELATIONS

The Constitution outlines that parents are to protect and educate their children. They are to oversee their development "as useful and well-prepared citizens for life in a socialist society."[14] The duty of children, in turn, is to respect and help their parents.

EQUALITY OF ALL PEOPLE

The Constitution promotes equal rights and equal duties for all people. Discrimination because of race, skin color, sex, national origin, religious beliefs or any other form is prohibited and punishable by law. Discrimination is harmful to human dignity. The state institutions educate children in equality from the earliest possible age. Women are to have the same rights as men in economic, political, social and family areas. The state provides employment, paid maternity leave before and after birth, day care, and boarding schools.[15]

The Family Code of 1975

The objective of the Family Code of 1975 is to regulate the institutions of the family: marriage, divorce, paternal-filial relations, the obligation to provide food, adoption and guardianship, with objectives to contribute:

- to the strengthening of the family and the bonds of affection, mutual aid and respect among its members;
- to the strengthening of the legally formalized or judicially recognized marriage, founded on absolute equality of rights of man and woman;
- to the more effective fulfillment by parents of their obligations with respect to the protection, moral training and education of their children so that they are developed fully in all aspects and manner of worthy citizens of the socialist society;
- to the full realization of the principle of equality of all children.[16]

In 1975, The Family Code sought to correct the unequal burden for women who had to work both inside and outside of the home.[17]

THE FAMILY CODE AND EQUAL RIGHTS
OF MEN AND WOMEN

Several factors increased women's participation in the work force: a change to an urban industrial economy from an agrarian one, women's rising education level and lower fertility and the government's encouragement. In 1980, women's participation in the work force doubled to 26.7 percent and in 1990, the percentage again had risen to 34.8. Men's participation decreased only slightly from 78.8 percent in 1955 to 61.0 in 1980 and 67.8 percent in 1990.[18] The position of men in the work force remained relatively stable because of the gradual decline in agrarian work and increasing opportunities to work in the import substitution industry and sugar exports. Cuba's redistributive mechanisms reduced the need to rely on wages and purchasing power as key factors of standards of living, and made it easier for women to raise children on their own. Women's lack of dependence on men to earn the income resulted in more single female parent households.[19]

Women are not expected to stop working. They expect their children, boys and girls, to study and work to have better jobs than they have. Men's roles within the home have changed little, according to Helen I. Safa. Younger nuclear families idealize the concept expressed in the Family Code. They are independent from the extended family, their marriage is stable, they are better educated and hold technical or supervisory positions. Men not only accept but welcome their wives working. Added income is welcomed.[20]

The presentations at the XII International Congress on Family Law in Havana in 2002 provided spirited debate. A male Cuban presenter explained that male equality is another reason men accept and welcome women working. A delegate from another Latin American country asked whether, in Cuba, free men and single women had plurality. By plurality the questioner explained that he meant the right of a woman, when one relationship fails, to get into another. In his country, a study found that for a woman, plurality was a means of survival, because by herself she cannot survive. So, women get together with a man to make it in life.

The Cuban presenter responded that his answer was no. "In Cuba thanks to the [progress] made, the women have become fully independent human beings since 1959. Often times we men have the main economic responsibility as the husband. So, specifically, no, we men do not have to get into common law or de facto marriages to help women survive economically."[21]

Women who are faced with the dual burden of home and family do not look to their husbands, but to the state to provide services as mandated by the code.[22] One author writes, "Private patriarchy was replaced with public patriarchy, which the centralization of the state and services under socialism made all the more powerful."[23]

Family Life

The changing economic climate has affected many areas of Cuban family life. Sociopolitical factors, too, have changed the way families make their living and conduct their daily lives.

MARRIAGE

Marriage rates in Cuba have traditionally been irregular. In the 1980s and early 1990s, due to socioeconomic factors, marriage rates were high, 15.1 and 17.1 marriages per every 1,000 inhabitants. Women who were university educated or economically stable tended to elect stable relationships, but they also had fewer children.[24]

Consensual free relations and nonlegal marriages have been a part of Cuba's history and accepted by the rural and economically disadvantaged since the 19th century. One source offers the following statistical profile.

> [An informal relation of a married man with an unmarried woman occurs in the group of] very young women. Some 28 percent of women below 30 years old maintained that kind of relation in the late 1980's, while married women stood for only 23 percent in that period. Adolescent women (under 20 years) were reported at a higher figure, 21 percent against 7 percent of legal marriages. Bearing in mind the amount of fertile women (15–49 years), matrimony has prevailed at 35 percent in respect to non-legal marriages at 28 percent. However, concubinage [an informal relation of a married man with an unmarried woman] has increased over the past few years. A 1987 survey showed that 4 for every 5 legally married women had chosen this form of marital union.[25]

Alex, a young Cuban, reflects on family types and fluctuations in male-female relationships. We asked, how many children are there usually in a family? He replied, "Commonly? As Cuba has developed a lot in terms of education and some technology, so typically they will have one or two, but mainly two children, a boy and a girl."[26] We asked, "Do most Cubans, as a society, adhere to the institution of marriage or do they, like citizens in our own society, have more single parents? Do you see any trends as a citizen of Cuba?" Alex replied,

In Cuba, in the 1980s, some people would get married when they were 19 or 20 years old. Now, with the development, people are studying a lot, so women in Cuba have a lot of independence now because they make money, they work in good jobs and have some other opportunities, so, for some women, they don't have to accept the machismo or macho man a lot. So they have a kind of independence. From 1994, people are getting married when they are 30 or 35. Some people live together and are not married. They live together for a while. If everything works out, they get married. If not, they just split up their relationship.[27]

Historically and presently, the stigma of a failed marriage is not evident. Before 1959 common law marriages were common because people could not afford weddings. In the 1960s, the Cuban business people who could afford a ceremony fled the island to Miami, Florida. The coming of communism liberalized divorce laws as a forceful reaction to Catholicism.[28]

DIVORCE

In 2002, the Heritage Foundation released a study based on recent data from the United Nations and other sources. The foundation found that Cuba's divorce rate stood at 3.54 for 1,000 people.[29] Another study indicated, "An increasing tendency of the island's gross divorce rate has been observed over the last 30 years. In 1960, this indicator reported nearly one divorce per every 1000 inhabitants, while in 1990 it increased to 3.5, with variations during some periods, for example, during the 1980's when the indicator reported figures exceeding three divorces per 1000 inhabitants. Divorce rates reached 4.1 in 1991 and 5.1 in 1992."[30] In 1998, the divorce rate returned to the low 1990 rate of 3.5 percent.

In current divorce law, one parent is permitted to waive parental rights in favor of the other. Family law professionals have recommended that modifying Cuban divorce law may help protect the family unit. In 2002, in its closing session, the XII International Congress on Family Law recommended, "It is necessary to give a new concept to parental rights, by giving it a new content in terms of obligations and duties. Parental rights are not something that can be waived. Therefore, the divorce law in Cuba should be modified because it allows for a parent to waive his or her parental rights in favor of the other."[31]

ABORTION

Newsday reporter Ron Howell has observed,

Cuba's families, to me, seem different from those of other Latin American countries, in the sense that they are perhaps more modern in their attitude toward certain things. In this way, again, they show a kindred spirit with their counterparts in the U.S.A. One important issue that comes to mind is that of abortion and birth control. The attitudes toward both are very liberal in Cuba. That has helped to keep family sizes relatively small and, I guess you could argue, has even helped make them cohesive. There is a sort of 1960's U.S.-style aspect to many Cuban relationships, in that they often appear open and unencumbered by the Catholic conventions of the rest of the Spanish-speaking region. Folks pair up and live together. Divorce is very much an accepted fact of life. And, unlike anywhere else in Latin America, abortion is available for unwanted pregnancies. Contrary to the impression some may have — that Cuba and the Catholic Church are drawing closer — the bishops of Latin America must still see Cuba as a version of the End of Days, a place where authorities give a stamp of approval to acts seen by the Church as most evil.[32]

ONE-PARENT FAMILIES

The support of the state and extended families gave impetus to single motherhood. The state gives no special privileges to this status, but does provide services for their children.[33] Some scholars point out that while single mothers are an emerging concern for the state, they are not an emerging phenomenon.[34]

In 1992, Marguerite G. Rosenthal found trends in single motherhood difficult to discern, but there was an increase in single mothers. Single mothers in her study did not include widows, but those who were separated, divorced, deserted and never married. The birth rate had declined and the divorce rate was high, impacting about 50 percent of all marriages in 1987. Since remarriage and recoupling were common, divorce rates reflected a minority of Cuba's population as divorced. Couples under 20 years of age were more likely to divorce, as were couples in urban areas. Estimates of single parents were at 200,000. Rosenthal concludes, "It seems safe to say that virtually all single parents are single mothers and that a large percentage of divorced and separated women are mothers; at least 10 percent — and more likely between 15 and 20 percent — of households with children are headed by women alone."[35]

Cuban authors have concluded that the one-parent family began in the ancient classical societies as accidental. This family form gave rise to a plurality of family types. Lic. Consuelo León Valle and Lic. Samuel Morales Castro believe there is no one model of the one-parent family. They also demonstrate that the change did not occur due to education or gender alone. One-parent families are not only "the result of changes brought about through education, or the particular gender of the responsible individual, they represent differences with respect to its economic status, ethnicity, and culture; and not only within each other, but also with respect to traditional families."[36]

The state's interest in women's participation in the Communist Party supercedes its interest in gender equality. Another result is that, although women are committed to work, they see their primary role as a mother. Thus, women discriminate against themselves in this way. But women also do not have the same opportunity as men to advance in the work force, nor do they have the support services to do the work they are allowed to do. In labor's need to cut costs and in men's resistance to incorporate women into higher working positions, women receive lower priority in housing than men. Single mothers, in particular, end up living with relatives. Fewer women with young children are on fixed shifts and therefore have difficulty in the area of child care. Women are undervalued in the work place in comparison to men.[37]

The Cuban government supports women being economically independent, but dislikes the results of more divorce, more teenage pregnancy and more female-headed households. The Family Code gave shared responsibility in the home, but it is also aimed at strengthening the family and helping the state.[38] In 1992 Rosenthal wrote that teenaged mothers accounted for one-third of births. When teen unwed mothers give birth, they challenge the state's official model — the two-parent nuclear family. Reasons for teen pregnancy center around the clash of traditional and newer social and sexual values, a lack of opportunity to occupy the preferred work roles and social participation and a support burden of the state. Most teen mothers have been deserted by the fathers of their children.[39]

Rosenthal concludes that single mothers face all of the same challenges as other women in Cuba but under harsher conditions. They are likely to be young and economically distressed. Because they are young, they are at an educational disadvantage and may have difficulty getting child care. Many have support from their extended families, therefore, do not have to face these difficulties alone. In their favor is the state's system of provision of basic support for food, housing, health care, and education. Not in their favor is the state's ideal of the nuclear family consisting of mutually supportive spouses sharing in familial responsibilities.[40]

CHILDREN OF SINGLE PARENTS

The Constitution protects children by abolishing illegitimacy of children — all children were declared to have the same rights regardless of being born in or out of wedlock.[41] In 1985, the *Gaceta Oficial de la República de Cuba* formulated the organization and functions of the Civil Registry in Cuba. Births, deaths, marriages, acquisition, reacquisition, loss of citizenship or any other circumstance that affects an individual's civil status are recorded in the registry as are pertinent documents. No distinctions between illegitimate births are to be made in the registry. Procedures are also included for persons named as parents to challenge birth entries and for appeals.[42]

León Valle and Morales Castro write that perhaps their study on one-parent families can appear ambitious because it is based on a questionnaire given at a Popular Council, a social-legal analysis, legal framework and the present trends and predictions. Yet, they believe that their partial results, when integrated, reveal the normal development of the one-parent family and its influence in modern society. Thus, the survey of the Popular Council Free Cuba of the municipality of Pinar del Río serves as one source to reach their results. The authors surveyed 54 heads of households. Their survey revealed 55.5 percent were single mothers, 25.16 were married, 11.1, divorced and 7.4, couples who lived together.[43]

They conclude that children will grow up following the traditions of their childhood family form. As an adult, the child reproduces this family form. In addition, due to society's more liberal thinking, individuals born into traditional families may also elect to have the one-parent family form.[44]

Legislation has not kept pace with the unprecedented worldwide presence of the one-parent family. León Valle and Morales Castro conclude, "In our country, even though this type of family is afforded legal protection, it is done in a general manner, through different legal channels; without the existence of specificity that it should have, nor is it mentioned in our Law of Laws."[45] Among the authors' recommendations are: more multidisciplinary study to understand the true conditions of the one-parent family; that the Constitution acknowledge one-parent families by providing special protection through its different legal bodies, so that the one-parent family's protection is equal to that of the nuclear (traditional) family; these family types should have those benefits related to the right to work, for example, in social security, equal benefits should be given to the widows and the widower alike; and offer special attention to children of one-parent families who may upon occasion exhibit unacceptable societal behavior that could lead to delinquency.[46]

The government is concerned about the economic well-being of one-parent families. During the Special Period crisis, women raising their children alone in Marianao had only social assistance. The Municipal

Directorate of Work, Social Assistance and Social Security, the Popular Council, the Federation of Cuban Women, and the neighborhood community development organization identified the needs of these families. Some of the mothers were trained in interviewing techniques and sent to interview other mothers. The interview results of 29 mothers receiving social assistance were as follows.

> [A]ll had children between ages 0 and 16; only 26 percent received support from the children's fathers, with half reporting very little support from [the] other family. Most lived in very precarious housing. Most women had worked, but not in stable jobs; most were willing to work if child care was provided. Together, the different institutions set out to provide some relief. Eight mothers were found jobs, most of them providing services to elders in the area. Three were referred for appropriate medical care, and three were placed in courses to prepare them for work.[47]

PROTECTION OF MINORS

Lic. Rosario Marquetti Perez and Lic. Lidice Crespo Sosa, Cuban jurists, presented a paper on legal protection of minors without shelter. They mention there are important international precedents for legal protection of minors, the Declaration of the Rights of the Child of 1924, the United Nations Declaration of the Rights of the Child in 1959, the United Nations Universal Declaration of Human Rights of 1948 and United Nations Convention on the Rights of the Child in 1990.[48]

Perez and Sosa write that care of abandoned orphans in Cuba goes back to 1687 when the "House of Abandoned" was founded. Later, the House was neglected. In 1705 new management named it "Foundling House," but this House also fell into disrepair. Other facilities were built early in Cuba's history. Before the revolution the children were taken care of in the famous "House of Charity," but protection was not guaranteed and conditions were not good. The revolution brought the beginning of new laws and norms to protect children and youth. In 1959, the Ministry of Social Welfare was created and houses became state property. It was then the obligation of the state to provide for minors in need.[49]

In 1960, the government assigned the Federation of Cuban Women to create institutions for the education of children. The new conception for the homes was the obligation of the socialist state to guarantee the education of the new generation. In addition to the homes there were four types of centers classified by age, 0 to 3, homes with cradles; 3 to 6, prescholastic farms; 6 to 12, scholastic farms and 12 to 18, youthful farms.

Internal day care centers also began with the purpose of assisting children 0 to 6 whose parents could not fulfill their paternal role. In 1970 the Institute of Childhood unified the direction of day care centers and institutions related to children so that they would receive early and prescholastic education.[50]

The law continued to be refined. In Cuba the Family Code of 1975 regulates marriage and spousal relationships. The Constitution also clarifies the state's role of protection as does the Code of the Childhood and the Youth, approved in 1978, the Code of Family. The Decree Law 76 of January 1984 complements the code by creating a national network of centers to take care of minors without shelter. The centers were to be like a home until children placed there were adopted or became of age. The centers consist of mixed day care centers (0–5 years) and the homes of abandoned minors (6–17). Mixed day care centers are open to workers' children up to 5 years old during the labor schedule as well as to children without shelter. These two care centers are supported by collective family substitutes and houses. Care in either facility ceases with adoption or formation of a trusteeship. In the case of homes of minors, children are also released when they reach labor age (17), are not studying or have completed their studies, marry or become active in the military.[51]

In Cuba a qualified substitute family is an institution under certain conditions, mainly the ability to provide care both in the terms of economics and affection. These families take care of minors on weekends, vacations and other periods. The minors coexist with the substitute family and the people at the institutions.[52]

ADOPTION

Perez and Sosa say that the welfare network they described cannot replace "the life of the natural and common home ... the attention by the State to the abandoned or abandoned minor, still with the support complementary of the families substitutes is not sufficient."[53] The Family Code supplemented by Decree Law 76 of 1984 eliminates legal differences between blood related children and adopted children. Some children must remain institutionalized, for example, children of physically or mentally disabled parents. Others must remain for an adaptation period of six months to a year with their future parents in order for adoption to be considered. Perez and Sosa say that adoption is one of three ways to enter a family (the other two being marriage and procreation). Because adoption is an irreversible judicial process, the period of pre-adoptive adaptation is beneficial to the minor.[54]

M.Sc. Irma Renee Fernández Guerra and M.Sc. Luís Palenzuela Paéz, Cuban jurists, presented a paper on adoption at the XII International Congress that shows how legislative changes pertinent to adoption reflect the social and democratic movements. Private and contract adoption seen to make children available to childless families is giving way to social adoption with the purpose of the satisfying the adopted child's interests. The law interprets adoption as: simple, complete, complete or semi-complete, adoption legitimization, privileged, or relinquishing of parental rights. Adoption's purpose through a judicial process is to incorporate the minor into the adopting family. The authors address another very important aspect of adoption: the international adoption.[55]

The Family Code of 1975 makes adoption legal as a way to protect minors. Childhood development is a priority in Cuba by the state, society and community. The adopting parent(s) must be 25 years old, economically capable, "in complete exercise of his civil and political rights," morally sound and have conduct that demonstrates he or she can fulfill the parental obligations of Article 85.[56] (See Appendix 2.)

In addition to the Code, Law Decree 76 of 1984 provides for institutions to assist children without parental support. The Department of Education directs this help through centers where a child can have a good home until their legal status is decided, for example, adoption, foster home placement or reaching legal age.[57]

The prevailing type of adoption in Cuba is the complete adoption. Complete adoption severs all ties with the adopted child's biological family. In the adoptive family, the child has the same rights and responsibilities as biological children. Relatives and descendants of the adoptive family are looked upon the same as those extended family members who are biological. Legally, adopted children are to be viewed as biological children.[58]

Simple adoption or semi-complete provides that the adopting parents are guardians. The adopted child stays in contact with the biological family and keeps all natural rights of that family. The adoptive parents have no right to inherit from the adopted child nor does the child have the right to inherit from the adoptive parents unless those rights are stated in adoption documents. Some Cuban jurists hold that classical or simple adoption used in some countries could produce a "discriminatory status" for the adopted child. On the other hand, having both types of adoption provides the opportunity to deal with social problems.[59]

International adoption is not prohibited. The option for international adoption should be kept as an alternative, but regulation is needed by all countries. Although Fernández Guerra and Palenzuela Paéz are not opposed to international adoption of Cuban children, they believe civic duty demands that minors should remain and be able to grow up in Cuba. Their concern for Cuba's children is based on "painful" activities in the second half of the 20th century when many parents lost their children and do not to this day know where or how they are. Fourteen thousand Cuban children were taken to live in the United States. Campaigns and propaganda about the revolution led Cuban families to think that by sending their children to the U.S., they would be safe. In reality the children were placed in orphanages or emergency centers for minors. Some were adopted by North American parents and thus became a legal part of a new family. This emigration is known as Operation Peter Pan. Fernández Guerra and Palenzuela Paéz point out that these activities were not in keeping with National Cuban Law, International Private Law and the United Nations Declaration of Rights of Children of 1959. More recently, Somalia and the United States are the only two countries that have not ratified the 1990 U.N. Convention on the Rights of Children.[60]

Because of these laws and Cuban law, the social programs in place in Cuba are in the best interest of children, provided that they remain in the country to take full advantage. Cuba is also concerned with the country's current economic crisis that prohibits them from following up on international adoptions to see that they are beneficial to children, and to ensure that children are not trafficked for their vital organs. Emigration of children for satisfaction of material and spiritual needs is unnecessary because of Cuba's programs in place.[61]

Consensual Unions

The consensual union between a man and a woman is a reality and a product of a natural impulse. Historically, these unions are as old as the marriages originating in old Rome, but have lacked legal character. In Roman times, the unions were not punished by law or censured by social conscience. Germanic law also accepted unions legally and socially. Down through time, descendants of these unions were discriminated against until social values produced laws that recognize them as legitimate. The taboos that remain and the controversy that surrounds consensual unions led Cuban author Lic. Xóchitl Aguirre Tamayo to analyze consensual unions in Cuba, historically to the present time.[62]

Under old Spanish law unions took the name concubinage. Laws begin to consider it a mortal sin and declared a concubine must be single. The Spaniards wished to protect the Catholic religious marriage. Cuba moved forward in recognizing unions with the Constitution of 1940. The

Constitution recognized unions through a married comparison, but it was limited by old social morality, classist principles and in part, the Spanish law.[63]

The laws of the new socialist regime after the revolution established the equality of children and ended the discriminations toward women. Free unions are legal but are not totally accepted.[64]

From 1961 to 1967, marriages decreased on the average of 3,635 unions each year. The Ministry of Justice carried out a campaign called "Operation Family" to legalize consensual unions, and laws were passed. In 1976, modifications in the Family Code legalized the recognition of unions. Marriage remains the most important institution for family and society.[65]

Lic. Xóchitl Aguirre Tamayo writes that marriage in Cuban society is the primary link of formation and support of family. However, formalization of marriages has decreased. In 1999, formal marriages numbered 40,710, compared to 39,220 in 2001. He says, "To the closing of the year 2000 the gross rate of marriage was of 5.1 per million inhabitants. Nevertheless, the importance that comes from gaining the consensual unions is not despicable if we are told in addition that from 1987 for every 5 women who live in pair, at least 4 exist united without interval of the law, which is not anything rare nor escapes to the new tendencies worldwide."[66]

Consensual unions in Cuba are, in part, a product of urban expression of the intellectual class that has a freer life than the religious sector. Sixty-eight and a half percent of children are born of consensual unions. Although the law does not discriminate between children born inside or outside of marriage, Aguirre Tamayo writes that having children outside of marriage can bring difficulties in the family and in society.

Aguirre Tamayo writes that the law strikes a note of ambivalence as it addresses the reality of numerous consensual unions of historical permanence in Cuba and the intention of the legal system to place them at the same level as formalized marriage, considered the preferable family form. The author concludes that Article 18 of the Family Code *"will have all the desired effects of the formalized marriage legally when it is recognized by a competent court."*[67] Article 18 can be established under two conditions. The first is when one of the spouses dies without having produced the formalization of marriage and the heirs of the deceased promote the recognition request. The second is when one of the spouses refuses formalization, without breaking the union. In these cases, the recognition will have to be promoted by the other spouse. If the union is not singular (one of the spouses is married to another person), desired legal effects will be in favor of the spouse who acted in good faith. The court promotes the recognition.[68]

Aguirre Tamayo writes that good faith is nowadays widely discussed. A person who is already married and enters a consensual union does so illegally. Thus, the family budget can be used by only one of the interested parties. So, good faith is closely related to singularity of bonds. The spouse who knows he is already married is counterproductive because he knows that the relationship lacks the requirements that are built on good faith.[69]

To legalize a relationship of one man and one woman in singular form (no formalized marriage to a third person), the spouses declare the union in front of witnesses. This formalizes or gives judicial recognition to the Cuban marriage, "because it gives the possibility of formalizing marriage with retroactive character at the time of initiating the consensual action."[70] The positive element most certainly offers stability in a lasting relationship, including support and education of resulting children.[71]

Aguirre Tamayo explains that the married union in Cuba is like the formalized marriage. The members must be of different sexes. Homosexual unions cannot be legalized as the foundation of the family. Nor are they considered suitable socialization for children brought into the union whether by adoption, birth or assisted reproduction. Both genders must keep their identity within a family so that the two parent family is one that is complementary.[72]

Dr. Olga Mesa emphasizes that certain effects of the judicial recognition of nonformalized marriage are equal to formalized marriages. These effects protect the survivor's rights in case of death, such as pensions and community property and with the rights of the children.[73]

If an innocent woman is in a putative married union, unlike the widow, she is considered a beneficiary. If one is in coincidently married unions, then both the married woman and the woman in the union are treated as beneficiaries. Sometimes absolute identity is arrived at through legal requirements.[74]

In October 1996, a project of modification of the Family Code provided recommendations that reflected the new political and social realities of types of family form.[75]

THE HOMELESS

Even though Cuba's elaborate welfare system is strained from economic crisis, few children live in the streets. The commercialism introduced during the Special Period (the economic crisis of the 1990s) gave rise to the tourism industry. This change created markets for illicit street life such as young female and male prostitution. More children beg from tourists or hawk merchandise or services. But children are not homeless unless they are unable to take advantage of the welfare and educational system, are orphaned or abandoned. In 2000, research on children in the streets was limited. One study "counted about 40 street children per week in the tourist sections of Old Havana, and about 20 identified in other areas of the city."[76]

The state has growing concerns about life in the streets of Cuba. The state's primary concern is not over increased prostitution, but the growing number of children in the streets. Three problems emerged: begging, working and sexual activity. Tourism, parents and schools were targeted causes. Sheryl L. Lutjens concludes that Cuba did not ignore the circumstances of children and the family in the 1990s. The Special Period has called for reforms. Unpredictable weather, the U.S. embargo and the outcome of the reforms affect Cuban choices.[77] New groups and new inequalities challenge the Cuban policies that prevail, "social justice in general, and child welfare in particular." As for children of the streets, "the state has not resurrected the repressive treatment typical of its capitalist past, nor lessened its commitment to education as the key to the futures of Cuban children."[78]

DOMESTIC VIOLENCE

The United Nations has criticized the United States' embargo for its effects on human rights in Cuba. In 2000, Radhika Coomaraswamy, a United Nations expert on violence against women, criticized the United States' sanctions as having "a significant impact on the social and economic situation of Cuban women."[79] She said the embargo results in a lack of medicines and promotes hardships in the home which could lead to domestic violence.

Asley L. Marmol, who emigrated to the United States in May 2001, believes that the economic conditions in Cuba affect the relationship within a marriage. He says that the social and economic conditions such as the lack of living space make violence more likely than in a society like the United States, "where you have your own space, your own possibilities, your own economy. You can plan your life. You can take your life as far as you wish if you are capable enough. If you don't want to go that far, you can live in a different way. That has made us more responsible people. I think that is very positive. We have learned a lot from this society."[80]

Social and economic conditions have an effect on domestic tranquility. But in spite of the effects of societal conditions, multidisciplinary studies since the late 1980s conducted by the Minister of Justice, Attorney General's Office and the Federation of Cuban Women along with other institutions demonstrate that there is a low incidence of domestic violence in Cuba. The studies also show that "among the key causes of family violence in Cuba is the continued existence of patriarchal family laws."[81]

Conclusions

Cuba's socialist government is wrestling with many of the same challenges to family life as the rest of the world. Family form is not consistent and is in a state of flux. Perhaps the Cuban American Alliance Education Fund's report described the country's emphasis best. Social concerns are prioritized within the structure of the political system and directed toward different sectors of society —children, youth, women, seniors, and the disabled. The legal emphasis on equality of men and women and of children and the obligation of parents to provide for their children is basic to a better life for the families in Cuba.

Politics, Emigration and Families

*I am that old tired woman nearly blind who must
hide like a criminal and circumvent U.S. laws in
order to nourish with love the daughters and
grandchildren left in Cuba.*

I am the rafter who risks life and limb in open seas to
come to the "Promised Land", but once there, must
break ties with loved ones back in his land of birth.

*I am that exile, who from the "Land of Liberty" is
not allowed to send assistance to the family that
nurtured him with love.*

I am the child trapped in my adult self traumatized and
torn from a loving home by a cruel campaign against
my family under the innocent name of "Peter Pan."

*I am that old man with calloused hands, who after
years of daily toil for his United Fruit Company
bosses, dies without ever receiving a cent from his
usurped retirement pension.*

— Delvis Fernández Levy[1]

Dr. Delvis Fernández Levy, president of the Cuban American Alliance
Education Fund, knows much about the healing process Cuban families
must go through and the need for understanding of future generations.
The relaxing of some of the standards set by law and doing away with
some others are parts of that healing process. He says,

> The first step towards healing is the recognition that there is pain, that
> there is pain on both sides. There needs to be availability of movement,
> that is, that you on one side can move to the other to engage and start
> a conversation. Right now, there are laws in the book that prevent Cubans
> with families in Cuba from going back there, unless there is a family

75

emergency. That certainly is not encouraging to any healing process. Secondly, the restrictions placed on family remittances also are not encouraging to building a healthy family unit. We need to start from the legislation in lifting all the restrictions or all the impediments to normal human engagement.[2]

There are close to twelve million Cubans on the island. Here in the United States, there are between one and two million Cubans. The majority of the Cubans in the United States are undergoing the process of assimilation into American society.[3] The U.S. has laws that affect Cuban families beginning with the Embargo of 1959. The sanctions were made stronger with the Cuban Democracy Act (CDA) and the Cuban Liberty and Democratic Solidarity Act or Helms-Burton legislation of 1996. On the other hand, U.S. policy supports the Cuban people through private humanitarian donations and U.S.-sponsored radio and television broadcasting to Cuba. Even though President George W. Bush announced new measures to reach out to the Cuban people, he has rejected loosening the embargo.[4]

U.S. policy appears to have as its goal to help bring democracy and human rights to Cuba. Opinion differs on how the goal should be accomplished. Some believe pressure should be kept on the government, but support helping the Cuban people. A second group believes in lifting the sanctions that hurt the Cuban people and to work toward more dialogue with the government. Others believe in lifting the embargo to normalize relations. Policy debate has recently centered on whether to keep restrictions on food and medical exports and on travel to Cuba. Legislative efforts in the 107th Congress reflect these three views.[5] The goal of this chapter is to examine U.S. law and policy and its effects on the Cuban family.

U.S. Law

Delvis Fernández Levy gives specific examples of how the power of the United States influences Cuban society. The impact of the U.S. is perhaps more tremendous than that of the Cuban government itself, on families, both in Cuba and the United States.[6] Fernández Levy explains,

> First of all, we have a law called the Cuban Adjustment Act that has been in effect since 1966. It is part of a policy that originally was in place to fight communism or tyranny. It gave a privileged status to Cuban immigrants, unlike anything that is given to immigrants from other parts of Latin America or other parts of the world. The law has gone through

transformations, but as it stands today, there is a wetfoot/dryfoot policy meaning that if a Cuban manages to reach dry land in the United States, that person is given pretty much a legal immigrant status. That person then doesn't have to go through the trappings, for example, that a Mexican immigrant or a Haitian or any other immigrant from any other part of the world would. That person has access to the political system. That person can come out and demand and request and ask for attention to his or her needs, can come out into the open. The person from another country that comes without papers would be in a different situation. How is this related to the family? At the same time that this privilege is granted to Cubans, that person has no legal bindings with the country of origin, in other words, that person perhaps left a child, a dependent child, a family dependent, and we, in essence, protect that person from legal prosecution. I can give you names and anecdotes of people who have family dependents in Cuba, who do not meet those responsibilities. At the same time that we protect someone from prosecution, we also prevent those who want to take responsibility from doing so. We limit assistance to Cubans from the island to only 300 dollars or less every three months. So let's say I am a father, I leave my wife, my children, my grandparents or my parents in Cuba, I can only send them, by U.S. law, 300 dollars every three months, which is a limitation that is not placed on any other immigrant in the U.S. Things like these need to be brought out. Another aspect of U.S. law that I think is very divisive to families is the fact that we, by U.S. law, can travel to see our loved ones only once a year, once every twelve months. We cannot go today and then return next month. We have to wait twelve months before we can go back to see our families.[7]

When I told Mr. Fernández Levy that I was not aware of the law's impact on families, he responded,

> Most people do not know these things. Moreover, and this is what I think is ethically unacceptable, is the fact that when we go back to Cuba to visit family, we have to sign an affidavit saying that we have a family emergency. Even that one every twelve months visit is not just to share good times with your family. It is not to attend a wedding or a baptism or to enjoy and build family relationships. It is to take care of an emergency. We need to really look at that as we deal with issues of the Cuban family.[8]

Several legal acts on the part of the United States have impacted the family either directly or indirectly. The challenges began with the 1959 embargo. Subsequent events produced more restrictive legislation regulating activity between Cuba and the United States. Through it all and beyond Elián, the Cuban families who have members in both countries have had to face the many challenges.

THE EMBARGO OF 1959

The U.S. policy through the Embargo of 1959 is to isolate Cuba through comprehensive economic sanctions, including medical exports and global trade.[9] In 1963, the Treasury Department's Cuban Assets Control regulations outlined the basic features of the embargo. The embargo includes "a freeze on all Cuban owned assets in the U.S. and a prohibition on all non-licensed financial transactions between the U.S. and Cuba, and between Cuba and U.S. nationals, including the spending of money by U.S. citizens in the course of travel to the island."[10] The *La Alborada* explains that the Carter Administration relaxed restrictions on travel by U.S. citizens and the Reagan Administration tightened them.

Delvis Fernández Levy works extensively with Cuban families, helping them heal from the painful separation from loved ones. I said to him, it seems illogical that we are one of the few countries that does not trade with Cuba. Fernández Levy's response to my comment was,

> Congress has voted now several times, if not to lift the embargo, to allow freedom of movement to travel to Cuba and yet we have not been able to get that bill through because of maneuvering in the Congress, in the House of Representatives in particular, by the leadership. There is a bipartisan group of forty Representatives, 20 Republicans and 20 Democrats, who are working very hard to see changes in U.S.-Cuba policy [107th Congress, 2nd Session]. One of the sad things is that, in poll after poll, most Americans are in favor of changing and so it is Congress that now must make changes. There is a lot of ignorance now because the press and publishers do not bring out certain things about Cuba policy that I think would be embarrassing to our country, speaking as an American, to the United States. The family restrictions I find abhorrent. I can't imagine the United States going to an international forum defending human rights and having this type of policy imposed on its people.[11]

THE CUBAN ADJUSTMENT ACT OF 1966

The Cuban Adjustment Act of 1966 (CAA) grants privileges to Cuban nationals not offered to immigrants from other countries. According to Nicanor León Cotayo, the law exists "because of Washington's interest in encouraging illegal departures" from Cuba.[12] It "provides for a special procedure under which Cuban nationals or citizens, and their accompanying spouses and children, may obtain a haven in the United States as permanent residents."[13] This act supercedes section 245 of the Immigration and Nationality Act. As amended, the act provides "that certain Cubans who have been physically present in the United States for at least one year may adjust to permanent resident status at the discretion of the Attorney General."[14] Spouses and children accompanying Cuban immigrants are also covered by the CAA. This act gives an opportunity to the Cuban immigrant that no other group has.[15]

Eligibility

Cuban nationals or citizens can apply for adjustment of status if they have resided in the United States for at least one year since admission or parole and are admissible as immigrants. If the applicant is inadmissible on any other ground than public charge or arrival at a place other than an open port of entry, "the applicant is not eligible for adjustment under the CAA unless the applicant is eligible for, and has obtained, a waiver of inadmissibility."[16]

Family Status

The CAA applies to the alien's spouse and children in spite of their country of citizenship or place of birth. Certain provisions must exist, according to the Law Offices of James G. Beirne:

- the relationship existed at the time the principal alien obtained lawful permanent residence;
- the relationship continues to exist until the dependent spouse or child adjusts status;
- they are residing with the principal alien in the United States;
- they make an application for adjustment of status under the Cuban Adjustment Act;
- they are eligible to receive an immigrant visa; and
- they are admissible to the United States for such permanent residence.[17]

Beirne's firm notes that "the Immigration and Nationality Act defines 'child' so that a person's son or daughter must be unmarried and not yet 21 years old to qualify as that person's 'child.' Step-children, adopted children, and children born out of wedlock can qualify as 'children' for purposes of CAA adjustment, if the claimed parent-child relationship meets the requirements specified in section 101(b)(1) of the Immigration and Nationality Act."[18]

An immigration attorney should be consulted to determine family status. But in general Beirne's firm suggests that aliens who think they meet the Cuban Adjustment Act eligibility requirements should apply to the district director having jurisdiction over their place of residence. Application may be made "to adjust to Lawful Permanent Resident Status under the Cuban Adjustment Act one year after the date he or she was granted admission or parole."[19]

Fees and several documents are required, such as: the application form, copy of a birth certificate or birth record with translation, two photographs, biographic information for people between 14 and 79 years, medical and vaccination information and evidence of arrival and departure record or inspection and admission or parole into the United States and one year's physical presence in the United States.[20]

The Mariel Boatlift

The significance of the 1980 Mariel Boatlift is that the immigrants were given the label of "Cuban-Haitian entrant — status pending" instead of refugee status.[21] The time of unrestricted admission and preferential treatment based on political consideration all but disappeared. Instead of granting political asylum, the United States grants more immigrant visas. This in-country processing is known as managed migration. Recently released political prisoners or those who have relatives in the United States can apply for asylum.[22]

Refugee Act, 1980

The Refugee Act of 1980 fills a gap left by the CAA. It incorporates refugee and asylum principles into Immigration and Nationality Act (INA). In 1996 Congress stipulated that CAA would be repealed when Cuba became a democracy.[23]

Torricelli Act or Cuban Democracy Act of 1992

The purpose of the 1992 Torricelli Act, also known as the 1992 Cuban Democracy Act (CDA), was to strengthen the economic blockade and put more pressure on Cuba. The CDA prohibits U.S. subsidiaries from trading with Cuba and prohibits entry into the United States for any vessel to load or unload freight if it has engaged in trade with Cuba within the last 180 days.[24] Track 2 of the act was designed to bring internal change. The act was debated in U.S. electoral campaigns, evidenced by the passage of the Helms-Burton Act in 1996.[25] Track 2 originally was not implemented because U.S. policymakers predicted the end of the Cuban Revolution.[26] Track 2 was designed as support for the Cuban people. It included U.S. private humanitarian donations and U.S. government support for democracy-building efforts.[27] Cuba survived the prediction, but not the economic challenges. The policymakers also believed the blockade wasn't enough to overthrow the revolution and the economic disrepair of Cuban society could bring about large-scale emigration.[28]

MIGRATION AGREEMENT, 1994

On September 9, 1994, the United States's policy changed considerably. Safe, legal and orderly immigration was the new policy goal. Two important points of its six points included that the United States no longer permitted Cubans intercepted at sea to immigrate. These immigrants would be placed in a third location. The United States agreed to admit at least 20,000 immigrants a year, not including immediate relatives of U.S. citizens. The United States could not meet the minimal level of 20,000. The U.S. established a "visa lottery" to randomly select who received a visa. Beginning in 2000, the number who qualified for the visa increased each year.[29]

MIGRATION AGREEMENT, MAY 1995

The United States allowed most of about 33,000 Cubans camped at Guantánamo to immigrate. Cuba agreed to allow these numbers to be applied to the 20,000 minimum. Cubans intercepted at sea would no longer be placed in safe haven camps, but repatriated to Cuba. Cubans who express fear of reprisal would be brought to the United States. This wet foot/dry foot policy evolved as a result of the various migration agreements.[30]

As of the year 2000, since the 1995 agreement, the U.S. Coast Guard had interdicted and returned to Cuba over 3,500 emigrants. As of 1999, no reprisals by the Cuban government against repatriated citizens had occurred. Smugglers, however, faced prison terms. From 1995 to 1998, over 95,000 Cubans became legal permanent residents of the United States.[31]

ILLEGAL IMMIGRATION REFORM AND IMMIGRANT RESPONSIBILITY ACT, 1996

On September 30, 1996, Congress enacted the Illegal Immigration Reform and Immigrant Responsibility Act (IIRIRA). IIRIRA stated that when an immigrant arrives at a point other than an open port-of-entry, it is grounds for inadmissability. After evaluating this act, the immigration service "established that a Cuban national or citizen who arrives at

a place other than an open port-of-entry may still be eligible for adjustment of status, if the Service has paroled the alien into the United States."[32]

The Helms-Burton Act or the Cuban Liberty and Democratic Solidarity (LIBERTAD) Act of 1996 "creates a federal cause of action, on behalf
of U.S. citizens whose property was confiscated without compensation by
Cuba, against those who 'traffic' in that property."[33] The principal cor-
porate traffickers are Canada and Mexico. The governments of these countries have denounced this legislation, saying that Title III of the act violates
international law and is outside of the United States's jurisdiction.[34] This
act increases pressure on Cuba and provides for a plan to assist Cuba when
it begins a transition to democracy. One of its sanctions falls under Title
III that "holds any person or government that traffics in U.S. property
confiscated by the Cuban government liable for monetary damages in U.S.
federal court."[35]

Cuban Government Perspectives

The Cuban government has long resented United States's policy of
accepting antigovernment exiles.[36] Castro's early policies did not permit
anyone who left illegally or many who had met all legal requirements for
emigration to return. As time passed, the Cuban government began to
ease restrictions. In the late 1970s, it allowed return visits by large numbers of Cuban exiles who had been living abroad for years. Mariel Boatlift
refugees were first allowed to return to Cuba after 12 years. The 1993 rafters were allowed to return after spending five years out of the country.[37]

Over time President Castro either turned his head or, as in the case
in 1994, he announced that his government would no longer stop citizens
from emigrating. At the time, some believed Castro used the illegal emigration issue to ease the embargo. Others believed that his goal was legal
emigration, to encourage the United States to prosecute Cubans who made
it to Florida in stolen aircraft or boats and the return of permission for
Cuban Americans to send money to relatives in Cuba. Some believed that
Castro did not care whether angry dissidents left the island, but was interested in preserving his image by not having citizens leave in an unsafe
manner.[38]

In September of 1999, to discourage illegal emigration and demonstrate its determination to uphold promises to Washington, the Cuban

government announced that any Cuban who left illegally after September 9, 1994, would not be allowed to return. The ban ended Cuba's 1993 policy of allowing those who fled illegally to return home after they had spent at least five years abroad.[39]

In 2000 after the Elián González event, Cuba tightened its emigration policy that increased the likelihood of high-risk escapes by boat.[40] All in all, the emigration issues have presented challenges to the Cuban government which, in turn, has approached them with a variety of responses.

Migration and U.S. Domestic Influences

U.S. policy toward Cuba is also influenced by U.S. domestic elements. A link between the Cuban issue and the U.S. electoral process is evidenced by the impact of the Cuban vote in Florida and New Jersey. Also, "The influence of the Cuban far-right lobby induced a relative disconnection of the Cuban case from general U.S. foreign-policy objectives."[41]

Executive Order, 1995

In 1995, a preelection year, an executive order (1) allowed Cuban immigrants living in the U.S. to travel to Cuba once a year without a special license from the Treasury Department (2) authorized the exchange of news bureaus between the U.S. and Cuba, (3) permitted donations to nongovernmental organizations (NGOs) in Cuba, and (4) allowed money transfers made for visa procedures or emergencies. It did not remove restrictions of Cuban-Americans' travel to Cuba or sending funds to relatives without a license from the Treasury Department.[42]

The Elián González Case, 1999

On Thanksgiving Day, November 26, 1999, five year old Elián González from Cardenas, Cuba, was rescued from the sea after the boat in which he was sailing to the United States with his mother, stepfather and 12 others capsized. Eleven people died. Elián was found floating on an inner tube.[43] Elián's event is important because, "Like the majority of Cuban families, the Gonzálezes are a family divided by the Florida Straits and by irreconcilable politics."[44]

The Immigration and Naturalization Service gave Great Uncle Lázaro González in Miami, Florida, temporary custody of Elián. Lázaro's wife, Angela, worked as a seamstress in a factory. The daughter, Marisleysis, who proclaimed herself as Elián's surrogate mother, worked as an assistant loan officer in a bank. The son lived close by in an apartment. The Lázaro González family also had other members still in Cuba. Juan Miguel González, Elián's father, was one of the family members "who never had any serious quarrel with the Cuban government and had no interest in leaving."[45] The family in Cuba and the family in the United States were tightly united, but with an understanding that politics was not to be discussed. When Elián met his destiny at sea, politics forced into the forefront tense family relationships.[46]

When Juan González spoke with his son and his Miami relatives, part of his Miami family said they wished for Elián to remain with them and for Juan to join them in Miami. The next day, Juan petitioned the U.S. government. "It soon became clear that more than just family members had stepped into the decision-making process on both sides of the Florida Straits,"[47] wrote Ann Louise Bardach.

The debate involved government officials, family members, church leaders, Cuban exiles, news commentators, talk show hosts and many others. The González family members in Miami filed lawsuits.[48] Differences of opinion developed in Elián's Miami family, specifically from the Great-Uncle Lázaro González, who had been in Spain at the time of Elián's discovery.[49] In January 2000, Elián's grandmothers arrived in New York City from Cuba on behalf of his father.[50] Then on April 6, 2000, Juan Miguel, with his wife, Elián's stepmother, and infant child, arrived to claim his son. On April 12, U.S. Attorney General Janet Reno, U.S. Justice Department, ordered the uncle to give up temporary custody. Except for the great-uncle and a few others, Elián's Miami family disapproved of Reno's ruling. Tensions mounted.[51]

Since the voluntary relinquishment of Elián was not occurring, on April 22, Reno ordered that Elián be removed from his Miami home and turned over to his father. The Miami family had time to be heard and had not turned Elián over to his father. Elián was returned to his father five months after he was rescued on Thanksgiving Day, November 26, 1999. No one was hurt in the raid.

Andrew E. Taslitz writes the raid "was not done for the purpose of the United States government limiting free movement, but rather to protect fundamental American principles of parental autonomy and family unity."[52] Further, "in liberal legal theory, it [the fundamental right of parents to raise their children] is considered one of the most important of inalienable rights."[53]

Taslitz writes, "Taken in its best light, therefore, the Miami Cuban-American position was that political ideology trumps the parental bond."[54]

Geri Díaz, an Operation Peter Pan child, asks us to examine all facts. She says,

> What we have gone through is very difficult to grasp. My husband is American. We never argue. The Elián González thing?—We had our first fight. He kept saying, "The child belongs with his parents," which is right. My answer to him is, "You're thinking, this country. What if that child went to a father who was a pornographer or a child abuser, would you still say that?" He said, "Yes, but his father's not that." I said, "No, but the atmosphere that he is going to go back to is very detrimental to his growth."[55]

Christopher G. Blood maintains that Elián's case had international overtones that should have been recognized. He writes, "If it was determined that Elián's life or freedom would be threatened by a return to Cuba on account of race, religion, political opinion, etc., the United States would be under international law obligations to allow him to stay or to find him an alternative country of safety."[56]

Elián's case made the international scene underscoring two things: the emotions of separated Cuban families and that no one family form exists in Cuba. Roger Fontaine, a reporter for *New World Communications*, puts forth a description of family life today for many Cubans.

> So can Elián González have a normal life once he undoubtedly returns to Cuba? Of course not. But then his life on the island was hardly normal in the first place. His parents had been divorced, and he spent most of his time with his father. Not apparently because his mother loved him any less, but the small apartment she lived in along with her boyfriend was too small for even a small boy to fit in comfortably. Such are the ways of today's Cuba.[57]

Newsday reporter Ron Howell says that the Elián saga definitely touched a deep collective nerve in Cubans. He explains,

> It highlighted two things: one, the instinctive bonds of family that exist within Cubans. Many were deeply repulsed at the idea that someone beyond their boundaries could keep a minor child from his legitimate next-of-kin. Legitimate, in this sense, having to do not so much with legal codes, but with the natural recognition that a father or a grandmother has more rights than a cousin or an uncle. Aware of the sentiment of his people, Fidel easily picked up on it and organized some of the biggest down-with-the-Yankees demonstrations of recent times. The Cuban community in Miami did more damage to itself, with its specious arguments and its strident, almost loony behavior, than it could have done with anything short of placing bombs on airplanes.[58]

The Elián saga secondly showed the extent to which families have been torn apart since the 1959 revolution. On the simplest level, you could say that the richer ones and fairer-complexioned ones were those who left for Miami. But even within nuclear families there are some who left behind siblings who remained more or less faithful to the ideals of the revolution, suffering through very difficult times. There is a kind of sadness, a divided quality of the soul that characterizes Cuba of the past forty years. And, in a sense, it is reflected in the divisions within Cuban families.[59]

Delvis Fernández Levy believes the decision to allow Elián's father to decide where his son should live was correct. Elián is surrounded by his father, stepmother, two little brothers, four grandparents, and one great-grandmother. But the schism in the bosom of the González family remains, writes Fernández Levy. Further, "It is a microcosm of the divisions within each Cuban-American family."[60]

Legal theory is often contradictory, as is legal practice. Blood writes, "The name 'Elián' has been etched into America's consciousness."[61] And Díaz asks us to remember the Cuban-American's struggle. Both elements place the bonds of family under duress.

The Cuban View of the Elián González Case

A stabilizing factor in Cuba is "the collective will to preserve *national independence*."[62] The Cuban people have withstood double colonization by Spain and the United States. At the Fifth Party Congress in 1997, party, state and nation became identical. The most intense expression of that new doctrine was the handling of the events surrounding the fate of the Elián González. A populist campaign mobilized all political and honorary leaders to demonstrate their loyalty to the government. This self-styled state of emergency became a pleading for national unity made "possible through subtle appeals to the Cuban sense of family and to national pride to sideline all other topics and demonstrate the persistent threat of the United States to Cuban national sovereignty."[63]

LEONEL CORDOVA CASE

In 2001, another case involving an effort of family reunification surfaced. In 2000, Dr. Leonel Cordova defected to the United States after escaping from a Cuban medical mission in Zimbabwe. He had two children: a stepson, eleven year old Yusniel Hernandez, from a previous marriage, and a four year old daughter, Giselle Cordova. The daughter's mother, Dr. Cordova's second wife, Rosalba González, was killed in a motorcycle accident in Cuba. Cordova had obtained visas for his wife and two children before she died. At that time the exit process slowed. Two Florida members of Congress, Ileana Ros-Lehtinen and Lincoln Díaz-Balart, and the Havana U.S. Interests Section tried to help. Since the children were Cuban nationals, they needed to get a white card, which is the exit visa to get out of Cuba. Congressman Díaz-Balart made a humanitarian case to get the children out of Cuba. The boy's natural father, Lazaro Hernandez, gave legal authorization for the son to live in Miami with Cordova. Exactly one year after the Elián González case, the Cuban government issued passports and travel permits.[64]

Miami Cubans and anti–Castro Cubans were saddened by Elián's return to Cuba. Moderate Cuban Americans elected to work to change the United States's old policy toward Cuba. "A year after Elián's homecoming, U.S. policy still fosters family divisions," Delvis Fernández Levy said of the case in 2001.[65]

THE 107TH CONGRESS' CHANGES IN U.S. CUBAN POLICY

On July 24, 2002, the U.S. House of Representatives voted to lift restrictions but the president said that he would veto a bill if passed. Travel, remittances and agricultural restrictions would be eased.[66] The House took five votes that signaled a change in Cuba policy is needed. First, the House passed by voice vote an amendment increasing agricultural sales to Cuba. Second, the House passed an amendment by a recorded vote of 251–177 to permit Cuban-Americans to send money to their relatives in Cuba without restrictions. They are now restricted to remittances of $100 a month. Third, an amendment conditioning travel restrictions failed by a recorded vote of 182–247. Fourth, an amendment ending the travel ban on Cuba passed by a recorded vote of 262–167. Last, an amendment opposing the entire embargo failed by a recorded vote of 204–226.[67]

United States citizens are not permitted to travel to Cuba or to import Cuban goods such as cigars. Citizens who break the embargo face prison or fines. People with family in Cuba are allowed one visit per year.[68] A United States political reality is that President George W. Bush is backed by the Cuban American community in the key electoral state of Florida. As of December 2002, Bush has vowed to veto any further easing of the sanctions.[69] Another reality is that perhaps the president is his brother's (Governor Jeb Bush of Florida) keeper. Specific political issues related to United States and Cuba are reflected in the president's flight to Miami to assure critical Cuban American voters that he will never ease the embargo on Castro even though some Republicans would like him to.[70]

I asked Alejandro Concepcion, "How do you think the Cuban family has been affected by the policies of the United States government?" He replied,

> I think this is a case of the other way around. The old establishment in Miami is wagging the tail and they are the ones who are driving the U.S. policy. I personally don't agree with it. I think we would probably be better served by opening up the trade, because once you start trading, once you open up the government and start having exchange of goods and commerce and people and visitors and things start to flow, it is like opening the flood gate. I think the government will have to change because you will never be able to go back, the same thing that happened in Russia. I grew up here in the States and I didn't lose my fortune. We never had anything. A lot of the people in Miami, the old-timers, lost their family fortune, their property and all this other stuff. They're still resentful.[71]

Beliefs depend, in part, on the generation of the Cuban American. When and under what conditions emigration occurred determine views of United States policy.

The Cuban American Alliance Education Fund (CAAEF) believes that the prohibition for U.S. citizens to travel to Cuba without a special license from the U.S. Department of the Treasury is a policy that isolates Cuba, is an anomaly and is unconstitutional. The inconsistency regarding travel is amplified because our foreign policy has always included person-to-person diplomacy. To normalize relations in other countries in 1972, President Richard Nixon traveled to China; in 1977 President Carter removed restrictions on travel to Vietnam; Reagan and George H.W. Bush allowed travel in European nations including the Soviet Union. Today, U.S. citizens can travel to most places, but cannot travel to Cuba, Iraq and Libya.[72]

The CAAEF makes the following argument why U.S. travel restrictions are unconstitutional:

1. The Constitution gives every individual the right to travel. In three Supreme Court cases, *Kent v. Dulles, Aptheker v. Secretary of State* and *Zemel v. Rusk*, the court upheld Americans' right to travel as guaranteed by the Fifth Amendment.
2. In *Zemel*, however, the court found the Cuban travel restriction was not unconstitutional because it was supported by the "weightiest considerations of national security."
3. In 1994, the State Department recognized that the right to travel is constitutionally protected and may only be limited in "extraordinary circumstances."

4. With the Soviet Union's collapse, Cuba's military has been dramatically reduced and no longer is a threat to U.S. security. Accordingly, in 1998 the U.S. Defense Intelligence Agency reported that Cuba is no longer a military threat to America.[73]

Other U.S. Programs, Laws and Policies

Interactions between Cuba and the United States have been addressed in other ways that make the relationship between these two countries unique.

OPERATION PEDRO PAN PROJECT, 1960S

Fernández Levy explains a program in place in the early sixties called the Peter Pan Project, or Pedro Pan, that impacted a lot of Cuban families.

> There were fifteen thousand children that were sent out of Cuba in the early sixties. The children were as young as six years to as old as fourteen. They were in their formative years. They stayed in the United States for long periods of time. Some of them never got to see their parents again. That had a tremendous impact on a sizable population of Cubans in terms of their family. There have been certain laws or tools of U.S. foreign policy that have had a tremendous impact, always under the guise of protecting the family or not doing any unintended harm to the family unit.[74]

Fernández Levy says that, in his case, he didn't see his sisters for twenty-two years. He tells that "there was a time when you actually had to rebel to go to Cuba. It was not easy at all. It was during the Carter administration in the late seventies that there was a chance to legally go back to Cuba and visit and share time with your loved ones there."[75]

UNITED NATIONS

On April 19, 2002, the United Nations Commission on Human Rights approved a resolution by a 23–21 vote calling on Cuba to improve its human rights record "in accordance with the Universal Declaration of Human Rights and the principles and standards of the rule of law."[76] On June 26, 2002, Cuba's National Assembly approved amendments to the constitution that said, "Socialism and the evolutionary political and social system in the Constitution ... are irrevocable; and Cuba will never again return to capitalism."[77]

In 2002, Fernández Levy reviewed United Nations activity as follows:

> Every year, for the last seven or eight years, the vote has been over-
> whelming. Only two votes against, one is the United States and one is
> Israel. In the last vote, there was the third country, the Marshall Islands.
> There is strong condemnation about the embargo. The aspects of the
> embargo that affect the most human beings are the restrictions on travel
> and on the people-to-people type engagement where you [a writer], for
> example, might be interested in doing research for your book and meet-
> ing people in Cuba and asking them questions. You have to jump
> through quite a few hoops to get there to do that.[78]

VISA POLICY

Dr. Leonardo M. Marmol, professor and chair of the Department of
Graduate Psychology at Seattle Pacific University, explains that getting a
visa to visit Cuba has evolved. Sometimes problems are also created by
the Cuban government.

> When the Castro government allowed exiles to visit in 1979 and 1980,
> people received the exiles with open arms though Castro had called them
> worthless worms, the word is *gusano* (worm), and people who left the
> country are called *gusanos*, worms. Yet, they were welcomed with open
> arms.
>   Now, Cuban families are allowed to visit their relatives in Cuba, but
> they have to go through a process to get permission from the Cuban
> Interests section in Washington. There they get a travel permit that allows
> them to go visit Cuba. Even if we have become U.S. citizens, the Cuban
> law and constitution does not recognize that you can lose citizenship
> ever. So the minute you hit Cuban soil, you are a Cuban again. The U.S.
> passport for entering Cuba is no good for entering Cuba for any one of
> us. You have to have that permit from the Cuban Interests section. This
> is one of the hypocrisies. There is no Embassy, but there is an Interests
> Section. There are American officers in Havana in the Interests Section
> who issue visas for Cubans to come visit here. One of my cousins vis-
> ited me in Oregon two years ago. Then the Cuban Interests Section in
> Washington, which is housed at the Swiss Embassy, issues these permits
> for us to go or American groups to visit Cuba, like religious groups,
> education and research people that have to visit Cuba.[79]

RAFTERS AND THE IMMIGRATION AND
NATURALIZATION SERVICE

Betsy Campisi, anthropologist at the State University of New York
in Albany, conducted life history interviews of 12 Cuban rafters, and has

done participant observation in Miami. The results of the early August 1994 rafter exodus led the Clinton Administration on August 19 to reverse a 28-year-old policy. Rather than follow the previous policy of admitting all Cubans as escapees from communism, the United States sent them to join the 15,000 Haitians already being held at the U.S. Navy Base at Guantánamo Bay, Cuba. Campisi writes, "With the stroke of a pen, they went from welcome refugees to illegal immigrants. Eight months later, it [the Clinton Administration] decided to admit only the Cubans as special Guantánamo entrants, and then took nine more months to fly all of them off the base.["][80]

Campisi became interested in the Cuban rafters when she worked in the refugee camps as a temporary employee of the Justice Department's Community Relations Service. For four months, she conducted intake interviews for the Immigration and Naturalization Service (INS). Over 600 families were eligible for medical parole. For nine more months, she worked inside three camps as a mediator between the Cubans and the United States military. Campisi says, "My job was to identify factors that could increase social tensions and to work with the military and Cuban camp leadership to mitigate them."[81]

Campisi is highly critical of the treatment of the rafters by the INS:

> I really was appalled at the entire INS operation in Guantánamo. I see this culture being supported by [U.S. Attorney General John] Ashcroft right now. The INS culture is, to me and this is my impression from Guantánamo, that it is some kind of crime to want to come to the United States. Therefore, people who do want to come and do not have all their paperwork in order, are, in the INS employees' minds, criminals and don't have to be treated with due process.
>
> The reason I am saying this is: you wouldn't believe the unprofessional behavior of the INS employees toward a lot of the Cubans. There are two different kinds of interview processes that happen in Guantánamo. From September or October 1994 until May or June of 1995, the only way you are going to get out of Guantánamo then was through medical parole. On May 4, 1995, President Clinton announced everybody would be let in, but there were still some sick people that they hadn't gotten off the base yet. Sick people were allowed to take family members and care givers. So they had to convince INS that people were care givers. The Cubans saw this as: Let's get as many people out here as we can and figure out how we can convince the INS that these people are family members. After they were all supposed to be admitted after May 4th or 5th, then that was just kind of a routine criminal background check of who are your family members. There weren't so many problems with those interviews. In the medical parole interview, a lot of the pregnant Cuban women came back crying. They had been accused of

being street sluts who had gotten pregnant just to get out of the camp
and the man with them wasn't really their husband. One man who was
a camp leader in one of my camps was strip searched because he had a
tattoo. He had been a prison guard in Cuba and that is why he had a tattoo. People getting harassed for their tattoos started other people in the
camp to try to burn their tattoos off before they went to their immigration interviews.

Then I personally witnessed a guy from INS who would introduce
himself to the Cubans as the jackal. It was very verbally abusive. They
brought in the Border Patrol to do these interviews because no one wants
to go to Guantánamo. Just the worst Border Patrol people were there.
He was Mexican-American and he resented the fact he had to detain
Mexican-Americans at the border so he was going to give the Cubans as
much hell as possible before they could get into the country. Anybody
that he thought was making up a story was really subject to any kind of
abuse he could think of. He told me this. This is apart from women
coming back crying and people getting all upset after their interviews.
When I see the treatment of the Iranians and things like that now, I think
back to that culture in Guantánamo that somehow it is a crime to want
to come to this country. I don't know what kind of people are attracted
to be INS interviewers to have this very punitive nature just because
people want to come here.[82]

If you could get that across somehow [in your book] that a lot of
people in Guantánamo really went through some abuse, not only by the
INS but also by the military. There was a lot, in the beginning, of ter-
ribly unsanitary conditions. Terrible medical care in the beginning. I am
going to make sure that I put in my book ... this example — I had to get
people to think, they don't like to think about these bad things a man
had a really bad kidney infection and they couldn't get the camp commander to get the person to medical care, so they had to literally throw
this person over the fence and then the military would come and throw
the person back over the fence. They would go back and forth until the
people were saying, "No, you take this person to the hospital. We're not
going to be responsible if this person dies. You are the ones who are
responsible if this person dies." Things like that really drove me crazy.[83]

There was another really terrible instance of abuse in Panama that
also really needs to get out. There were riots in the Panama camp. After
the riots, what they did was, in the one camp that rioted, the people who
were in that camp who were not accused of rioting were sprinkled
throughout the other four camps. Because the rumor was that some
women had instigated these riots because they were bothering their husbands so much about when they were going to get out of Panama that
the men had gotten so agitated. One incident happened where the people they thought may have had something to do with the riots and who
had been put in camp by mistake were beaten by Green Berets who were
dropped in the camp from helicopters. They beat a bunch of people and
threw them in a big pile in the lower pit area of the camp. They broke

bones, beat up pregnant women, and they left all these injured people in a pile without giving them medical attention. The people who they did think had something to do with the rioting were taken in their underwear in flexicuffs and put in the equivalent of Camp X-ray in Guantánamo for two weeks and not allowed to bathe or shave.[84]

The worst incident to me happened on another day. The woman [who] told me the story said that early in the morning this group of women was rounded up from the back of one of the camps, stripped and made to march around the camp naked. Everybody was forced out of their tents to look at them and people were doing such things as trying to throw towels and clothes over them and not look. Then the women [were] brought over to the cafeteria and to sit down and breakfast was put in front of them and they said, "Now you eat." That to me was like a semi-rape experience. The woman who told me this was a psychologist who had to treat them after that and some of those women were suicidal.

In February 1995 all the Panama people were transferred to Guantánamo. After they arrived at Guantánamo, they were spirited off to other places because nobody ever heard from them again. That was the most incredibly hideous example of abuse by the military and no one has ever investigated that. What is the long term effect on these women? I want to know who these women are and how that's affected their adjustment to this country. No one has compensated them for that — given them special therapy or extra therapy. I will bet you that no camp commander ever reported that they did this to this group of women.[85]

Before the incident the relationship between the Cubans and the military was really very good. There was a spirit of cooperation. They formed schools and churches. They planted little gardens and things like that. [Until] those riots happened, which could have been instigated by fake Rafters sent over by Castro, as military intelligence implied. Then all these people got beat up and thrown into the brig for two weeks. Then the military policy was cold shoulder, we're not going to talk to you if we don't have to. Everyone got really depressed.[86]

Campisi, who was a mediator in one of the camps, continues that the abuse of the Rafter population in general is not acknowledged. Though abuse was not systematic, there were definitely instances of abuse and other demoralizing things, depending which branch of the military was rotated in. The Rafters really went through a [painful] life psychologically. Campisi says she gave me the worst, the most extreme examples, and concludes,

> It is traumatic enough to be exiled, but then to be put in these camps where you are abused by the military or the INS or have to keep your head low or, if you are a woman, you have no privacy in the showers because people are always peeping at you including the soldiers. What

is not acknowledged about this population is these people were really traumatized by this whole experience and they have not gotten the attention from the psychological community and have not gotten the acknowledgment that they went through that coming here.[87]

Conclusions

Incremental improvements in U.S. attitude toward the embargo can be seen through the successful legislative efforts in the House in 2002. The piecemeal changes affect issues of citizenship for Cuban Americans. In turn, the wearing away of the embargo favorably affects the Cuban family. The executive branch vacillates from administration to administration. Although the George W. Bush administration has held firm to his belief in favor of the embargo, the Carter and Clinton administrations worked to ease sanctions. In May 2002, a Gallup poll showed that 71 percent of Americans are in favor of reestablishing diplomatic relations with Cuba. Of the 200,000 Americans who travel to Cuba, 130,000 were Cuban Americans who returned to visit their families under the auspices of dealing with a family emergency.[88] In addition, Cuban Americans are limited in the amount and frequency of money they can send back to their families in Cuba. Further, "a Cuban in the U.S. who abandons children or family dependents in Cuba is exempted from prosecution by U.S. law, on the other hand a person in the U.S. who takes responsibility for his children in Cuba is not permitted to claim deductions from his/her income tax reports."[89]

6

Emigration to the United States

by Rosemarie Skaine and James C. Skaine

Let the sea part our ashes, if it must.
— George Santayana[1]

Over the years, between one million and two million Cubans have emigrated to the United States.[2] The emigration periods and methods are identified with political and economic conditions at the time.

Number of Emigrants

Although a relatively small number (about 3,000) of the first politically motivated migrations from Cuba began in the 1830s with the rebellion against Spain,[3] the Immigration and Naturalization Service (INS) did not separately report data on Cuban migration until 1925. In 2000, 19,322 people with their last residence in Cuba emigrated to the United States. From 1925 to 2000, the INS reports 918,032 migrated.[4] (See Table 6.1.) However, in 2000, the Service admitted 20,831 immigrants bringing the total for the decades to 191,506.[5] (See Table 6.2.)

The population of Cuba in 1959 was 6,901,000 people; in 1960 their number had grown to 7,027,000, and in 1961 the population climbed to 7,134,000 people.[6] In 2001, the population of Cuba had increased to more than eleven million.[7] With the Cuban economy faltering from 1990 to 1993 and its slow recovery due to a drop in production, from 1990 to 1994, emigration figures topped at 105,000. In 1994 during the rafters crisis, approximately 50,000 people illegally emigrated. As a result, Cuba and the United States signed two accords. The United States agreed to provide 20,000 entry visas a year, and repatriate any illegal emigrant intercepted.[8]

TABLE 6.1
IMMIGRATION FROM THE CARIBBEAN REGION WITH CUBA SELECTED AS COUNTRY OF LAST RESIDENCE

1921–1930	15,901[1]
1931–1940	9,571
1941–1950	26,313
1951–1960	78,948
1961–1970	208,536
1971–1980	264,863
1981–1990	144,578
1991–2000	169,322
1997	29,913
1998	15,415
1999	13,289
2000	19,322
Total 75 years 1925–2000[2]	918,032

Notes:
1. Data for Cuba not reported separately until 1925.
2. Data for Cuba not reported separately until 1925.

Source: U.S. Immigration and Naturalization Service. *Immigrants, Fiscal Year 2000*, a report to appear as a chapter in the forthcoming *Statistical Yearbook of the Immigration and Naturalization Service*, 2000, 1–67. July 7, 2002 http://www.ins.usdoj.gov/graphics/aboutins/statistics/IMM00yrbk/IMM2000list.htm.

From 1995 to December 2000, legal Cuban emigrants numbered 133,800. Applications to emigrate indicated interest to come to the United States. One hundred thirty thousand applications were received in 1994, 438,000 in 1996 and 541,100 in 1998.[9] In 1995, the U.S. and Cuba signed an agreement that Cubans camping at the U.S. Guantánamo naval base could emigrate to the U.S. legally, up to 5,000 to be included in the 20,000 figure of the 1994 agreement. Cuban immigrants intercepted at sea or who had gained entry to the naval base would be returned to Cuba.[10]

Why and How Cubans Emigrate

Lisandro Pérez reminds us that the exiles from revolutionary Cuba are not the first to establish communities in the United States. In the 1840s and 1850s Cubans rebelled against Spanish authority and settled in New York and New Orleans. The intellectually elite comprised many of this

TABLE 6.2
IMMIGRANTS ADMITTED WITH CUBA AS
COUNTRY OF BIRTH, 1990–2000

1990	10,645
1991	10,349
1992	11,791
1993	13,666
1994	14,727
1995	17,937
1996	26,466
1997	33,587
1998	17,375
1999	14,132
2000	20,831
Total, years 1990–2000	191,506

Source: U.S. Immigration and Naturalization Service. *Immigrants, Fiscal Year 2000,* a report to appear as a chapter in the forthcoming *Statistical Yearbook of the Immigration and Naturalization Service,* 2000, 1–67. July 7, 2002 http://www.ins.usdoj.gov/graphics/aboutins/statistics/IMM00yrbk/IMM2000list.htm.

group who came without their families and intended to return. Cigar manufacturers comprised an increased number of single, male migrants during the insurrection in 1868. The manufacturers settled in Key West, New York and Ybor City bordering Tampa, Florida. Pérez explains that the temporary nature of migration, the nearness to Cuba and absence of immigration restrictions contributed to the high proportion of single men (120 men for every 100 women). Yet, mostly men made up migrant workers, a group that crossed and recrossed the Florida Strait. Cuban cigarmaking shifted back to Havana in 1930 and immigrants returned.[11]

Cuba rapidly modernized during the first half of the twentieth century. Since the revolution in 1959, estimates show that more than a million people or one tenth of the total Cuban population emigrated.[12] Pérez describes the three major waves of migration that took place,

1. 1959 to 1962, when regular commercial air traffic moved between the United States and Cuba;
2. 1965 to 1973, the years during which an airlift, or "freedom flights," operated between Cuba and Miami; and
3. nine months in 1980, when the notorious Mariel Boatlift took place.[13]

Research demonstrates that early emigrating Cubans were Cuba's displaced elite who then had economic success in the United States. Pérez refers to that emigration period as the "golden exile."[14]

UNITED STATES AS A BASIS FOR EMIGRATION

The nations of the Caribbean are diverse politically, economically and culturally. They share some of the same problems and opportunities. The countries are small, open and vulnerable because they border the world's richest and most powerful country. They all face the strategic dilemma of "how to elude the dominance of the United States while securing improved access to the U.S. market."[15]

Delvis Fernández Levy, president of the Cuban American Alliance Education Fund, says, "The United States is such a large and dominant country with so much power that we sometimes forget that, meshed within that power, we might have more influence on people in another society than we give credit to ourselves."[16] Fernández Levy firmly believes there are specific ways that the United States has a tremendous impact, perhaps more than the Cuban government itself, on Cuban families, in Cuba and the United States. These ways include the Cuban Adjustment Act, cumbersome requirements for Cuban Americans who wish to return to Cuba to visit family, and the effects of the Peter Pan Project.

Cuban emigrants have made great efforts to stay in touch with and help support their families remaining in Cuba. They send $800 million a year in food and medicine. Many would go home if they could, because they never planned to stay in the United States. Others believe, however, that uprooting their children makes it undesirable to return.[17]

Emigrating Cubans are at risk. Nicanor León Cotayo believes that the United States's Cuban Adjustment Act of 1966, retroactive to 1959, is the key reason for the travel between Cuba and Florida. Cotayo believes that repealing this act is a critical step toward ending the deaths of the many people who die fleeing hardships resulting from the U.S. blockade. The University of Havana's Center for Political Alternatives found that "among more than 100 citizens who tried to immigrate illegally in 1993, 82.3 percent did so 'to alleviate the family's economic situation.' Regardless of how they tried to leave, 50.3 percent, when asked what kind of society they preferred, responded, 'Cuba before the Special Period' (austerity period declared in 1990)."[18]

There are many examples of attempts to flee to the United States that end tragically. On December 24, 2000, two adolescent students at a military school, Alberto Esteban Vázquez, 17, and Maikel Fonseca, 16, hid in the landing gear of an airplane they believed bound for the United States. Instead the British Airways aircraft departed for London. The altitude of 32,808 feet, with an inadequate oxygen supply and temperatures at minus 58 degrees Fahrenheit, ended their lives. Again some media in Cuba held the Cuban Adjustment Act responsible. At a panel discussion, President Castro, on the other hand, placed the responsibility on the families for giving the boys an unrealistic view of the United States. Journalist Arleen Rodríguz commented, "It is the siren's song. A call for exodus, to die in order to be used against the Cuban Revolution [of 1959]."[19]

PETER PAN PROJECT OR PEDRO PAN, 1960S

Operation Pedro Pan was conceived when Miami relatives could not support 15 year old Pedro Menendez. A benefactor took Pedro to the Catholic Welfare Bureau (CWB), later renamed Catholic Charities. Father Bryan O. Walsh headed the bureau. The headmaster of Ruston Academy, an American School in Havana, Mr. James Baker and members of the American Chamber of Commerce of Havana — Mr. Kenneth Campbell, Mr. Bob O'Farrell of Esso Standard and Mr. Richard Colligan of Freeport Sulphur Company — wanted to provide shelter and education for children who did not have relatives or friends in the United States. Mr. Baker and Father Walsh joined in their efforts to assist the children. Mr. Baker was to help the children out of Cuba. Father Walsh was to meet them once they arrived in Miami and provide proper care. Operation Pedro Pan, the very complex project which flew children out of Cuba, was launched.[20]

The first "camp" or "transit center" set up to house children until they could be placed was located in Kendall, Florida, and owned by Dade County. Camp Matecumbe and other foster care facilities grew in number. Non-denominational, denominational, Jewish, and various private groups and agencies helped find foster homes. In 1961, President John F. Kennedy ordered the Cuban refugees be taken care of under the Department of Health, Education and Welfare. To find good homes, ads were placed in newspapers and magazines that stated, in part, that "none of the Cuban children could be adopted (custody remained with their parents in Cuba.)"[21] Children were placed in foster care in 35 states through 95 agencies.[22]

Over 14,000 young people of Cuba migrated to the United States in the early 1960s as a part of "Operation Pedro Pan." Some children never saw their families again. The name came from the play *Peter Pan* by Sir James M. Barrie that told "about the legendary boy who could fly and taught his friends to fly away with him to Never-Never Land."[23]

In 1960 and 1961, rumors in Cuba and United States media reported that Castro planned to make every Cuban child practically a ward of the state. Some reports indicated that children would be required to give information about the activities and beliefs of their parents. Other rumors were that Castro planned government nurseries and dormitories that would separate children from their families and that some young people were sent to Russia without their parents to study collective farming methods.[24] Some Peter Pan children witnessed televised trials and executions with firing squads. One fifteen year old said that it was only when he became an adult "could he really comprehend the great sacrifice his parents made."[25]

In 1960, about 60,000 upper and middle class families had left or wanted to leave Cuba. The emigration affected Cuba's supply of professional people. Castro canceled all existing exit permits. Many parents that were involved in counterrevolutionary underground efforts feared for their children in three ways. They feared their young children would be taken from them, their teens would follow their counterrevolutionary example or their sons would be drafted into the military. Parents sent their children to the United States through what was then the "secret phase" of Operation Pedro Pan. "They trusted that their children would be cared for in the Cuban Children's Program initiated in Miami."[26]

As a result, Miami became overextended in its ability to assist the great number of refugees. The U.S. government set up a Cuban Emergency Center in Miami in 1960. Geri Díaz, a Peter Pan child and now a Miami resident, explains the operation's reality and how, ultimately, her extended family "claimed" her.

> I came to the United States by myself under the auspices of the Catholic Welfare Bureau and Monsignor Brian Walsh's signature was on my visa waiver. I was 11 years old, almost 12. I was picked up at the airport by the personnel from the Peter Pan movement. I was taken to a refugee camp that had been set up in Florida City. There were houses versus a dormitory. They had couples that acted as surrogate parents to the Cuban children. Where I was, there were boys up to age 12 and girls up to age 18. It was a very difficult experience, but my parents sent me because they thought, as a lot of Cubans thought, that Castro would be overthrown momentarily. By 1962 there would be no communism and no Castro. They didn't want me to be in Cuba in case there was bloodshed. So, they sent me to the United States for what they thought, a very short period of time. It has turned into 41 years.[27]
>
>   In addition to concern for my safety, anytime anyone left Cuba for the United States or for any foreign country, unless it was a Soviet bloc country, what would happen is that all of your belongings, furniture,

whatever, in your house were inventoried by Castro's police. The belongings would be confiscated, including your car; everything. You couldn't sell it. Say, you had a car and you were coming to the United States and you decided to sell your car and get a little bit of money, you would have to pay for the value of the car because they know everything. They have a very extensive police network. My parents, thinking that Castro's demise was imminent, didn't want to risk losing what they had. We were middle class in Cuba. We were not wealthy by any stretch of the imagination. We lived very well. My Dad had a business. When they nationalized businesses, his business was nationalized even though he was Cuban. So, that makes no sense. So, that's how I got here.[28]

After not quite a month, so many children were coming to the United States in an unprecedented number, a little under 15,000 unaccompanied children. The program was busting at the seams. There was no place in Miami to put them. So children were relocated to different places. Some went into foster homes all over the United States, others into different institutions. Unfortunately, I landed in an orphan home in Helena, Montana. It was the first time I had ever seen snow in my life. It was not a very nice place. We missed our parents. It was a Catholic orphanage. There was a lot of communication problems. A lot of the nuns were not very nice. They were strict disciplinarians and couldn't understand how we were homesick and that we were totally fish out of water. I was there from January 19, 1960, through March 6, 1962. I wrote to every single individual in the United States whose address I had, begging them to get me out of that hell hole. My cousin in New York claimed me. She became like my foster parent.[29]

In the meantime, I had a sister 11 years older than I who was married. She had left with her husband from Havana via Panama. She had gotten her residency in February 1962 to enter the United States and then joined me in New York in February. So, I at least had my sister and my brother-in-law. I lived with them in New York from 1962 to 1966. In September of 1966, we moved to California which was horrible for me, because after thoroughly hating New York which was so new to me, I had gotten acclimated and made friends. Then I was uprooted again. It turned out good, like most things in life.[30]

The experiences of the children of Peter Pan varied depending on their age, where they were placed, time spent separated from family and the trauma of being in a strange country, according to Victor Andres Triay. Because most of the children were from middle class families representing economic comfort and close ties, foster care impacted them strongly. Most children thought the situation was temporary and that they would return to Cuba. Some became confused, shocked or surprised. Children placed in orphanages suffered more. Most children realized they were being sent to escape with their lives in an uncertain Cuba and from required communist indoctrination. Many children saw their schools closed and their parents' businesses taken over, had relatives in prison or in exile and were told to keep their departure secret.[31]

Triay profiles children who found the glass-enclosed Havana airport like a fish tank and painful because they were separated from their parents. For many, it was the last time they saw their parents. The many stories of older siblings protecting the younger children were very "poignant and powerful."[32] The caretaker role gave the older brothers and sisters a purpose. Children very often identified with their adult caretakers once placed. They came to love them like parents. The parents of the children of Pedro Pan also suffered from estrangement and found comfort in the Cuban adults who cared for their children. Triay writes that, in letters to a particular nurse, "parents thanked her graciously for the love, affection, and guidance she gave their children. They frequently expressed their love for their children and their longing to be reunited with them."[33]

Although Pedro Ferreira, who holds a doctorate and master of business administration and is now a licensed psychologist, in Wilmington, Delaware, did not realize it at the time, he also was a child of Operation Pedro Pan. He tells his story.

> It is interesting that we are talking here in July, on July 15. It will be July 27 in a few days and that will be the fortieth anniversary of my arrival and my brother's and a few other boys and girls to Wilmington, Delaware. We had been in a refugee camp in Miami. One of several run by the government, I believe, with the help of the Catholic Welfare Guild as Catholic Charities was called in those days. Monsignor Brian Walsh, who died within the last year, was the basic impetus, the basic head of the church in those days and for many years later, assisting the children who were coming out of Cuba in Operation Peter Pan. Operation Peter Pan is something that I didn't know I was a part of until probably in my forties. My birthday is June 29, 1946, so I just turned 56 years old. I learned that the refugee program was called Peter Pan while attending an American Psychological Association meeting, I cannot remember where it was exactly, but there was a psychologist, a woman, I cannot remember her name, I do remember that she was Cuban-American and she had a poster on some social psychological issue, the title escapes me. What was remarkable to me at that time was I realized that there was a more organized program than I ever knew existed concerning bringing children out of Cuba. I read later that between October 1960 and October 1962 during the missile crisis that President Kennedy so skillfully managed for the United States, certainly for Cuba, for our relations here with the Soviet Union. I read later that between October 1960 and October of 1962, over 14,000 Cuban boys and girls came to the U.S., the program ended around the time of the Cuban Missile Crisis.[34]

My brother and I left Cuba on Friday, March 23, 1962. In those years there was a series of rumors that came flooding through the Island of Cuba, particularly Havana and the larger cities, that the government of Fidel Castro was going to take away the rights of parents to control their own children, something called in Spanish "patria potestad." There is a concept in law where parents have the right to take care of their children and manage their children. The Castro government has always said, "No, we are not going to do that," but we were from a Spanish family on my father's and mother's sides. My father had been born in Spain. On my mother's side, my grandfather had been born in Spain and he married my mother's mother who was born in colonial times in 1882. My mother was born in Cuba. She was the child of Spanish immigrants to Cuba. So we were, to a large degree, tied into the Cuba-Spain story. During the Civil War in Spain between 1936 to 1939 (I had been hearing about that all my life), to the best of my knowledge it is accurate that a number of children were taken to Russia for whatever purposes, but, certainly at that time, the thought was that these Spanish children had been taken to Russia for indoctrination. And that, of course, some twenty years later, the Castro government was going to do the same thing. I remember very clearly that sometime late in 1959 or sometime in 1960, my parish priest, a father by the name of John McKniff, who spent some time in jail in Cuba for his activities against the government, was very worried that he had seen or he had heard that there was a Soviet ship on the Bay in Havana and that was the signal for worse things yet to come. Whether this was a rumor (some people say the CIA did this) or whether this was true that the Castro people were going to do it, it was not very difficult for parents to believe that, unless we do something about it, we will lose our children. And the best thing to do, then, is to send our children to Europe or to the United States. In our case, we had gone to an American Catholic school in Havana run by Augustinian (Order of St. Augustine) priests from Villanova, Pennsylvania, Media, Pennsylvania area. The way to get to the U.S. was, either you had a visa which you obtained prior to the break-up of relations between the U.S. and Cuba in January 1961 when Eisenhower broke relations or you were given a letter sent from somewhere in the United States that said you had a visa waiver to come into the United States. You were instructed by that visa waiver document to buy airline tickets either at Pan-American Airways or KLM (Royal Dutch Airlines). You also had to have the money in American dollars. In the case of my family, my mother had a cousin who worked in the bi-lingual typing pool at the U.N. in New York City and he sent us the money via some kind of transfer. I think the cost was $25.50 for the round-trip.[35]

I saw the piece of paper that said $25.50. I cannot remember whether that was one way or not. It seemed to me that it was pretty reasonable. It was very difficult in those days if you did not have a relative or if you did not have dollars. By then, unlike now where people are authorized in Cuba to have American currency, I think it was already illegal to have in your possession American money, which was punishable in some way.

In any case, the whole process of leaving Cuba was one where you had a visa or a visa waiver, you would write a letter to the appropriate office, you would get your ticket and you would be an unaccompanied minor. I was already 15 going on 16, my brother was 13 going on 14, but we also had younger cousins, one of whom is a medical doctor in Northern New Jersey and the other one is a dental hygienist in Orlando, Florida, who were only 11 (not quite 12) and 10 (not quite 11). They came in a few weeks later than we did, in April 1962. They were put in a camp for younger boys and teenage girls. There were several camps. I cannot remember now how many there were.

The idea was that this would be a short trip and we were going to come back to Cuba at some point and we were going to go to a Catholic school and everything was going to be wonderful until communism would be defeated and everyone would be happy again. That was not quite the way it worked. I have no regrets. I never saw my father again alive. He died in 1984. My brother would tell you the same story. My brother and I lived together in a refugee camp called Camp Matecumbe. Matecumbe is one of the keys of Florida. The camp was originally a summer camp for kids in what was then a very remote site off of Kendall Drive in Florida. Today, it is surrounded by housing and is urbanized and is unrecognizable, unless you really were there and remember. It became a very crowded place. There were wonderful things and not so wonderful things. There are books available in the United States and in Cuba that mention what we experienced. I think we are all real people.[36]

I am married now. I have my own profession. I finished my education here in a Catholic high school for my sophomore, junior and senior years. I went to the University of Delaware. I have a bachelor's degree and a master's degree from there. I went on to get a Ph.D. from Temple University in Philadelphia. Four years ago, I finished an MBA at Northwestern University.[37]

Ferreira said that one reason he wanted to have experiences beyond the east coast is that he had been doing some work for the federal government in the Leavenworth prison. He had traveled in other places as a consultant in the Midwest. He said, "It is very interesting the way people act out there in Chicago and all those places. They are different than here in the east coast." Ferreira was accepted and finished his program at the Kellogg School of Management. He believes his experience in the United States has been wonderful. In fact, he thinks that the entire Cuban exodus of about 14,000 boys and girls has within it a lot of success stories. He adds, "Another important thing is that most of us are giving something back, not just to the U.S., but to Cuba also."[38] On balance, he says,

It is a remarkable aspect of a very difficult situation. There are a number of people that, I am sure, continued to either curse the Cubans or curse the U.S. or feel that they were trapped in a tunnel without hope.

> Not everything that I saw or my brother saw was wonderful. I will never, never forget, for example, the fact that Cuban children who were black or who had African looking features were sent to somewhere in Portland, Oregon. I know that there is a group of Cubans in Portland, Oregon, today who reflect back to those days forty years ago. Most of them were Cubans who were bi-racial or who were black. Why there was segregation at that time, who can answer that? We were in the middle of a civil rights movement in those years.[39]

I attempted without success to locate and interview people who had been sent to Portland, Oregon, during those days of forty years ago. That period in United States history was a highly volatile time. Segregation was wrongful, people were rising up. The probability that those children were sent to Oregon seems high, because they were caught in a society that was working through the racial issue in very violent ways. Dr. Leonardo M. Marmol, professor and chair of the Department of Graduate Psychology at Seattle Pacific University, has learned from African Americans who have experienced this placement as children that black children that arrived under Operation Peter Pan were routinely sent to black families in Portland through either a church or agency in Portland that was willing to place them. But he adds, "That's all I know."[40]

Castro did not stop flights between Cuba and the United States after the "bungled" 1961 invasion backed by the U.S. in the Bay of Pigs.[41] But in 1962, the Cuban Missile Crisis brought an end to all flights from Havana to the United States. Operation Peter Pan had lasted 22 months. Even though exile continued in other ways, many parents were not able to leave Cuba. Thus, many children of Peter Pan grew up in foster care.[42]

Children who were reunited with their parents viewed the reunion differently. Some saw it as a dream that had come true. Others considered their parents unfamiliar. Some resented the situation. Triay says that whatever view they held, children felt great joy at the time of the first reunion.[43] Sometimes reunions were awkward because parents did not recognize their children who had become young adults. Some children had become proficient in English. Still others had forgotten their Spanish and could not communicate with their parents without an interpreter.[44]

Some parents were able to reunite with their children quickly before the Cuban Missile Crisis. Others fled to third countries to apply for a U.S. visa. Many were reunited in 1965 or soon after. In September 1965, the Cuban government allowed anyone with relatives in the United States to emigrate after October 10. Castro opened the port of Camarioca to boats from the United States. The U.S. Coast Guard accompanied the boats. The onset of the hurricane season ended the boat lifts.

EARLY INDIRECT THIRD COUNTRY FLIGHTS

Regardless of when Cubans emigrated to the United States, some had to do so by circuitous routes. By the mid–1960s, the Cuban government began to limit funds and resources that emigrants could take with them.[45] Some had to come to the United States by way of third countries. First, a family often applied for a visa to travel to an acceptable country such as Spain or Russia. Then, some traveled to a third country before coming to the U.S. In 1964, Adelfa Fernández and her family applied to travel to Spain, but first traveled to Czechoslovakia because it was the fastest way to leave Cuba. The final destination was Madrid, Spain. She recounts how she emigrated.

> I left Cuba with my husband and his parents in August 1964. My mom, my two brothers, their wives and my nephew remained in Cuba and left in March 1965. My father never left Cuba. He was a self-made man, was forced to drop out of school after completing the 5th grade and worked very hard since age 12, became accomplished in business and bought a pharmacy in the little town of San Luis in the Pinar del Río province. His dream became a reality. He was well known and respected. Under the Cuban law, even when he owned the pharmacy, a licensed pharmacist had to be appointed and will appear as the registered "owner," despite the fact that she just received a salary. I was very young at the time, but the government found out that the "owner" had left Cuba and technically they now owned the pharmacy even when the real owner was living in the country. They came and took the business away from my father. As a result of all that, he became very depressed and committed suicide. That was in 1961. After that the whole family began considering to leave Cuba.[46]
>
> Once you decided to leave, you had to resign from whatever job you had and remain unemployed until you left. Unless you had a lot of savings, it was financially difficult because you had no income.
>
> When we left Cuba, we had to leave everything. Before you left the country, you presented your documents to the country to notify your intentions and someone would come to your house to take inventory of all your possessions, meaning from glasses to silverware to a furniture, just everything. The day before you were to leave the country, they would come back, check again and go over the original inventory. If you broke a glass, you'd better have saved it to show that it broke. Everything belonged to the government. And that day, the house's front door would be sealed. You were not allowed to go back inside. Things like your family pictures I mailed to the United States to my uncle's house and they got here before I did. I left Cuba with five changes of clothes.
>
> Living in Spain was great because we were free, but we had no money. So my brother-in-law who was already in Miami sent us money. We rented a room in Madrid. We had a little breakfast in our room,

went for lunch to a public dining facility and at night a dollar and some change would buy a small meal. That was how we survived there for two and a half months until all the requirements for residency were met and we could enter the United States.

From Spain we came to Miami on November 4, 1964.[47]

FREEDOM FLIGHTS, 1965 TO 1973

The Cuban Adjustment Act of 1966 allowed Cubans to become legal residents without going through the process required of refugees from other countries to become citizens. President Lyndon B. Johnson signed the immigration bill that allowed Cuban refugees special status to live in the United States. Since many parents died at sea while sailing in inadequate vessels, the two governments signed an agreement for airlifts of Cubans who wished to come to the United States. These airlifts became known as the Freedom Flights. Most Pedro Pan children were united with their parents through the Freedom Flights.[48]

The flights brought very few Afro-Cubans to the United states because relatives of children in exile were given preference. Most relatives were white. Since the 1960s were racially volatile in the United States, Afro-Cubans were reluctant to emigrate. When they did emigrate they settled in the north in cities like New York, Detroit and Chicago. The Jewish and Chinese population also settled in the north.[49]

Alejandro Concepcion of Waterloo, Iowa, who came to the United States on a Freedom Flight in 1970, relates his experience. "We weren't really allowed to take anything with us. A lot of the pictures we have were sent over after we left Cuba by family members. They came through the mail, because we weren't allowed to take anything out of the country — just the clothes that you were wearing. That's it."[50]

Concepcion's mother, father, youngest sister and an older brother emigrated with him. His oldest brother had to stay because he was of military age. His grandmother also remained in Cuba along with other extended family members. "My mom and dad just didn't agree with the political system and my dad's oldest sister had left in 1960. She lived in Miami and was the one who sponsored us," he explained.[51]

The brother who stayed behind shared with Concepcion's wife, Gretchen, that the whole time he remained in Cuba, he knew that he wanted to come to join his family. He knew everything was on hold. He couldn't fall in love or get married. Concepcion agreed, "That would have made things a lot more difficult for him. While he was there, he was pretty much unable to do anything. It makes it more difficult because suppose you marry someone who doesn't want to leave their mom and dad. He didn't want to get into that situation."[52] The oldest brother now lives in the United States. Concepcion doesn't think remaining behind for a period of time had an ill effect on his brother. "He's really pretty well adjusted. As soon as he got to the States, he was hard working. He got married and has three children. He works for Fidelity Investments in Cincinnati and he's enjoying his life."[53]

Since Concepcion had a sponsor, emigrating to the United States was legal. He explained other conditions that were necessary for Cubans to leave.

> We were almost the last [of the Freedom Flights]. In 1973, they canceled the Freedom Flights. They used to give a certain amount of visas for political refugees. I don't know the exact number, but each year so many people who did not agree with the political system could leave and the U.S. government accepted so many people. But you had to have been sponsored by a relative that lived in the States.[54]

He had memories of actually emigrating:

> The day that we left, it was in the afternoon. I don't really remember, but every three or four months, my dad would go to some Cuban government office to check to see if it was our turn to go yet. Then one day, my dad just showed up with this taxi which is very unusual because they don't have many taxis there. He said, "Pack up. We're going." We just had to pack up what we had and left. We drove all night to the airport and the next morning, we were in Miami.[55]

Concepcion, who arrived during the summer, says that the flight to the United States was short, not more than a couple hours. He stresses the importance of family and the Cuban American community in the achievements his family has made.

> We stayed with relatives in Miami for a couple of months while my dad was looking for work. He couldn't find work there at that time. The economy was doing real well in California, in Los Angeles. The INS [Immigration and Naturalization Service] people offered to relocate us to Los Angeles. My dad had a nephew and a niece who agreed to help us out, so we moved to Los Angeles and that is where I grew up.[56]
>
> It was a combination of family and the other Cubans who had already been established here [who helped us achieve]. We quickly made friends with them and through their networking, my dad was able to find work at Martin Marietta, now it's called Lockheed Martin. He worked as a steelworker there for twenty years until he retired.[57]

MARIEL BOATLIFT, 1980S

The Mariel Boatlift of the 1980s consisted of 125,273 people who fled Cuba for the United States. The Mariels were the first wave of immigrants that were strongly differentiated by class and racial characteristics. Seventy-eight percent of Cubans identified themselves as white, compared to six percent as black and sixteen percent as another race. Most were single males without relatives in the United States. Emily H. Skop maintains that the early group of Mariels from April 21 to mid–May were distinctly different from later arrivals. Early arrivals resembled immigrants of the early 1970s, but later arrivals had few social networks to assist them. Early Mariels were mostly white while later Mariels were about 50 percent white. Both groups were largely of the working class.

There were five reasons why they immigrated. The group included those people who never believed in the revolution and who were left behind in previous emigrations; those citizens who were disenchanted with the revolution; those who were neutral toward the revolution but emigrated because of the appearance of the well-being of Cuban Americans; those people the Cuban regime forced into the boats and those from the prisons and the streets.[58] Two to three thousand were criminals or people with severe mental illness.[59] The quota for Cuban emigrants was 19,500. The United States government said that most Mariel Boatlift persons were motivated by economic interests, and were not asylum seekers. President Jimmy Carter created a temporary classification under the Cuban-Haitian Entrant Program in 1980. In mid–May Carter stopped the freedom flotillas by announcing that Cubans landing in Florida would be treated as applicants for asylum rather than refugees.[60] Mariels continued to come to the United States. It wasn't until President Ronald Reagan's term in 1985 that the Cuban government took back 2,746 patients and prisoners and the United States agreed to give visas to 3,000 political prisoners and their families and 20,000 other Cubans.[61] After the 1980 Mariel Boatlift of about six months, arrivals of boat people from Cuba dropped until the numbers rose from a few hundred in 1989 to a few thousand in 1993.[62]

From May 1979 to early 1980 Cubans sought asylum in Latin American embassies. Hector Sanyustiz drove a bus with five passengers through the gates of the Peruvian Embassy. Guards shot and wounded some and the Peruvian Embassy sent them to a hospital. The Peruvian Embassy did not allow Cuban soldiers to arrest the intruders, so Castro withdrew his guards. As a result, 10,800 people crowded the embassy until an emigration plan was worked out. Castro responded by allowing all Cubans to emigrate from the Port of Mariel provided they had relatives to pick them up. At the port, emigrants had to wait days for relatives, resulting in their having to take in strangers. These strangers were, in part, prisoners or institutionalized mentally ill.[63]

RAFTERS (*BALSEROS*), 1990S

Cubans emigrating in rafts was not a new phenomenon in the 1990s. But in August of 1994, Castro threatened in speeches to unleash an exodus of Cuban boat people. As a result, riots occurred in Havana. The number of people leaving Cuba on makeshift rafts increased. The Coast Guard and Border Patrol intercepted a post–Mariel high of about 40,000.[64] Saul Landau describes what preceded the mass emigration of the summer of 1994, known as the rafters or *balseros*.

> The Cuban government could no longer fulfill its pledge to provide each citizen with basic needs. Even the famed health and education systems had begun to show signs of serious deterioration. Power outages lasted up to 20 hours a day. Imagine the summer heat and humidity without the ability to turn on an air conditioner or even a fan! In parts of Havana, residents had no water for much of the day. Food had become scarce. And what the government did make available often lacked proper nutrition.[65]

The summer of 1994 saw *balseros*, Cuban people on makeshift rafts, going north to Florida. Some stole boats. Landau describes an event after which the Cuban government discontinued policing illegal emigration and permitted rafters who wished to leave for the U.S. to do so. A policeman shot an ex-offender, Gabriel, who was trying to steal a boat. An angry crowd consisting of between 700 and 900 men began to throw rocks, sticks and whatever they could find. As they marched a mile along the Malecón, which borders the sea to K Street, they shouted "Down with Fidel!"[66]

When the crowd reached the construction workers who were building the five-star Meliá Cohiba, the workers threw tools and wood chanting revolutionary slogans such as "¡Viva Fidel!" "¡Patria o muerte!"[67] Although the police were to use no weapons, they tried to stop the conflict. Landau writes the following,

> Fidel emerged, wearing his usual sidearm. The ubiquitous two bodyguards trailed him. He peered up and down the street as, according to observers, everyone almost froze in position. Fidel strode toward a group of policemen and conferred with them and then walked, by himself down the street. Some of the very people who had been screaming "Down with Fidel!" from apartments and from the street level now began to chant

"Fidel! Fidel!" The word spread: "Ahi está Fidel." He had again arrived and placed himself in the front line, where the danger was.[68]

The U.S. was faced with a wave of panicked Cuban rafters. Some 40,000 were tended to at the Guantánamo naval base. When the refugees began to riot, the U.S. and Cuba reached agreements. The immigration accords granted those Cubans at the base to come to the U.S. Permanent residence visas up to 20,000 a year were to be granted to other Cubans.[69]

In the 1990s Cubans used homemade rafts to emigrate. In 2001, another method used was by speedboats that charged up to $8,000 to smuggle one person.[70] In 1994 Castro allowed over 35,000 Cubans to leave by rafts and homemade boats, hoping to clear out dissenters. According to the United Nations, of the 25 Cubans that left each day, at least six died in the Straits of Florida.[71] About 30,000 rafters succeeded in arriving in the United States. Many others did not. Exact numbers are not known. In some cases, they were washed overboard. In others, they became dehydrated and died.[72] Catherine Moses, who was in Cuba in the aftermath of the rafter emigration, writes about its effect on families.

> Family members who stayed behind hoped and prayed for news that loved ones had successfully made the crossing. Often that news did not come. Individuals seemed to simply have disappeared and there was no real way to mourn. There was no funeral mass. The nation had to swallow its tears. People grieved silently for the sons, daughters, and friends who had been consumed by an unfriendly sea.[73]

Moses maintains that people left Cuba not so much because they wanted to. Rather they could not earn a living, even though some young Cubans knew English and in some cases, a third language or they had earned degrees.[74] Consuelo Martín found that emigration has become a survival strategy to confront the effects of the crisis on their daily lives. Research shows that most people "are seeking a home, the means to develop personally and professionally, and to a lesser extent, a way to satisfy their desire for personal freedom."[75]

The migration accords of 1994 and 1995 between the United States and Cuba attempted to end rafter migration.[76] Both countries were concerned about the loss of life. The United States agreed to admit 20,000 people a year and Cuba agreed to monitor its emigration. Rafters were to be returned to Cuba. Some rescued rafters were taken to the Guantánamo naval base. From there, many were taken to the United States for medical or humanitarian reasons. In 1995, all women, children and elderly had been transferred to the United States. Approximately 20,000 young men remained, of which, the United States accepted 15,000 later as part of the accords. Moses writes that three days after the accord was announced some rafting occurred.[77]

A group of 139 teens who came to the U.S. without their parents had a difficult time adjusting in foster homes because in Cuba at age 14, they are considered an adult. They were not used to laws controlling their behavior. Neither were they used to the family structure of foster care and schools. For this group, refugee workers placed them in subsidized apartments while they worked and attended part time adult education classes. If they chose not to work or go to school, they were denied federal aid.[78]

Her curiosity, the intriguing stories the Cubans told about their experiences and the extraordinary amount of creative expression in the camps at U.S. Navy base at Guantánamo Bay, Cuba, led Betsy Campisi, an anthropologist at SUNY-Albany, to conduct life history interviews of Cuban emigrants.[79]

Those that Campisi interviewed tended to be more on the professional level, but some were average Cubans. She talked to hundreds of people at Guantánamo for a year. I asked Campisi what their lives were like in Cuba. She said,

> The people in Cuba seemed to have happy childhoods and very good memories of their experiences in school, kind of up to the university level. Some of them, when they got to the university level and started questioning things, would have run-ins with authorities, but as they used the rhetoric of the revolution, they seemed to be able to get around some of these run-ins. As far as materially what their lives were like, they had materially very modest lives. The people who actually I interviewed, because they tended to be professionals, [said] there was a lot of scarcity during the Special Period, which was one of the reasons they fled Cuba, but they didn't seem to feel the scarcity quite as much as a lot of people I talked to in Guantánamo, although that could have been because I was talking to them about an experience that was seven years behind them.[80]

Campisi says that scarcity wasn't the only reason people fled Cuba. People had a combination of reasons. She compares the people on Guantánamo and professional Cubans.

> The people on Guantánamo talked about how there's no soap, there's no shampoo, the rationing card hardly had ten days worth of food in it. They had to steal from work in order to get enough food and clothing and, at the same time, they could be turned in by anybody at any time. It kind of made them all really neurotic. So people fled Cuba for a variety of reasons and some of them were more economic and some of them

were more political. A lot of the people that I interviewed who were professionals had tried to leave before and had gotten caught and either sent to jail for a short period of time or reprimanded or lost their job. So, when the opportunity came to leave freely, they left freely. The rafters left Cuba because in the Special Period, the economic problems were accompanied, it seems to me, by increasing government vigilance of people's behaviors. So, there was more frustration by the economic situation and also more instances of government coming down on people. When I was in Guantánamo, I distinctly remember a man who said he had been in jail for three months because he took a lobster tail home from work.

Other professional people talked about it as over a period of time, they became disenchanted with the revolution and had increasingly done things to get around it or had been laid off from work or gotten in trouble. One man left because he was trying to get permission to go on a fellowship to study overseas. He really wanted to go and he knew the person who was supposed to sign his paperwork probably wouldn't let him go. So he went over the person's head to somebody else who he was more friendly with and had him sign. That was really improper and he was about to be fired from his job. He resigned. Apparently it is better if you resign before you get fired. He had to go all the way to the end of the country, to Santiago, and get some paper signed. In this whole process of losing his job, being pursued and having the guy who signed the paperwork get in trouble, then the exodus happened and he got out of the country. Other professional people had actually tried to leave the country before, they had been frustrated with the whole system.[81]

Campisi believes that it is frustrating for people to have economic hardships and try to do things that are entrepreneurial to try to make up for that and can be sanctioned by the government. People's efforts are a vicious cycle. When they get more and more disenchanted, they take extreme measures and then want to leave.

I asked Campisi how the Cubans reacted when they were treated as illegal immigrants. Since she interviewed mostly people in Miami, one man in Rochester, New York, and another in Pennsylvania, she points our that seventy percent of Cubans end up living in Miami and their community in Miami is really strong. They were not treated like illegal immigrants. When the United States issued the decree on August 19, 1994, that immigrants were going to be detained, Campisi says,

Some people were in the middle of the ocean and were picked up by the Coast Guard. They didn't realize that they were going to be sent all the way back to Guantánamo. One woman made it all the way to Key West to the land, she was put back on the Coast Guard cutter and sent to Guantánamo. When they arrived in Guantánamo, the Justice Department read a statement to them that said, something to the effect, that you are illegal immigrants or illegal migrants, which is what Janet Reno said. If you want asylum, you are going to have to go back to Havana and apply for asylum through the Special Interest Section. You are not going to the United States. And then with that, they were let off the boat and put into the camp. In effect, their identity was questioned from the minute they arrived on the base. They all had to face this issue: "But we're not, we have always been welcomed with open arms. What is this?" Some of their reactions to being detained were: "This must be a test." I don't know how this comes from growing up in Cuba. "This must be a test. The government is testing us to see how badly we want to go to the United States. They must think we are like the Mariel people, a lot of criminals. We are not. We are good people. We left for political reasons."[82]

Campisi holds the rafters believed they were being detained because of the United States. "They felt like they were pawns in a chess game between Fidel Castro and Bill Clinton. They felt like they were victims caught in the middle of diplomatic problems between the two countries. They didn't really see that they were going to overwhelm Florida again."[83]

In addition to being detained, the rafters had difficult experiences at sea. Campisi says the way one rafter told this story "is sickening:"

The rafting experience depended upon two major things: how strong the raft was or whether it was a boat and the weather. The worst case was: people left on a raft that wasn't well constructed, a storm hits and the raft starts to break apart and sharks come. When I was there, I felt sick to my stomach hearing the worst case ... a family with a nine year old boy and a seven year old girl in the middle of the ocean and a shark comes by the raft. The boy tries to scare it away by hitting it with the oar and the shark flips around and knocks the little girl out of the raft. They have to watch the little girl get eaten by sharks.[84]

Campisi says that other people had similar frightening stories. The worst stories are of rafts breaking apart or getting caught in bad storms in the middle of the pitch black night with giant waves upon them. One story is "The rafts break apart. They tie them together. The stronger raft goes to get help. When they come back, nobody's there anymore. The occupants of the raft are gone."[85] Campisi says because a lot of people went through traumatic ordeals before they were picked up by the Coast Guard, when they were put in Guantánamo, the trauma was compounded.[86] A third traumatic experience awaited them when their situation was not addressed by appropriate organizations.

The trauma they went through was never fully addressed by either their relief agency, World Relief, or the military. World Relief was not given the resources by the government to address that and the military was unprepared and unwilling to address those issues. On top of the rafting trauma, we have the trauma of being detained and nobody is there to hear their trauma stories and help them process that and really do things to make it so the trauma does not continue for a year and a half.[87]

Campisi heard many stories. She shares two others.

> One woman I interviewed said they got on a boat with a bunch of people. It's got a motor and zooms out until the Coast Guard intercepts it. When Coast Guard picked up people in the sea, they always sank the ship. They shot at the ships until they sank, no matter whether they were a ship, little boat or a raft, so they could tell that the people had been picked up, so they wouldn't find things floating without occupants and not knowing what happened to the occupants. That was the least traumatic scenario.[88]
>
> The most amazing survival story that one man told me while I was in the camp was: He had been in prison for some minor offense, there was some kind of thing called dangerousness that they would put you in jail for. I don't know [what] made you become dangerous. Anyway, he was told by the guard in the jail that you're in jail, we are letting you out, you are going to leave the country right now. So he got a little cushion or raft and he was on his stomach lying on this raft for two or three days and he thought he had drowned and he was still alive. He finally got picked up before he was too dehydrated or sunburned or anything. He was a black man. But his nerves were so shot from the experience that his hands and feet just dripped sweat constantly. I interviewed him for medical parole and he would be apologizing because his hands were all wet. I just thought a lot of people are nervous. He said, "No, look at my hands while I am talking." You could just see little drops forming they were sweating so bad. His nerves were destroyed.[89]

Campisi says the people had a lot of faith that the United States was going to save them.

ENTERING THE U.S. BY LAND, 2001

Cubans are increasingly entering the United States by land, crossing either the Mexican or Canadian borders or by air with falsified passports.[90]

A study by Antonio Aja, Center for International Migration Studies at the University of Havana, revealed that in 1990 immigration took on economic influences due to Cuba's financial crisis. Economic reasons are intertwined with political reasons. Citizens wanted to be reunited with their families overseas or they believed that the revolution's social project held no hope for improvement in the economic situation.[91]

EMIGRATING TO A THIRD COUNTRY FIRST, 2001

In 1964, Adelfa Fernández, now a Miami resident, emigrated to the United States with the help of two other countries. Since her family had to become U.S. residents before they were allowed into the United States, they did their application for U.S. residency in Spain. By way of a Czechoslovakia airline, her family eventually got to Spain, but first stopped in Czechoslovakia.[92]

Thirty-seven years after Fernández arrived, Asley L. Marmol came to live in Miami. He tells his emigration story of 2001 with a great deal of passion. Asley and his wife, Yeni, emigrated first to Holland. He explains.

> I remember being in a strange country asking for asylum in a different culture with no guarantees of any success at all. I remember in Europe, Holland in this case, a very, very large sad procedure of asylum which was denied in the first instance. We appealed it and remained over there, but it was very, very dark. We had the possibility of coming here and getting together with the family, but it is very hard to leave your normal, natural world and restart it in a place where you do not know what is going to happen.[93]

I asked Asley whether there were any problems leaving Holland to come to the United States. He said,

> It was difficult, but with the help of the family we could get all of the support needed to come over here. It was not easy. There was a lot of waiting and uncertainty. The Dutch didn't deport us to Cuba, but also didn't open the door for us. They let us stay, but with a legal status that didn't allow us to have our own house or rent a house, to work. There was a procedure that you were inside the country, but you had barely rights to remain there but not to live there as the rest of the people there. Even still we are appreciative and are very in debt to them. They allowed us to stay there and to have shelter.[94]

Holland was a stop in Asley's and Yeni's journey to get where they wanted to go, the United States. I asked, "What made you decide to go to Holland first? Was that the safest route or the way open?" He replied,

> That was the way open. It was the only way possible at the moment I was trying to find a way out. Originally, we were traveling to Russia. Cubans at that time didn't need a visa to access the country, but we made a transit [transfer or connections] in Holland. Of course, we were looking at that transit [transfer or connections] as a democratic nation where we could ask for asylum. We knew that it was a country that was part

of many international agreements that would help refugees. Russia is not the best example of that given all the convulse [political upheaval] of the last ten years they had had. So, Holland was a better place to restart. That's why we did it.[95]

I ask Asley whether he was trying to get to Russia or trying to get to Holland. He replied that that he was trying to get to Holland. Russia was just the formal destination, but in his mind it was Holland. I asked whether that made his journey easier. He replied,

> Yes, because Russia was the only country at the time that did not ask Cubans for a visa. So, we were able to live outside. We pretended that we were going as tourists invited by a Russian family that never existed. We just used this plan as a way out and bought a ticket with transit in Holland, so we ask for asylum in Holland.[96]

Asley and Yeni faced many challenges before they left Cuba on their indirect route to the United States. Before he left Cuba he spoke of not telling his family because he didn't want to be discovered and that might keep him from departing. I asked him if his family in Cuba knew he was leaving, would that put those family members in harm's way. He replied,

> It would, but it — I don't want to say that I don't trust my mother, but I was pretty sure that they would not tell. At least my closest relatives would not tell, but I didn't want the possibility of a mistake or a word passed to the wrong person at the wrong time. It was one shot. If we missed that shot, there probably wasn't going to be another possibility like that to leave in a safer way other than getting into a raft into the sea. A raft was not safe enough, let's say that I was not able. I was brave enough to do it, [but] it is very risky. So, that was our only shot, my wife and I together, to leave in a safe, not totally safe, but a safer way, and I was not going through any major risk. If it would have failed, I knew that I was going to be expelled from the university and I would have to restart another way. My personal history inside the country, my fissure with the country would have made it more difficult because of that intent of departure. They consider that treason and all those medieval concepts that you have of mankind and people, that certificate of ownership the government has on Cubans. If you intend to do something different than that, they say that you are a traitor. They will mark you with a scarlet letter. Let's say for the next ten years, you have the scarlet letter everywhere you go. If you get lucky, maybe when the situation changes, you can go ahead with your life, but the most important thing was my career. I was going to lose it. I didn't want to put my family in that position of sharing my secret. Also, I didn't want any possibility of mistakes. I was trying to have everything perfect.[97]

I asked Asley, "Could we say formally that you left in a legal way because you were going to Russia?" He said,

> I think I left in an illegal way because first of all, I had to somehow misinform or change my identity by hiding the fact that I was a student of the university. The way the system works is if you are in any intellectual or professional institutions, you have to have permission from those institutions in order to go outside the country. For teachers, it is very difficult to get those permissions. In our case, we were not teachers yet, but we were studying for that. Also, it was not possible to get permission from them, so we first had to bribe the immigration inspectors and second, go to the place where they keep the records and pretend that we lost our documents. When they reissued our documents, we didn't say that we were students of the university.[98]

Thus, even though Asley was going to Russia, technically, his migration was not considered legal because he was affiliated with the teaching profession. He explains, "They wouldn't have allowed us, because they're very strict [about] that. They are afraid of losing professionals. They keep very, very tight measures not to lose professionals, [especially] teachers and doctors...."[99]

Conclusions

Although Cuban emigrants used a variety of ways to emigrate, none was without challenges. Some early emigrants left in relatively safe circumstances, but even their travels were not without a great deal of uncertainty. As time passed and events posed new challenges, Cubans emigrated in greater numbers in the ways that posed a threat to their physical existence. Whatever way they chose, it was not without risk. To those Cubans who took a risk or had the risk thrust upon them and survived, one result remains clear, they rose to the challenge and the new life in the United States.

7

Cuban American Families

*Let not the waves of the sea separate us now, and the years you
have spent in our midst become a memory.*
— Kahlil Gibran

In the United States, the dominant minority populations are African
Americans, Hispanics and Asians.[1] The Hispanic population has become
the largest minority population at 37 million, superceding that of African
Americans at 36.2 million.[2] McLoyd *et al.* predicted that by 2050 the U.S.
population will be 25 percent Hispanic. The United States will no longer
be predominately white, but will be multicultural. Asian American and
Pacific Islander populations will also increase. The increment results from
increased fertility rates and younger average ages of African Americans,
Hispanics and Asian Americans. For Hispanics and Asian Americans, the
increment also results from increased immigration. The changes predicted,
however, "are scarcely reflected" in quantitative research in the social science journals of the 1990s.[3]

Cubans in the United States at the Beginning of the 21st Century

The Pew Hispanic Center in Washington, D.C., sought to improve
upon the Census 2000 regarding the Hispanic origin question. Believing
the Hispanic population was undercounted, their goal was to understand
its composition. Their study reports on an alternative estimate of the
breakdown of the Hispanic population according to national origin
groups. Census Bureau data reduces the "other" category by more than
half. Pew's estimate does not change the overall size of the Hispanic population, but it does offer a new calculation of how national groups are dis-
tributed within that population.[4]

In 2000, Cuban Americans numbered 1,241,685 and represented four percent of the Hispanic or Latino race.[5] Most of the population was born in Cuba and came to the United States after 1959 when the revolution brought radical change.[6] In the 1980s, Cubans in the United States settled predominantly in the urban areas of Greater Miami, southern Florida, Greater New York and Los Angeles.[7] In 2000, Cubans were highly concentrated in the South (80.1 percent). They were most likely to live outside the central city within a metropolitan area (76.0 percent).[8] In 2000, slightly over eighteen percent of Miami's population was Cuban American, the highest number by far than any other location in the United States. A little over five percent of Florida's population was Cuban American, far higher than the percentage in any other state.[9]

Cubans are still the third largest single Hispanic group in the United States, at 1.3 million. There are nearly as many Dominicans and Salvadorans, 1.1 million each.[10] On the national level, Cubans living in Florida are the best known of all the Hispanic population. They are still the largest group, with nearly 900,000 residents statewide. Their growth has been slower than the other groups, and nearly an equal number now are New Latinos (850,000), weighted toward South American origins. There are also over half a million Puerto Ricans and close to 400,000 Mexicans.[11]

Most Cubans, 68 percent, are foreign-born. Few entered the country in the last ten years (27 percent). Most represent a pre–1990 immigration stream.[12] They average 11.9 years of education, and are economically successful with the mean earnings of those employed being above $13,500 and only 18 percent falling below the poverty line.[13]

As a part of the Hispanic population, Cuban Americans are often statistically analyzed in relation to the Hispanic or Latin group. The 2002 National Survey of Latinos by the Pew Hispanic Center/Kaiser Family Foundation uses the terms Hispanic and Latino interchangeably.[14] Five percent of adult Latinos originate in Cuba, a similar percentage for all countries of origins except Mexico, which stands at 64 percent. Seventy-eight percent of Cubans are foreign born compared to 63 percent for the total group of Latinos.[15] Fifty-three percent speak Spanish as the dominant language while 30 percent are bilingual and 17 percent speak English as the primary language. Among Latinos as a whole, 47 percent speak Spanish, 28 percent are bilingual and 25 percent speak primarily English.[16]

Fifty-five percent of Cubans prefer the racial category of white and 24 percent prefer Hispanic or Latino. The preference is reversed in all other country or area comparisons.[17] Forty-two percent of Cubans believe that Latinos discriminating against other Latinos is a major problem, 38 percent, a minor problem and 15 percent, not a problem. When compared to the total Latino population, the results are 47 percent, 36 percent and 16 percent respectively.[18]

Concerning reported reasons Latinos discriminate against each other, 45 percent of the Cubans said it is mainly because they come from different countries. Thirty-six percent believed discrimination was because of different income levels while only seven percent believed it was due to skin color. Thirty-one percent of the total Central Americans believed discrimination existed because of country origin, 41 percent, income levels and eight percent, skin color.[19]

Only 20 percent of Cubans reported not having health insurance compared to 35 percent of the total Latino population group.[20]

MIGRATION AND SOCIOECONOMIC STATUS

Cubans came to the United States in different immigration waves. They represent different ethnicities. Dr. Delvis Fernández Levy, president, Cuban American Alliance Education Fund, Inc., explains,

> The first wave is the historical émigré or exile. In the early sixties, right after the Cuban Revolution, these tended to be people associated with the previous government. In the majority of cases, they came with their family unit (mother, father, children, even grandparents). Another wave was in 1980 when a massive number of Cubans left Cuba in boats. These were boats that came from the United States. These Cubans represented a different class (class in terms of ethnicity). In the 1990s, there was the rafter crisis. A lot of people just took off.[21]

The largest emigration of Cubans to the United States has occurred since 1960. Political and economic developments in Cuba influenced their emigration, but their leaving Cuba was, in most cases, voluntary. In the 1960s and 1970s, the emigrants were mostly middle and upper class professionals and business people. In the late 1980s, most people were working and lower class. The Cuban government also released from prison thousands of criminals who came to the United States.[22]

"In the longer course of history, human migration and economic development will shape the region more than any transient breakdown of political order in a particular country, even the exceptional case of the Cuban Revolution,"[23] writes Ronald L. Taylor. The Cuban family and its uniqueness in the United States is best understood within the context of the progressive family law in the first half of the 20th century, which is reflected in the high level of modernization of Cuba by the mid-twentieth century. Lisandro Pérez writes, "The more privileged and modernized segments of that society formed the catalyst and the core of the post revolutionary exodus to the United States."[24]

In 1986, most of the Cuban population in the United States were immigrants. In 1980, three-fourths of the 803,226 Cubans living in the United States had been born in Cuba. Cubans had a higher level of family income than the other Spanish-origin populations and only a slightly lower level than the U.S. population.[25] More people in the Cuban American group had a variety of skills, aspirations and experiences.

The demographic differences of the later arriving Mariels made resettlement difficult because sponsors were hard to find. Emily H. Skop maintains, "The popular misconception of exiles as criminals also hampered the relocation process."[26] She explains that the negative images encouraged fear among older immigrants that the Mariels would not blend into their community. Age, class, race and 20 years of ideological differences made the Mariels too different. The Mariel Boatlift complicated the success story image of earlier Cuban immigrants. Forty-three percent were resettled in Florida and the remaining in New Jersey, New York and California. White Mariel immigrants tend to successfully return to Miami compared to nonwhite migrants. White Mariels tend to be more accepted by Cuban immigrants in Miami and they tend to have more extended family to join in Miami. Skop concludes that race may be a factor, but lack of access to a supportive network is more important to attaining upward mobility economically.[27]

Time of arrival is a particular indicator for Cuban Americans of diverse family type. The first wave of immigration in 1959 consisted of highly trained professionals and their families. They left for political reasons. In 1965–1973, a large number of immigrants were elderly. They contributed to the three generation Cuban American household. In 1980, the Marielitos and, in the 1990s, the *balseros* or rafters contained mostly young males of lower socioeconomic status.[28]

Family Types

Just as there is no one family type, no single Cuban American family type exists in the United States. The structure of a family is formed by immigrants' reactions to specific contexts and contingencies. Time of arrival, poverty, resources, family cohesion, acculturation, biculturalism, and generational status influence family structure.[29] But whatever form the Cuban family becomes, Leonardo M. Marmol, professor and chair of the Department of Graduate Psychology at Seattle Pacific University, sums up Cuban family characteristics this way:

> We are a collective culture as opposed to an individualistic culture, i.e., the Harry Triandis distinction between allocentric and idiocentric cultures. In the Cuban culture you have a business and you have jobs, you give them to your family first. It is expected that your oldest son is going to take over the business. My cousin is now looking to retiring and turning the business over to his son. His two daughters also work in the business. The daughter's husband works in the business. It's that kind of familial support. Then we get together on holidays, anniversaries and birthdays. It's always a big thing. My cousins' homes in Miami are always full of people coming in and visiting. I'm the one who is isolated here on the West coast because of the fact that I came out here to go to college and then I stayed in California all of my life until I started moving further and further north.
>
> My wife's mother lives in Boynton Beach, Florida. At Christmas time as soon as school lets out here, wherever I am, we get on a plane and we go and spend our Christmas in Florida. We get to visit with my relatives there on Christmas Eve and my wife's mother on Christmas Day. We stay very much in touch with the family. Whenever anyone in the family has any trouble, everybody rallies around. Anybody who needs money, other people jump in and help.[30]

Helping, Marmol says, includes assisting family still living in Cuba.

FAMILY CHARACTERISTICS

Persons of Cuban origin had the lowest proportion of individuals younger than 18 (19.2 percent), according to the March 2000 U.S. Census report. The proportion of elderly, 65 years and older, was 21.0 percent. Cuban family households were most likely to have only two people (41.3 percent). Cubans were least likely to have never been married (20.4 percent).[31]

Cuban Americans are proportionately well educated, with 73.0 percent having at least a high school education; 34.4 percent are employed with earnings of $35,000 or more a year; 17.3 percent live below the poverty line and 14.0 percent have households with five or more people.[32] (See Table 7.1.)

Daniel T. Lichter and Nancy S. Landale found in the 1980s that marital bonds have been historically strong for Cuban Americans and most live in two parent families. While parental employment status has an effect on child poverty for Latinos in general, Cuban American women had rates of labor force participation parallel to non–Latino white women and rates lower than those for other Latino women. Seventy percent of Cuban American

TABLE 7.1						
FAMILY HOUSEHOLD CHARACTERISTICS BY DETAILED HISPANIC ORIGIN AND NON-HISPANIC WHITE TOTALS, 2000						
In percentages						
Characteristics	*Central and South American*	*Cuban*	*Mexican*	*Puerto Rican*	*Hispanic*	*Non-Hispanic White*
Five or more people	27.9	14.0	35.5	18.1	30.6	11.8
At least a high school education	64.3	73.0	51.0	64.3	57.0	88.4
Full-time, year-round workers with annual earnings of $35,000 or more	24.5	34.4	20.6	29.6	23.3	49.3
Living below the poverty level	16.7	17.3	24.1	25.8	22.8	7.7

Source: Melisa Therrien and Roberto R. Ramirez, 2000, *The Hispanic Population in the United States: March 2000*, Current Population Reports, P20-535, Washington D.C.: U.S. Census Bureau, 4–6.

families had a full-time employed father. In female headed families, only 34 percent of the Cuban American children had mothers who are not employed. Moreover, the mothers of Cuban American children in female-headed families are more likely to work full time.[33]

Because of the special refugee status of Cubans, children in families are immediately eligible for and will receive higher levels of public assistance. The 1996 welfare legislation affects eligibility once Cubans have been in the United States for five years. Thus, the high rates of public assistance prevail in the first two generations. By the third generation, these Cuban Americans will have become integrated into mainstream society, in part, due to the assistance they received.[34]

BONDS OF FICTIVE KIN OR FRIENDS AND FAMILY MEMBERS

Kin is most often defined by blood or marriage. But kin can also be formed by the concept of "fictive kin." Fictive kin refers to a family-type relationship based on "religious rituals or close friendship ties, [which] constitutes a type of social capital that many immigrant groups bring with them and that facilitates their incorporation into the host society."[35] The most common fictive kin that duplicates many of the rights and obligations accompanying family ties are religious institutions. In the case of Cuban and Cuban American families, those institutions are Catholicism and Yoruba. These institutions give individuals social capital or access to opportunities. The ways that social networks facilitate immigrants' settlement and assimilation are widely shared, but have not been studied extensively.[36] Helen Rose Ebaugh and Mary Curry maintain their findings are applicable to immigrants of all ethnicities. Perhaps of great interest is their finding regarding the relationship of the immigrants' new country to their previous country.

> The expectation that one who 'makes it' in America will support not only fictive kin within the immigrant community but also family and fictive kin back home is a strong norm among both Hispanic and Asian immigrants. Among all of the Hispanics we interviewed, the sense of responsibility to routinely send money to relatives in the home country was very strong.[37]

Dr. Consuelo Martín Fernández, Training Center of International Migrations, University of Havana, wrote in 2002 that the results of recent investigations in Cuba demonstrate that to emigrate is one of the strategies of the family to face problems generated by the country's crisis. The solution of emigrating, in turn, generates other personal, family and social problems and conflicts. The family forms a network with those members that live in Cuba and those who live outside the Island. This networking is done to the extent that members assume functions of physically absent members, for example, economic assistance. The center studied Cuban families to find out what duties and rights were assigned to the emigrated Cuban family in daily thought. They found that the best emigrated family is one that maintains the bonds of relatives, has a positive relationship with Cuba and has successful adaptation in their new society.

The center compared its 2002 study to its 1997 study. They found that the initial emphasis was on economic assistance from the emigrating family. The later study also emphasized expression of family bonds and connection with Cuba. They conclude that the emigration of a single family member always impacts the daily life of the group.[38]

In addition to the bonds with their homeland, once new immigrants receive help in their new home country, they establish the expectation to return that assistance. Bonds of solidarity and reciprocity become a part of the social network and support system of the immigrant community as well.[39]

Adelfa Fernández, Miami resident, explains why and how her culture is caring for both family and friends. I asked whether Cuban Americans combine both cultures in their lives in so doing. She says,

> Yes, and because of the inter-marriage we want to be polite with each other. Actually, we all enjoy it. My son-in-law kills for the pork that I make. I have adopted what I like of each culture. We are a very close knit family. If I know someone in my family is in trouble, I drop everything and I go to their side. That is how most Cuban families relate. The same applies to close friends who become an extended family.[40]

ECONOMIC SUCCESS

Lisandro Pérez's research gives several reasons for individual economic adjustment and upward mobility. The first reason is the person's socioeconomic level in Cuba, age, father's occupation, satisfaction with occupation in the United States and ability to transfer skills. Other reasons are: the impossibility of returning to Cuba, the political nature of emigration and the middle-class ethic.[41]

Another factor in the economic success of immigrant Cubans is their "self-enclosed enclave in South Florida."[42] The enclave insulated immigrants from the usual processes of the segmented labor market. They entered the work force through many businesses in Miami owned and operated by earlier arriving Cuban immigrants.[43]

Pérez says the family bridges the individual and community sources that aid immigrant economic adjustment. In fact, household economic strategies are critical to understanding the economic adjustment of Cuban Americans. In the twenty years prior to 1986, most of the literature on economic adjustment lacked a household perspective because surveys interviewed only men or heads of households.[44] Pérez's research identifies structural features of the family that aid economic adjustment "High rates of female labor-force participation ... low fertility; and ... the importance of the three-generation family and economic contribution of the elderly."[45]

The high family income among Cubans is because they have proportionately more workers per family than other Hispanic and the general United States populations. Few families have only one worker. In 1983, the Cuban-origin population participated in the labor force more than Hispanics and the United States population. Perez concludes that the work ethic and cooperation of the family are the key reasons the Cuban immigrant is economically successful.[46]

Robert Suro writes that Cuban Americans are one of the most affluent Latino groups in the United States. Their success is due to geography, timing of migration, politics, policies of immigration and "massive public assistance" in education, housing and business. Suro says his position is not meant to diminish the resourcefulness and sacrifice of Cuban exiles, but given these advantages, any Latino group could have done well in Miami.[47] Important to note is that the focus of Suro's study is the Miami enclave. Suro agrees that the Miami Cubans who created the initial successful enclave or "builders of the barrio" managed to avoid one of the pitfalls of other groups. Cubans expanded out of Little Havana, leaving it at a working-class poverty level. The most successful Cubans migrated to the suburbs, taking economic and human capital with them. As they settled, they "stuck together" and created new economic enclaves. The left-behind *Calle Ocho* or Little Havana has "become the historic old town of Cuban Miami with its restaurants and bookstores, its ceiba trees and its memorial to those who fell at the Bay of Pigs. Now *Calle Ocho* is a place of memory and identity." Suro reminds us that Miami Cuba is not a "collection of urban neighborhoods."[48] He explains, "Cuban Miami is a barrio without borders because it is a frame of mind and a network of relationships that is interwoven throughout South Florida and that stretches across the water down to Cuba itself."[49]

The first immigrants, the builders of the barrio, came from upper and middle classes. Suro says their socioeconomic status does not entirely explain their success. Circumstances in the United States are also an element. The United States provided opportunities for growth of their capital. Nonetheless, Little Havana provided a place for Cubans to adapt to the United States, build networks and gain capital. The Miami Cubans never faced the challenge of continuous migration, thus they had time in between waves to assimilate newcomers and continue building the barrios. The fact that the migration waves were of different socioeconomic composition often filled new demands of the enclave. The United States provided more assistance to the Cuban refugees than it had to any other refugee program. Many Cubans worked or received income from the CIA or both. Law was on the side of Cubans. Regardless of whether they entered the United States illegally, they were allowed to live and work in the United States the rest of their lives almost independent of the U.S. economy.[50]

Suro believes that material success in the United States does not mean Cuban Americans focus their attention on life here. He maintains that wealth makes it easier to avoid "total engagement with a new land, while poverty sometimes focuses attention to one's surroundings."[51]

Zulema E. Suárez holds that stereotyping of the Cuban American group lacks evidence and puts the group at risk. First, successive waves of immigrants to the Golden Exiles were often perceived as successful. Thus, the needs of the lower strata of Cuban Americans has not been recognized or addressed. Suárez explains, "The economic success of the entrepreneurial segment of the Cuban American population has not been widely shared, as it has profited from the existence of low-wage, unskilled Cuban workers who have become the working class of the Golden Exiles."[52]

Betsy Campisi, anthropologist at SUNY-Albany, says a lot of the Cubans that she interviewed, especially the professional people, have adjusted very well. They have had to work hard, especially in Florida, because the salary base is low. Among the people she interviewed were a couple of engineers: "The wife was working on passing her boards and the husband was employed in an electrical company. They were both doing very well and they had bought a house. The people who were willing to adjust and really learn English have done really well."[53]

Campisi says that the lower skilled people have a much harder time because they come in on the low end of the income, often at the minimum wage. "There's a big shock in the beginning on the amount of work you have to do just to make ends meet and pay all the bills. In Cuba, you are not paying bills for all these things. You have free rent, next to free phone service, and next to free electricity. In Cuba, they are struggling to get food and here they're struggling to get their housing paid for."[54]

Campisi met people in extreme situations. The most extremely maladjusted people wouldn't let her interview them. She says that they would talk informally but once she wanted to formally interview them, they wouldn't do it. She explains,

> They had expected to make a lot more money and have less work. And they used the words, "I am not a slave. I am not a slave, why do I have to do this. I hate this system. I wasn't expecting this. I thought this was a free land and you are not free here. You are a slave to your employer." The people who are willing to adjust can do well and I have seen a lot of people do well. Because I interviewed mostly professionals, I can't say what the average experience is. There are time issues. Time is a lot different here. There's a lot less time. You don't have time for things and that's also hard to adjust to. And people really miss their families. They really miss their families bad.[55]

Political Activity

Ambivalence toward the United States is most recognizable in the political realm. Influence of Miami Cubans could have been exerted in a variety of matters on the national level, but instead they have focused on Cuba and, in some cases, its liberation. Dissent is not tolerated. Perhaps this position is due to the fact that Cubans have been unable to return home for visits during most of the building of the barrio. Building the barrio became a way of defeating Castro. Thus, while the Miami Cubans enjoy socioeconomic success and political influence, it is their shared historical adversity that politically energizes.[56]

Suárez reports that political views shift from generation to generation and within families and that views will continue to shift in future generations. The hard-line anti–Castro position has over time become more moderate. Despite their differences, the generations are bound by their love of freedom and longing for Cuba.[57]

Some political activity is focused on the United States' embargo provisions. Delvis Fernández Levy is the president of the Cuban American Alliance Education Fund (CAAEF), an organization that educates the public at large on issues related to hardships caused by current U.S.-Cuba relations. It works "outside ideological constraints, in compliance with U.S. law, and respectful of Cuba's sovereignty and independence."[58] CAAEF calls for a reassessment of U.S. policy that causes undue harm to both Cubans and Americans.

In 1991, Brothers to the Rescue, a Miami-based exile group, was founded to assist the Cuban people to bring about change and to bring democracy. In 1996, the group gained world recognition when Cuban military jets shot down two of its planes, which killed four pilots. The incident prompted worldwide criticism of President Castro. In 2003, Brothers to the Rescue suspended flights due to a lack of funds and a shortage of rafters. Founder Jose Basulto said, "The pilots flew more than 2,500 missions in 13 years, spotting and helping to save 4,200 rafters in their first three years alone."[59]

Cultural Traditions

Cuban Americans tend to hold onto cultural traditions and their language. These cultural traditions are often viewed as clannish when they are in reality a force for group cohesiveness basic to their adjustment and success. Some evidence to support the acceptance of their new culture is that they are more likely to marry outside their group than other Latinos and have the highest rate of naturalization. Suárez writes that the rate can be viewed that "Cuban Americans want to participate in and be part of mainstream society."[60]

Assimilation

As Cuban Americans become assimilated, will the division between birth heritage and new culture disappear? Perhaps not disappear, but blend, thus contributing a richness of diversity. Fernández Levy believes it is important to remember the following:

> There are two things that come to mind. One is the idealization of the Cuban family as a wide unit that is quite inclusive of different members of the family and different age groups. Some of the cohesion that we like to give to a family, both trans-generational and across age groups, is very healthy. To me, it is a sign of hope. So many times I see, in so-called advanced societies, families reduced just to children playing by themselves, so parents can do their thing, or children put in an institution. There tends to be a certain emphasis on dividing rather than in bringing together which I think, at least in the ideal, Cuba tries to promote. That is one thing. Another is the pain that the Cuban family is undergoing that needs to heal. If you could perhaps give some insight as to how the healing process can take place because, at the same time that we have this beautiful, idealized family, our families are highly divided because of politics or because of the impasse in the relations between the U.S. and Cuba. Families have problems. When you live under the same roof, you are going to have people who fight, people who have disagreements, but, because of their proximity, there is always hope that the problem will be solved. Now when the problem exists between Americans, you can talk about it, you can always come back to it. In the case of the Cuban family, we have this idealized situation of how wonderful we are, how much we love each other, but then we have time that separates us. We might not be able to see a loved one for years and years and years and years. In the meantime, you will have problems, just like you have with people that live in the same household. When you go back to visit the loved ones, you spend so little time. You have this joyful meeting at the beginning with the pain just left behind. You never quite deal with the festering issues that creates a tremendous source of pain between people that have been separated for many, many years and yet, in their vision, they see themselves as being together or in unison with those people they left behind.[61]

Adelfa Fernández, who arrived in the United States in 1964, explains how diversified her family became.

> When my husband and I went to California, my two brothers were already there, so, we all lived close to one another. We are lucky in the sense that we were able to raise our children close to each other. One of my brothers and I lived in the same town. His children and my daughters are very close. My other brother's children, three of them, lived

about an hour away and got together with cousins on birthdays and holidays, still remain close to this day also. But as they grew older, they have branched out. All of the children in our family that are married have married American young men and women. It has changed in some ways, but not really. The Americans they married have learned to understand the Cuban family culture, but the Spanish language is being lost. My daughters and my brothers' kids speak perfect Spanish, only one of my nieces is not as fluent [in] Spanish. None of my great-nephews speak Spanish, probably the only one that is going to speak Spanish is my grandson, because of his father, although he is an American, he learned Spanish after he married my daughter, Rebecca. The father wants Rebecca to speak Spanish to the little baby all the time so he can be bilingual. As far as other customs, I think that we have learned to respect each other. Sometimes there might be a little culture conflict there. Americans have their way of thinking. Cubans have their own way of thinking. On the other hand, what happened to me personally was that I went to California when I was 21. I lived there for 14½ years. At times I was living in a place where there were no Cubans. I was almost forced to become a culture myself. I find that, even to this day, in some ways I do not act like a Cuban. For instance, I do not pop-up at anybody's house without calling first. But Cubans just knock on your door and they are there. They just drop by, [that] kind of thing. Personally, I want to know when someone is coming to visit.

When I was recently watching a PBS documentary, I am reminded of how true dropping in is. Willy Chirino, a Cuban singer, said as he was being interviewed, "At my house, we opened the front door and it stayed open until 11:00 o'clock at night." I thought, "This is how it was at my house."[62]

Asley L. Marmol, a Miami resident and émigré of 2001, says that his memories of arriving in the United States are positive. He describes the importance of family. Asley already knew how to speak English, thus, language was not a communication challenge. But most of all, he expresses his happiness with the opportunity to make independent life decisions.

When I came here [from Holland], I was coming from a year and a half all alone with only my wife with no family around. When we came here to this country in which Cubans have a second home, it was like coming home, literally. We saw our family. I met relatives that I never knew in person, that I never spoke with on the phone because they were just the enemy. They were the other side so they were the enemy. I never had the opportunity to talk with them, to write to them. My mother's uncle was the only one we had contact with and we met; he visited once. My wife's family, I knew some of them because they had visited Cuba before, but not my family. I have more than ten relatives over here that I didn't know. So, it was very emotional to meet all of those relatives that I didn't know.[63]

We also knew that we were going to have the possibility of working. We had all of this energy and desire of progress that we had to start our lives. Our first days over here were very warm. It was very exciting to get to meet this big country, because this country is really huge in all senses. All the possibilities there are in this country are really amazing. Even though we had lived in Euro in a very, very developed nation, you can tell the difference between the societies. We had the valuable experience of Holland. We knew what the developed world was already. We had a command of English, so we could start our lives very easily. As soon as we got the legal situation in order over here, we were allowed to work. I remember that was the most happy days of my life when I had the possibility of going out and looking for a job. Eventually, getting everything we needed to be independent. It was our dream coming true, little by little.[64]

When we lived in Cuba my wife and I were married, but we were still living with relatives. We were not allowed to work while studying in the university. We did not have complete independence and we wanted that as a couple and as a family. So, when we had that possibility here, it was really marvelous. It was the best feeling ever. Nowadays, we've been here a year and a half, we are just like the rest of the people. Believe me, that's something you would not find in any other country. A couple of foreigners come in, and in a year, they have a normal standard of living. I saw families in Euro that lived five years without the possibility of renting the house and living in very, very small rooms in between hundreds of people for years. We are talking about 5 to 7 years and living like they were in limbo instead of a very, very rich nation. What this country does, not only for Cubans, but for a lot of immigrants is really amazing. That shocked me. We Cubans all know that because we have made this country a second home, but to experience that and to live that, when I saw Miami, I thought I was in heaven. It was a better heaven because of the conditions, but I felt like I was at home. I still go to Miami and I feel like it is a place that I have been forever. That's the feeling that brought us back to life. We were really depressed in Euro. We had a lot of doubts about the future. But now we know where we're going. Now we know that we are here to work, to live in freedom and to do whatever we want with our destinies.[65]

Cultural Beliefs and Families in Transition

Adelfa Fernández describes her experience in 1964 as simultaneous excitement and apprehension.

> I was excited. This was a new country. The first week we were taken in by a family. Then we had to move on and eventually into a furnished apartment. About a month later, I went into the deepest depression that

I have ever known. I think it was a combination of the separation from the family — now that I'm older I've been able to understand some of those things, but at the time, I could not put together why I was so depressed. I was 20 years old when that happened. It was not until that time that I realized the effect that losing my father in a tragic manner has had on me. I was the last person that saw him alive and all of a sudden, the past was overwhelming. To this day, I think it was a miracle that I survived that. I had a little medical help, but it was extremely expensive. We didn't have the money. By God's grace, I survived the depression. Through the years on and off, I had to use some professional help because I would have a flare up of the depression. Thank God, I haven't felt any of that in years.[66]

Families should be placed into their cultural context. Ethnicity and race coexist with class and gender hierarchies. Culture and context produce "interactive and joint effects."[67] Family climates should be considered. Researchers are often unaware of the perception that families have of them, and that that perception differs "within and between ethnic families or families of color, and the differences are as great as those that exist for all families."[68] Harriette Pipes McAdoo believes that Hispanic and Asian families may be open to higher authority and therefore, more receptive to receiving help from the larger society.[69]

MARRIAGE

Elizabeth Arias selected the Cuban American population for her study of nuptiality patterns from 1970 to 1990, because they have attained relative socioeconomic parity with the larger society. The majority, 64 percent in 1990, live in a rich ethnic community in Dade County, Florida. She believes their group circumstance should allow them to remain ethnically distinct in terms of demographic patterns and marriage partners, if they wish.[70]

The United States nuptiality patterns have changed greatly since the 1960s. Mainly the decline between marriage and fertility is evident in the low proportions of never marrying, late age at first marriage, high divorce rates and more consensual unions. These changes are due to more women in the labor force, increased educational and occupational opportunities for women, decreasing economic opportunities for young men, changes in perceptions of premarital sex and having children outside of marriage, and increased birth control.[71]

Arias writes that the pattern of Cuban nuptial customs in the 20th century is contradictory in that there is a prevalence of unions. Consensual unions are and have historically been a part of Cuba's nuptial pattern.

Sharp differentials by race for informal unions has decreased in more recent times. Arias explains.

> By 1981 its cause appears to have shifted to resemble more closely [that of the] U.S. case. For both segments of the Cuban population, for example, the differences between remaining outside any union and remaining unmarried increased substantially. On the other hand, the mean age at formal marriage decreased for both segments of the population — a trend that is rather distinct given the increasing prevalence of consensual unions and rising divorce rates. In the United States, rising levels of consensual unions and rising divorce rates are associated with decreasing prevalence of formal marriages and with rising age at first formal marriage. Thus, in some regards post–1960 Cuban nuptiality mirrors closely U.S. nuptiality and in others it appears to be embarking on a very distinct path.[72]

Arias maintains that the immigration period affects nuptiality changes regarding the relationship between socioeconomic and cultural assimilation. Cubans who emigrate in a particular period represent a particular class. Date of emigration affected patterns of nuptiality. The upper class that arrived in the 1960s could have already held the same nuptiality patterns as those of the United States. The nuptiality standards in Cuba may have differed with each wave of migration. Emigrants who left between 1959 and 1962 were not experiencing the sharp rise in divorce seen by those emigrants who left after the revolution. Emigrants of the 1980s witnessed high divorce rates and more consensual unions. Each wave was exposed as well to different social and economic constraints. The important considerations for marriage include education, race and place of residence. Arias's study found that women with higher educational attainment married later. Although living in a Cuban community within the United States could affect marriage rates, more study is needed to determine whether it does. Socioeconomic assimilation is closely related to and usually precedes cultural assimilation.[73]

Arias studied the changes in marriage within the Cuban American society. As Cubans intermarry they become integrated into the larger society. She discovered that both Cuban American men and women tend to marry outside the group with men doing so slightly more. The rates do not change significantly over time. By 1990, Cuban Americans living outside the United States with the highest concentration are more likely to marry non–Cuban people. Although those Cuban Americans living in Florida tended to continue to marry within their group, this trend was on the decline. Arias concludes that the prevalence of interethnic marriage in the Cuban American population is unprecedented.[74]

Men and women who marry out are usually young, more likely not residing in Florida, likely to have been residing in the United States longer and have a higher educational attainment. Arias concludes that selecting partners is based on socioeconomic status rather than on ascriptive characteristics.[75]

ABORTION

One analysis suggests that Cuban Americans are more pro choice than Mexican Americans. Attitudes of Latinos are influenced by the same factors as those beliefs of non–Latinos—religiosity, feminism and demographics. The authors of this study on abortion attitudes conclude that "abortion is not an 'ethnic' issue."[76]

Family and Parenting

The awareness of the dynamics of the family's religious, cultural and racial identity is especially critical during the period a family is in transition. Harriette Pipes McAdoo explains, "The existence of supportive links between the two settings increases the opportunities for positive development within the family. The existence of common values will enhance the process and conflicting values will impede."[77]

The saving grace, for example, for a family who is having conflict with a school may be the social support parents get from the family of origin or the extended family. In the case of the Cuban American family, these sources of support may be too far away to be of help.[78] In the case of motherhood, Cuban teens receive considerable support from their extended families within the States.[79]

Ethnic parents will often intervene in behalf of their children to enrich their lives, but they may need assistance to prevent becoming bitter or frustrated. These parents may need help in taking the long-range view of the society that influences their existence. The family's vocabulary and meanings of the events that happen may differ from those of the larger society.[80]

A study by Teresa W. Julian and her colleagues found a general lack of cultural differences in parenting in the United States when socioeconomic factors were removed. The Hispanic group studied included Mexican, Puerto Rican and Cuban families. Parenting techniques in two-parent families among ethnic groups are more alike than they are different. They agree that the cultural variations discovered in parenting are necessary to the ethnic community for survival. Therefore, ethnic parents tend to be more strict. Parenting is a more difficult task. Socialization requires a bicultural effort of promoting self-esteem within their own culture while at the same time teaching skills to live within the larger society. This effort also suggests that ethnic parents are highly motivated to insure their children's success and thus are more open to help.[81]

Julian *et al.* found ethnic groups share the same goals as the larger society, but sometimes do not have the economic wherewithal to realize them. Common to all ethnic groups studied "is their use of adaptive strategies including extended families, role flexibility, biculturalism, and collectivism versus individualism, including loyalty to the group."[82]

The study found that families of Spanish descent tend to believe in the integral nature of family, male dominance, a positive but traditional role of women, sex-role definitions through methods of parenting, strong kinship bonds, being children-centered, repressing feminine attributes in males and the precedent for the male as head of the household.[83]

Hispanic parents placed more importance on independence, self-control, obedience, getting along with others and success in athletics. Fathers to a greater extent than mothers placed more emphasis on getting along with others. Fathers are very interested in and are directly involved in their children's behavior. In general, differences between the involvement of mothers and fathers in all groups was minimal, and they were highly involved in parenting.[84]

Becoming Acculturated

Age at the time of immigration will affect acculturation. Within Latino families, children become acculturated faster than their parents. One wave of migrants perceives the United States differently than the last. Birgit Leyendecker and Michael E. Lamb maintain that first generation immigrants are more likely to compare their experiences and situation with their home country than with the United States. Basically, immigrants are "a highly self-selected, upwardly mobile, and achievement-oriented group."[85] Second generation immigrants and those individuals who immigrated as children, known as the 1.5 generation, are more likely to blend the two cultures and compare their situation with peers in the new culture. Some romanticizing the homeland exists.[86]

Scholars write that "the demographic revolution" in the United states already exists in the classrooms, schools and lives of our children.[87] Approximately 12 million people of color migrated to the United States during the 1990s. At the beginning of the 20th century most immigrants came from Europe and Canada. At the end of the century they emigrated from Asia and Latin America. The process of adopting the cultural traits or social patterns of another group can be stressful and can lead to family conflict that "when handled poorly, can engender increased problem behaviors among Cuban American and, more recently, non–Cuban Latino youth in South Florida."[88] Family therapy strategy at each stage of acculturation can help members through the difficulties.

It is helpful to examine first impressions and first experiences of the Cuban immigrant as a base for understanding more fully the process of acculturation. As we will see many factors affect successful assimilation into another culture, but perhaps no elements are more important than the positive attitudes of wanting to be in another country to have a better life and having the support of extended family.

Alejandro Concepcion, a Freedom Flight emigrant, was nine years old when he came to the United States with his family. He did not believe adjusting was a hard process. But rather, he says,

> It was like a new adventure every day. For example, just silly things that most people would take for granted. My dad didn't speak the language, so he went to store and, a funny story was, he wanted to get some beer, so he bought some root beer and he thought that was beer. Another funny story was: he wanted to buy tuna and ended up buying cat food.[89]

Concepcion said his family learned cultural ways by experience. Gretchen, his wife, tells how he told her a long time ago that the best sandwich he ever ate "was the ham sandwich the Americans gave him when he got off the plane."[90] Concepcion adds that lunch was provided for the immigrants when they got off the plane.

The Concepcions spoke freely about their "Cuban-Anglo" marriage. Alejandro says,

> We met soon after I got out of college. We worked for the same company. We met in Los Angeles in 1984. We knew each other not very long, just a couple of months, and we got married. Both of our parents thought it wouldn't last, because you can't marry a Cuban and an Anglo— it's too culturally shocking, I guess. They thought we were too different.[91]

Gretchen, his wife, responds, "We always thought we were exactly alike." Alejandro agrees as the children introduce themselves as Lucy, age 12, and Tony, age nine.

Education

In 1994, Trinidad Arguelles wrote about her experiences as a young Cuban immigrant in the American school system. Arguelles left Cuba on May 10, 1980, when she was 14 years of age. In Cuba, she had been eager to learn. She applied that eagerness in school in the United States. When she enrolled in school in the United States, she had to adjust. She had to interpret her performance in terms of the letter grades of A's and B's instead of percentages. She had to get used to wearing a P.E. uniform. She spoke only Spanish and had no friends.[92]

Following her parents' advice, Arguelles realized that educating herself "transcended all frontiers."[93] She says that her educational accomplishments helped vanquish the initial discrimination of compatriots. Although she eventually won the Foreign Language award upon graduation, she writes that at first, she refused to speak the English language. She also graduated as a "Senior of Distinction, a *Miami Herald* Silver Knight Nominee, and a member of the Math, Spanish, Science, and National Honor Societies."[94] She ranked 10 in a class of 545 students, yet her high school counselor implied she did not speak English well enough to succeed in college. In 1994, at the time she wrote an essay, she was working on a doctoral degree in applied psychology. She attributes her success to her parents providing her with philosophy to learn and to the education she received in the United States.[95]

Adelfa Fernández was 20 years old and married when she came to the United States in 1964. A year later she had her first child. She tells how she met life successfully in a new country.

> It was always in my heart that whenever I had a child, I wanted to raise that child. So, basically, I stayed home. I didn't speak any English when I left Cuba, so I went as a part-time student to learn English because I had no idea of how to express myself. I figured the only way that I could survive in a country where they spoke a language other than mine was just to go and learn it. After I learned English, then I began taking other classes. I completed about a year of college.[96]

Adelfa Fernández dedicated her life to her children, encouraging them to get their education. Both children graduated from college. She worked part time in a banking institution for 14 years. She stopped working for a while to fulfill a childhood dream, to study photography. She enjoys working part time for a health insurance company assisting with Medicare recipients. She says, "I love working with the elderly community."[97]

Asley L. Marmol arrived in the United States in May 2001. He tells how he and his wife met the challenges of a new country.

We have grown a lot. We've had to face a lot of responsibilities in all senses that have made us come closer together. Life here asks that you be very responsible and organized in order to succeed. You have to concentrate. You have to understand that immigrants have to concentrate double, two times more than a person that was born here. We are coming from a different world with a different education, from a society that cannot define itself yet. That's where we grew up. The United States is a very solid society. It has its defects like every other society, but it has its virtues and many of them.[98]

In the family unit in the United States that we have experienced, there are very solid values as a general rule. You have some issues, but there's a will and a law that backs it up. All of that is new for us. In Cuba, a person could beat the daughter or the son as many times as they wanted, and nothing would have happened. The police, if they come twice, the third time, they wouldn't come. The law in Cuba, its kind of a joke when it comes to social issues. Only when it comes to political issues they take it seriously. But over here, it's very sensitive. This is a bigger country. This is a more complicated country. We have more ground where [we can] grow as a family. That changed us a lot, because we are now thinking about being the perfect mirror for our kids. We want to give them a solid world where you could be strong enough not to go the bad way.[99]

Financial wherewithal, education, legal entry status, social networks and family structure all have tremendous effect on the success of the immigrant family. Whether the family's status is legal or illegal will often depend on a network of friends. Family networks and job availability tend to motivate immigrants to locate in a specific area. Cuban Americans tend to settle in southern Florida, close to their homeland. With the help of friends, some Cubans desire a new life and settle a greater distance from Cuba, for example, in New York City. Large metropolitan neighborhoods are ethnically separated and help new immigrants establish new networks.[100]

Associated with cultural identity is mastery of the Spanish language. Biculturalism and bilingualism allow basic skills as well as an additional language without giving up one's own culture. As initial immigration challenges wane, this allowance can add to an immigrant child's coping and learning skills, thus increasing opportunities. Some scholars believe that the benefits will not be realized until the larger society recognizes multiculturalism rather than assimilation is more desirable.[101]

Conclusions

Family success will depend on how flexible the members are in adapting to the new culture's challenging of traditional roles and to the changes that adaptation will bring. For example, jobs may be available for mothers and teenage daughters, but employment may not be attainable for the father. A central trait of the Hispanic-American culture is "a deeply ingrained sense of being rooted in the family to which one is oriented and obligated."[102] Leyendecker and Lamb believe that this quality decreases over time, but remains more important relative to other U.S. citizens. Sometimes a family who has shared the migration experience will cohesively and productively close ranks and achieve in exceptional ways. Southern Florida Cuban American families are financially secure and have bicultural lifestyles that permit them to be American without giving up their cultural identity.

Leyendecker and Lamb write that it is important not to confuse the effects of culture and poverty because to do so ignores the fact that the Hispanic American culture is heterogeneous and has uniqueness and strengths. The Hispanic American family is dependent on its extended family even when it can only do so with a part of the extended family, the members within the new culture. Immigration is central in the lives of most Hispanic Americans. And especially important to this book, Cuban American families in southern Florida have found their niches. They are financially secure individuals with a bicultural lifestyle.[103]

No single Cuban American family type exists in the United States. The structure of a family depends, in part, on the reactions of its members to specific contexts and contingencies. Time of arrival, poverty, resources, family cohesion, acculturation, biculturalism, and generational status influence family structure. Whatever the structure of the family, its members place a lot of emphasis on assisting each other. This emphasis includes helping family members living in Cuba. Thus, the bonds of solidarity and reciprocity become part of the social network in both the United States and Cuba.

8

Family Narratives of Life in Cuba

Seasoning the termless feast of our content
With tears of recognition never dry.
— Coventry Patmore[1]

The people of and from Cuba express themselves eloquently about relationships and events of their lives. The people I interviewed spoke passionately about their families and the lives they lived in Cuba. I have grouped their narratives around common themes they addressed.

Childhood Memories

Alejandro Concepcion, who came to the United States on a Freedom Flight, said that his memories of his life in Cuba were pretty happy.

> Thinking back: we were pretty poor but we just didn't know it. We went to the beach a lot as a family. We did things together. We played with the other kids. There wasn't much television or anything like that, so you made do with what you had. So, that created deep bonds between people because we were always doing things together.[2]

Geri Díaz, a Peter Pan child, speaks fondly of her eleven years of childhood in Cuba.

> I was very happy. I had a very, very happy childhood. I am very family oriented. Most Cubans are. We had a very close family. It was a large family. I remember birthdays and parties, or just every day, my school. Life in Cuba as I remember it was very much with the family. We were not wealthy, but we had everything we needed. My parents were anti–Batista, the dictator that was deposed by Castro's Revolution. We were

pro–Castro in the beginning. We thought that it was going to bring democracy, truth and honesty. For about a year, from January 1, 1959, we believed it. Then things started changing.[3]

Asley L. Marmol, who came to the United States in 2001, speaks affectionately of his life during his preteen years in Cuba. The 1980s was a time of prosperity, of ideas of progress and of satisfaction of basic needs. Marmol says,

> I grew up in the middle of this music of communism. My family was normally linked to the communism. My father was a sailor, a merchant marine. I lived most of my time away from him. He was always traveling. Thanks to that, he had access to a different world and brought things from the outside world. I had access to things in my childhood that many people didn't have. My mother is a very sacrificial person, very honest, very sensitive. She is also a writer. I think that I inherited that from her and my family on my mother's side. We were very close, being that she was almost a father and mother for me. My father was only in seasons with me. I have a very happy feeling of those years. I could say that I was some kind of privileged kid because I had toys that the rest of the people didn't have. My father had a car, which many families didn't have. I had a tape recorder and a color TV. Nobody had a TV in my neighborhood. Many people didn't have it. All they had were Russian black and white TVs. I was some kind of eccentric boy, not eccentric in a bad sense. I had a lot of friends and we lived in a nice neighborhood in the suburbs of the city. Economically, we were in good condition.[4]

Miguel Arguelles came to the United States in 1982. Now 17 years old and valedictorian of Miami Lake's Barbara Goleman Senior High School, Class of 2002, he is the first student in the schools' seven-year history to be admitted to Harvard.[5] Arguelles wrote college essays describing who he is, his troubled homeland and his new life in the United States. He writes freely and graphically of the problems that beset Cuba. But like most Cubans, he speaks warmly about his family in Cuba.

> It is there where I left my family — my grandmother Chucha's kisses, my grandfather Pape's stories, my aunt Lisette's hugs and tireless efforts to get my dad to take away my punishment when I misbehaved. It is in the Cuban soil where my roots can be found, planted deeply, where none can extricate them. It is there where I walked a great and key distance of my existential quest for an identity.[6]

Arguelles, like Asley Marmol, continues to say, among other illustrations, that it is also in Cuba where: he had to recite Communist pledges daily, a prostitute earns more than a professional, freedom of expression is silenced, and food is rationed.

The Afro Cuban Experience in Prerevolutionary Cuba

Dr. Alberto N. Jones, DVM-EH, Caribbean American Children Foundation, an Afro Cuban who lives in Florida, provides a penetrating view on life for Afro Cubans in Cuba in the middle of the 20th Century.

On August 1, 1975, in Helsinki, Finland, 35 countries signed what was known as the Helsinki Human Rights Agreement. The Agreement declared among other things, "the right to be free of governmental violations of the integrity of the person" and "the right to enjoy civil and political liberties." For myself and other Afro Cubans and millions of human beings, understanding the scope and morality of this agreement was very easy.

I was born on a hot and humid day of August 1938 in La Güira, Banes, Cuba, a community of transplanted emigrants, mainly from the English speaking Caribbean Islands and Haiti, lured to Cuba, by what was billed as "the Promised Land," by the United Fruit Company, Manati Sugar Company and others.

In this community, on the "other" side of the tracks, I learned early on, that the only homes we were allowed to build were the shack type homes, with thatched roofs, that defined our living quarters.

Sewer, running water, electricity, schools, jobs, hospital or medical services, were limited to people living on the "other" side of town.

What we did have, was a pervasive infant mortality due primarily to preventable diseases that touched the lives of every family. There were rampant pre- and postpartum deaths; hunger and malnutrition, seen predominantly in children with their disproportionate heads and distended abdomens, overflowing with such a variety of intestinal parasites, sufficient to produce our own Atlas of Parasitology. Another common landmark was the infamous gully with putrid drainage winding through our neighborhood.

The only schools in our community of approximately 8–10,000 people, were two or three mock-classrooms of 10–20 children in the living room of those slightly more enlightened members of our community. Two churches had what could be qualified as small schools, with approximately 40 children each. Because of our teachers own limited education, the level of training by those who were able to stay through the entire school program (3–4 years), was the equivalent of a low third grade.

But this vicious cycle got even worse, if we were to add, that living in Cuba, a Spanish speaking country, the teaching was in English and everything that was taught to us, was either pertaining to England, Ireland or Jamaica! We learned about Admiral Nelson but nothing about Marti, we learned about Pound, Shilling and Pence, but nothing about *Peso, Peseta* and *Centavos*. We learned about the Thames river but nothing about our own *Río Cauto!*

Unbelievable as it may sound today, most of the kids could not stay in school, either because their parent could not afford it or their helping hands were already required on the plantation.

As a direct result of this horrendous environment, our community, and tens of similar ones, dispersed [throughout] what was then the provinces of Camagüey and Oriente, did not produce in 60 years, a single person who had achieved a mid level or higher education. An exception was a lady who was able to complete nursing school, only because her parents had the vision and could afford to send her back to Jamaica.

The only job available was in the *zafra*, the 4–5 months sugar harvest, which was virtually slave labor, because it was not only the lowest paying job but it also kept the people in perennial debts: whatever income you made this year, was credited to debts incurred the previous year. This practice was so pervasive, that thousands of workers never saw or received money, they would only receive promissory notes (*vales*) from the landowners, who were often the same owners of the stores. That is why, 10–12 year-old boys went off to work in the fields, while girls in same age group became maids.

I will be eternally grateful for my grandfather George Jones. Pappi Georgy — as he was known — was a dignified man of enormous fortitude, respect, and deep religious beliefs, who kept our family together in spite of the most difficult circumstances, by always instilling in us honesty and moral values. My grandfather was among the fortunate few, because, as an orderly in the United Fruit Company's hospital, he had a year round job paying 50 cents per day.

There were always people sitting in my backyard, waiting for Georgy to get off his job. Some suffered from diarrhea, vomiting, fever or any sort of injuries. He would cleanse their wounds or give them medication he stored in a coffin-like cabinet he kept in his bedroom. As I pieced these events together, I concluded that this honorable man, who preached values to us, was forced by the brutal society in which he lived, to steal from his workplace, in order to serve those who were deprived of the most basic means of survival.

What can we say about the psychological trauma endured by unfortunate mothers, trapped in abusive relations, domestic violence and occasional life threatening situations, without anywhere to go, forced to live this hazardous existence, as the only means of feeding their hungry children.

For these and so many other reasons, none of us had to flock to South Africa to see what Apartheid was all about. We were born, lived and many died in our own Soweto!

That's why it is so painful to us, when we hear the likes of a Diaz-Balart attempting to apply the content of the Human Rights Declaration, to their narrow and selfish, self serving interest.

Where were these demagogues, hypocrites and frequently active perpetrators of the terrible conditions previously described, or when young people were beaten, tortured, disappeared or murdered and left by the side of the roads to rot by the military structure that they helped put in place to protect their illegal boot, stolen public funds or immoral business practices?

For us to have a clear picture about the real intentions and the interests that these individuals stand for, suffice to say, that Diaz-Balart's father was one of the highest ranking government officials in the Batista regime, while all of the above was happening, and today, his sons, one as a State and the other as a U.S. representative, both representing a Miami that has become one of the most politically corrupt, segregated, bankrupt, drug ravaged community in the nation.

I can only wonder, if the Cuba that U.S. Representative Diaz-Balart struggles fervently to recover — even at the expense of the country's sovereignty — may well be a Cuba reconstructed in his father's image or that of today's Miami.[7]

The Extended Family

Adelfa Fernández, who came to the United States in 1964, tells of the strength and beauty of the Cuban extended family.

> My grandparents were the center of the family circle. They created a family of four children. My mother was one of them. To give you an idea of the family closeness, there was a land lot, maybe the size of one acre where three houses were built: my grandparent's, one of my uncle's and my parents'. The three houses connected through their back yards. That brought great security growing up, knowing that these people were there. For a while we moved by the pharmacy that my father owned and every single night we would visit my grandparents and everybody would sit on the big porch to talk and share the day's experiences, and it is one of the things I value the most about my childhood.[8]

Holidays and Celebrations

Almost all of the interviewees would agree with Adelfa Fernández that one custom "that hasn't that really changed is the way we eat. We still eat rice and beans. At Christmas and all special occasions, the roasted pig is always present. We do not change that."[9]

Leonardo Marmol, Ph.D., American Board of Professional Psychology, professor and chair of the Department of Graduate Psychology at Seattle Pacific University, came to the United States in the mid–1950s. He explains the way the holiday was celebrated in Cuba.

We would roast a pig in the back yard, that is the Cuban traditional Christmas. We celebrated it on Christmas Eve, not on Christmas Day, *Noche Buena*. The traditional gift giving for children in Cuba was not Santa Claus at Christmas, but the wise men on Epiphany day, which is January 6. So we all waited for the wise men to bring the presents. By the time I was a late teenager, the American influence had started coming in. Christmas trees and Santa Clauses were in stores, and children began to want to have gifts twice. But that was not the tradition in Cuba, and that's the way it was in Spain and most of the Latin world.[10]

Geri Díaz, who emigrated with Operation Peter Pan in the early 1960s tells a similar story.

The tradition was that Christmas Eve and Christmas Day were family days. There were no gifts. We exchange gifts, January 6, the Epiphany. Santa Claus did not come to Cuba. The three wise men came to Cuba and they brought their gifts the morning of January 6. I like that tradition, maybe because that is how I grew up. Maybe because it made Christmas more of a religious focus. You were not running around buying Christmas presents. We were concentrating on getting together with your family. We would go to midnight mass. My generation were Catholics. We have different religions. We have a large Jewish community.[11]

Asley L. Marmol talks of the holidays that were observed in Cuba.

In the middle of the year, you have the political, governmental celebrations that became also a tradition, because that was the substitution. So, you had the 26th of July where you have one or two free days they give people time to get together, but because of the political motive. Then they have the CDR [Committees for the Defense of the Revolution] anniversary which is in September. People get together. Those were made afterwards. Those were used and the Cuban family saw it as a substitution of those that were erased at Christmas, Easter and all of those in between that I don't even know. It changed a lot with the new political situation. At the beginning, there was even a pressure put on those families that tried to keep the Catholic religious celebrations in general. After that, they were replaced. I remember the day for the magic kings to come and give gifts to the kids. That was substituted for the days of the children which is the 3rd Sunday of July. Normal, traditional celebrations were banned and replaced with the political celebrations scheduled by the new government. The bans have lessened over the years, but still the only natural celebration that we kept is at the end of the year that we celebrate the 31st of December.

Some people in Cuba still keep what they call Good Night. That is a literal translation from Spanish. That is from the 24th to the 25th and Christmas Day. They don't say Christmas anymore. They call it Good

Night. Some families kept that or not at all. My family didn't celebrate that at all. I knew some families that did, and they still keep it over here.[12]

Alex, a young Cuban teacher, says,

> On New Year's Eve, we join together. We have parties. In Cuba, we celebrate on December 24. We celebrate on the 24th, 25th, 26th, 27th, 28th, 29th, 30th, and 31st. January 1 we celebrate the revolution. January 2nd is another celebration. So many days of parties. My friends also have those celebrations.[13]

Education

In 2002, Alex had experience in the classroom that was part of his teacher training. He describes his educational process in Cuba as well as recent government efforts to improve schools.

> In fact, I didn't work as a teacher because it was my fifth year when I was teaching. During that time I was teaching at a high school. Education is very good on that point in Cuba because for a year, you go to school for practicing and I was in a primary school. Then I went to a middle school for the third and fourth years. When I was in my last year, fifth year, I went to a high school to teach. So you practice on all levels. It was good experience. The things you have been taught you have to practice. You have to make it perfect in the classrooms. So it is very good. Now it has improved a little bit because sometimes we have problems with the teaching aides. There has been a lack of teaching aides so it has been a little bit difficult. Now it has improved a little bit. In fact, the government has taken care of it recently. In July and August of this year, they were restoring all of the schools in Havana, the primary and middle schools in Havana. The government made a huge investment to restore the schools in the city.[14]

Asley Marmol recalled that his good life started to change when he had to leave his family to attend junior high school in a boarding school. He tells his story as a young teen required by law to leave his family.

> In those years and yet today, whoever wants to study in the university has to go to the boarding school in the countryside. I'm talking about schools in the middle of the countryside, miles away from the city. I had to leave my family. During those days, I was not with them for three years. I stayed 11 days inside of the school and then went home for a weekend and then came back to the school. I have to say all of the influence of my family was cut by that regulation of the government. Even

though you want to study outside in the city, that's not a possibility, because all of the schools that they have in the city are supposed to be for those people who have health problems. The truth is that many people with health problems end up in the boarding schools. Only the sons and daughters of the most politically elite are in the schools in the city. All the kids like me had to go to those boarding schools. I did 10th, 11th and 12th grade in that type of school. I started [school] in the morning and worked in the countryside in the afternoons doing any type of cropping, any type of work in the middle of the countryside. We were free labor for the government. We are not just talking about me. We are talking about thousands of students. Hundreds of thousands of students in the whole country were going through the same thing.[15]

That experience is very strong, because you are away from your family and I was a strong kid. It wasn't easy. It was not as difficult as for some other people. There are some people that get traumatized with that and can't resist the school and go through very hard times. I don't want to tell you about the conditions of those schools. I literally cried some nights because I was hungry.[16]

Asley Marmol was enrolled at the boarding schools during the 1990s. He explains that because the fall of the Soviet Union had come in 1989, "communist Cuba was empty." He describes this situation as "terrible."[17]

[There was] no light, no water, sometimes not even a phone, [and] not even gasoline to communicate with the city until the next day. So, we were like in the hands of God. We were supposed to get an education. We were separated from our families, the people who really knew what was good for us. At the beginning you miss your mother. You miss your family, but it comes to a point where you don't anymore. You get used to it. Then you start living a different life than what your parents wanted. Parents don't have another choice. Many parents are strong enough to have their kids give up the idea of going to the university so that they will not have to go through that experience for three years. I wrote a novel about that. It's called *Interdictus*. In Latin, it's *What the Teacher Commands*. My point is that it is a very tough moment for young Cubans when they have to go away from their families. Your book is about Cuban families—one of the factors that destroys Cubans families is that many people have to go away from their families. All the values that your parents wanted to pass over during a crucial age, [it] is not possible. The teenagers start living by a different code. It is a wild code. All kinds of crazy things happen in that kind of school because there is not the proper supervision. This lack of teachers, this lack of discipline would be content for two or three books. Maybe you haven't heard about this point. I have the conviction that it is one of the main strategies of the Cuban government to deviate any influence that the parents could exert on the teenager. That way the government can exert its own ideas. It is a governmental strategy that has been in effect for years. It started in the 1960s and 1970s. It is still in effect today. If your family doesn't sympathize with the government when you go away from them at 14 years old, it is a time when you start to develop profound ideas, principles and values. You don't have your family there to give those [principles and values] to you. You spend all of your time alone without them. When you go back home you say, "Yea, you don't tell me what to do and what to say. This is my time alone without you, so I can control myself. I know this is the right thing." They cannot tell you anything else, anything different, because it is out of their hands.[18]

Working in Cuba

Although Alex is a young Cuban trained as a teacher, he works in the new dollar economy. He tells how the economic situation presents conflicting values:

> Yes, I'm thinking [about going back into teaching]. I have been working here for some years as a tour guide. When our economic situation goes back normal, I don't know. Maybe if they can improve the standard of living, I could go back. You have to take into account that I am younger now and I can make some money. If I can make some money, I can have a better life for me and for my family in the coming years. In the future, the way I am thinking, the education system needs me because it is important to educate and to help your country be developed. That's a good thing. I think in some years I will be back in my former job because that was the thing I studied when I was at the university. I miss my former job. I like this too because you meet a lot of people and that's good. You make good friends but, on the other hand, the school needs me.[19]

Religious Freedom

Adelfa Fernández experienced the lack of religious freedom in Cuba in the early 1960s.

> The last years in Cuba I lived with a lot of fear, especially the last year. When I got married, my husband was a minister with the Baptist churches. When we were engaged, he was taken to prison twice. The first time, he was conducting a vacation Bible school. Every morning there is a parade and the children walk into the church carrying the Christian flag and the flag of their country, in this case, the Cuban flag. These were elementary school children and yet he was accused of using them

to protest against the government. He was taken to prison for three days and was tortured emotionally and mentally. He was forced to take freezing cold showers, constantly awakened for questioning that took place in a small room, surrounded by people smoking all over him, trying to get a "confession" admitting to their accusations.

The second time was when he was having a prayer meeting at a house, which was something they had been doing forever. And again he was taken to prison for having an illegal meeting at a church member's house. These meetings were something they had been doing forever. Again he was taken to prison for having an "illegal" meeting and was kept overnight. After these two incidents he said, "We are leaving the country." A year after we got married, we left.[20]

Conclusions

Cubans and Cuban Americans have vivid memories of their lives in Cuba. For some life in Cuba was happy. For others it was tragic. For others, it was harsh. Whatever lives they had on the island, memories of family were positive. Those early memories mark the beginning of their *Iliad*.

9

Family Narratives of Life in the United States

God offers us all a chain of opportunities and that each of us can be a link in that chain and that what binds the chain is love. If you are religious, it is the love of God. If you are not religious, as a human being, it is your love and respect for your fellow human beings.

—Pedro Ferreira[1]

The stories of the people of and from Cuba are indeed inspiring. Families in Cuba sometimes provided the avenues to come to the United States. Other families offered love and support. In some cases, extended family met and supported Cubans once in the United States. The family fortified the courage of the individual members to journey.

Coming to the United States

Leonardo M. Marmol, Ph.D., currently chair of the Department of Graduate Psychology at Seattle Pacific University, tells of emigrating from Cuba during when Batista was in power.

> I was invited by a big church in Los Angeles to come and study in a seminary. They helped me get started with a scholarship the first year. After that, I was on my own. Also, Batista had closed the University in Havana. So, after I finished my Bachillerato, which is kind of an equivalent to junior college, there was no place to study at the university. There was a Protestant seminary in Cuba, but I didn't want to go straight to seminary. I wanted to get a college degree first, but there had been so many students rioting as part of a protest against Batista. In 1955-56, Batista had closed the university, there was just no place to study. At that time there was just the one university in Havana. Since the revolution, there

are many more universities there than just Havana, but at that time, there was just the one national university. The motivation for coming here: I was pretty much an Anglophile ever since I had spent that year in Georgia. The university not being available, the invitation of the church with the lure of coming here with some support, I just came. I had been recently married. My wife and I just came and made our life here.[2]

Leonardo Marmol's emigrating experience was made easier by the fact that he had come to the United States for the first time when he was 14 years old. He says,

My father sent me to a boarding school in Georgia to learn English. Our families were Protestant, we were third generation Presbyterian. The Presbyterian Church, like the Methodist, Baptist and Episcopalians, came into Cuba after the Spanish American War when Spain was thrown out and the American missionaries were allowed to come in with the Protestant missions. Both my grandparents were converted. We were still a small minority. The American influence on the Protestant churches was very big. The missionaries ran the churches. The desire to learn English and look towards the United States as a great Protestant country was very important for a lot of professional and middle class Protestant people. They sent their children here to school so they could learn English. For one thing when you reached your teens, you could work for American companies if you were bilingual. I worked for the National City Bank of New York in Havana. I started working when I was 17 as an office boy. I worked there for five years until I decided to come here and go to college. At the age of 22 I came here more permanently and I've stayed ever since. I went to Pepperdine College in Los Angeles.[3]

Leonardo Marmol's intention was to become a Presbyterian minister in the United States then return to Cuba as a pastor. He adds, "But the revolution came in and everything changed. There was no sympathy for the communist developments there. Then also my family started coming out. So, there was no incentive for me to go back."[4]

Returning to Cuba to Visit

After the journey from Cuba, love for family still there continues a lifetime. Delvis Fernández Levy, Ph.D., president of the Cuban American Alliance Education Fund, writes vividly of his personal experiences visiting Cuba in 1996, entitling his trip "To Cuba with Love."

The serenity of a quiet Sunday afternoon is suddenly broken by the persistent ringing of a phone I try to avoid.

— Hello.

— Cuba calling ... accept the charges?

— Of course!

— Brother, *Tia* is not well ... sure would be nice if you could come ... but for now, I guess it's impossible....

Two days later, hours before leaving for Havana I run through the house opening drawers looking for things to take to *la familia en Cuba*—anything I can stuff into a suitcase before my dash to the airport. On the way there, I must stop at the Fed-Ex office for my permit to enter Cuba. Yes! I'm going home ... for my *once every twelve months* allowed visit to see a *close relative* in circumstances of extreme humanitarian need.

Hours later, in Mexico City, I'm taxiing to a hotel for a good night's rest before the final flight to Havana.

Tia, my *close relative*, is an aunt who remained in Cuba and is now living in *extreme humanitarian need* due to the lack of necessities and the ravages of her ninety years of life.

The dark green landscape dotted with swaying palms on a background of bright blue sky splashed with white puffy clouds fills me with intense emotions as the plane lands at Havana's José Martí airport. *La familia* is waiting to share hugs and kisses, laughs and tears, and stories to bridge years of separation.

The ride to *Tia's* home through the streets of Old Havana reveals baroque ornamented walls recalling the grandeur of a bygone era. Young and old in hues of colors are seen moving in every imaginable mode of transportation: a Chinese bicycle transporting a family, fiftyish-vintage American cars, and *guaguas* (buses) filled to capacity being pulled by tractors. Along Havana's 5th Avenue we pass grand old mansions being restored and store front signs of foreign companies doing business in Cuba.

Almost twenty-four hours since leaving New Jersey, I arrive at a house full of relatives I hardly recognize, although they all seem familiar. Tia's living room buzzes with conversations that at first are like incomprehensible sounds. But after a short time of acclimating to the fast pace of Cuban-accented Spanish I become fully engrossed in two or three simultaneous discussions. The hot topic is the recent downing of the planes from Miami and the ensuing tightening of the embargo. Will Castro be able to weather Helms' storm as it has Torricelli's and others for 37 years? (The embargo has existed through nine U.S. Administrations since President Eisenhower first imposed trade restrictions with Cuba in 1960. Torricelli's legislation in 1992 and Helms' in 1996 strengthened the trade embargo.)

My nephew José, a nuclear engineer laid off when construction at the Juraguá nuclear plant stopped, foresees hard times ahead for his family. He wants to leave Cuba but fears that his teenage son will be enlisted in the army. José thinks that the *patria-o-muerte* (fatherland-or-death) hard-core Castro supporters are consolidating forces under what they perceive as a reinforced economic war from *El Norte*. He waits for better times and for the present supports the family with odd teaching jobs.

Cousin Marta, who years ago had begged me to help her pregnant daughter to get out of Cuba after her live-in boyfriend took off for Florida in a raft, expressed indifference about the effects of the tightened embargo. A modest display of affluence was evident in her house since my last visit: new furniture and a fresh coat of paint — rare sights in any Cuban home. Marta proudly tells me, "I rent the place for 15 dollars a night and with dollars I buy anything I want."

While Marta enjoys the fruits of her tenuous capitalist venture (at the margins of Cuban law), her sister Maria, a teacher, lives on a meager salary of about 10 dollars a month plus the *beneficios socialistas* of free school and medical care — benefits that her "wealthy" sister Marta also receives.

Finally it was Sunday again and time for my teary goodbyes and hugs to Tia. This time, I was lucky to get ground transportation and connecting flights from Havana to Mexico City to Newark, all within a span of 16 hours.

The Continental flight touched ground in Newark after midnight Monday morning. Now only U.S. Customs stood between me and my wife.

What I expected to be a routine check turned out to be an unpleasant two-hour ordeal. Upon seeing "Cuba" written on my "Customs Declaration" form the officer in charge sternly warned me that travel to Cuba was forbidden and followed the admonition with a series of questions: Where is your license to travel? How much money are you carrying? How much money did you take to Cuba? Then he proceeded to place me at the mercy of two other officers who informed me that they were only following rules. A computer check of my passport was followed by more questions and photocopies of driver's license, business cards, and car registration.

I left customs with bags and passport in hand minus my two boxes of Churchill's *Romeo y Julieta* Cuban cigars. My wife, after two hours of waiting and being told that everyone had been processed, returned home thinking that I had missed my connecting flight from Mexico City.

At 2:30 am, in a nearly empty airport with no wife, no ride, and no cigars, I was filled with memories of *Tia* and *la familia*— my Cuban soul had been recharged.[5]

Helping Family Members in Cuba During the U.S. Embargo

If it were not for the family members in the United States, those members in Cuba with medical needs might be in serious circumstances.

But the method of helping one's family members in Cuba is indirect. Leonardo M. Marmol came to the United States after the revolution when he was 22 years old. He explains how he assists a family member in Cuba.

> The members of our family that are in Cuba are in dire need of U.S. dollars. Anyone in Cuba who has access to dollars can access a lot of things that people who live only within the Cuban economy are not able to acquire. So, we send money there. I have a cousin in Cuba who is dependent on medication for a chronic condition. The only way the medication can be bought is with U.S. dollars. So, I send him $100 every month to buy his medicine to keep him alive. This is just something we do. There are agencies here that for a fee, for money, they deliver in cash over there. I'm not sure exactly how that works, because I send this agency here $112 and they have the connection in Cuba. They go to my cousin's house in Cuba and deliver $100 in cash to him. I don't know how that $12 gets divided up and how they get the money because there are no banking transactions between here and Cuba, but evidently they get it from Mexico or Canada, but I don't know how they get the dollars in their national banks, but they have them.[6]

Marmol concludes that the embargo "is really a brutality."[7]

The Extended Family in the United States

Still other Cuban Americans haven't been in the United States very long. The ties to family members still in Cuba remain strong. Asley L. Marmol, who emigrated in 2001, says that his family in the United States helped him adapt successfully. He explains:

> Since the beginning when we were outside, my family was there for us. The Cuban family is very, very strong. Even the regime hasn't been able to destroy that even though they tried hard to split Cuban families. To split those families that had some members in the United States and some members in Cuba, like mine, there were 20 to 35 years where we barely had contact. My mother was not able or didn't want to contact all of them or at least some of them because of the political issues. Even though after that, look at me, I'm another generation that is just getting back together with family members. It's going to happen. In many families even though we are miles away, we overhear things about our families in Cuba and the other way around. We live for our families in Cuba and think of them every single day and what they need. Every time we buy something or see something, we think of them not having that possibility. When we came here, our family was like that. Our family was

very happy and welcomed us because we worked. [We had] the possibility of getting our of that inferno.[8]

Separation from Family in Cuba

With the strength of the Cuban family, separation from them is bound to affect members in both the United States and Cuba. Asley Marmol says,

> Emotionally, it's very, very sad to know that something could happen to my family in Cuba and I wouldn't have the possibility of going there and helping them directly, face-to-face. The system doesn't allow it. It is very hard for my mother, my sisters and my grandmother to see me departing, because we had a very strong relationship. They all know, and this is how the Cuban feeling is nowadays, that whoever leaves is lucky. Even though it is hard, it is for the best. At least somebody is living a different life. A life that is not [one] the rest of the Cubans inside Cuba can live. We've been trying to change that reality for years, but the people in power are still not willing to listen, to cooperate, to leave or to open up. For those who live over here on the other side of the world in the other Cuba, it is very sad to know that they are there and to know that what is happening is so illogical, that a small group is trying to impose a line of political ideas no matter what the cost is, even though they see all the pain going on all around, even though they see people dying or just people not having an actual life. People that are apathetic. People that do not want to participate — that just go in massive marches like robots. That's all they see — I'm sorry I'm a little off the line of questioning, but it also reflects how we feel over here and how they feel over there. In Cuba they are always thinking about the salvation; not only the source of material help but also the spiritual possibilities that we have over here that they don't have over there. Somehow there is a connection. We fit each other from the distance. It's sad, but it is powerful. I sometimes wake up or listen to the news and see what is going on in Cuba and say, "My God! When is it going to end? When am I going to be able to spend a weekend with my family and go whenever I want and come back whenever I want and not have this feeling something is going to happen to my family and I'm not going to be able to respond? I'm not going to be able to go over there and visit."[9]

The Question of Going Back to Cuba

In 1996 the Cuban *balseros* or rafters also came to the U.S. due to the economic crisis in their homeland. Sadiy Morales, president of *Cubanos Mano a Mano*, an organization working for normalization with Cuba and lifting U.S. restrictions on sending assistance to families, is also a rafter.

In 1996, Morales crossed the Florida Straits with his three brothers on a raft made with inner tubes and boards tied together with ropes. He came shortly after the Helms-Burton Act went into effect. He said, "I didn't come to the U.S. to break ties with Cuba or forget about my family. It's just not fair that Mr. Helms doesn't want me to visit and help my parents."[10]

Orestes Lorenzo was a fighter pilot in the Cuban military until 1991 when he flew to Florida in his MIG-23. His wife and two children had visas to join him, but the Cuban government wouldn't let his family leave. He flew back the next year in a private plane to bring them to the United States. Lorenzo had a friend who endured being separated from his children and who believed Elián González should be returned to his natural father. Lorenzo differed, saying, "I left my family to make a path toward freedom for them."[11] Lorenzo believed that his children growing up in freedom was more important than growing up with him, their father. He writes that when he was separated, "I offered to turn myself in to the Cuban government in exchange for allowing my family to leave Cuba."[12] Based on his own childhood in Cuba, Lorenzo believes that Elián, like all children there,

> will be forced to repeat daily that he "will be like Ché." He will be taught to hate those who disagree with communism and to adore a dictator. He will be forced to participate in demonstrations of intimidation organized by the regime....
> The government will decide for him what books he can read and what movies he can watch. The independent media will be prohibited to him forever....
> If he has the talent of an artist, he will have to suppress it or compromise it to fit in with the official ideology.[13]

Other Cuban Americans have no desire to return to Cuba as long as Fidel Castro is in power. Geri Díaz, a Peter Pan emigrant, says,

> I love the United States. I'm an American citizen, but I'm a Cuban. My dream is that the day that Castro is overthrown, I want to go back and help rebuild my country. I don't know whether I'll do it, but that's my dream. I've not been back to Cuba. If I had my mother or dad or somebody very close there, I would probably go. But I cannot go to a place as a tourist where my people are being enslaved and mistreated. I just can't.[14]

Food

Alejandro Concepcion, who immigrated to the United States in 1970 on a Freedom Flight, explained that, in Cuba on the night before Christmas, "we always roasted a pig when that was available. We really didn't have religious celebrations because that wasn't allowed. Any religious customs were frowned upon."[15] When asked whether any of these customs were brought over and continued into his new life in the United States, Concepcion replied that a blending of the two cultures has occurred.

> My mom and dad still celebrate the night before Christmas, where most American families celebrate the day of Christmas. The cooking is still Cuban tamales, black bean soup. They have rice with everything. The food is still with us. They are a lot more Americanized than when they first got here. My mom and dad love Mexican food. When we first got here, they wouldn't think about eating Mexican food because they thought Mexican food was pretty bad, but it kind of grows on you. They really love it now. The same thing with roast beef and gravy. Before they didn't think that was too hot. Now they like their American food. They make this little collard green, deep fried stuff, that we have every once in a while. But they spice it up a little, before it was pretty bland. Now they add a little of the American spices to it.[16]

Holiday Celebrations

Leonardo Marmol came to the United States in the mid–1950s. He explains that, although the U.S. culture has changed Cubans in many ways, the Cuban customs of food and holiday celebrations have remained constant. "On Christmas Eve, we gather in Miami. All 35–40 people, all cousins or children of cousins, or daughters of cousins and their fiancés or boyfriends." The Cuban custom of roasting a pig in the back yard is continued. "The celebration is one of those events where you eat late at night and at midnight people go to services, church or mass and sleep late on Christmas day."[17]

Geri Díaz, who emigrated with Operation Peter Pan in the early 1960s, tells a similar story.

> For us the big night is Christmas Eve, *Noche Buena*. That is when you have a pig, black beans and rice, [and] potatolike roots called yucca. We eat Spanish food like congri (black beans and white rice) and of course, wine. The family gets together and friends get together. The tradition which a lot of people have followed is to dig a pit in your back yard, 'though not everybody wants to dig a pit in their back yard, here, then you put [in] the whole pig, sounds like a Lua pig, but no apple. That's Hawaiian, no apple. It is seasoned before. Usually, the men are the ones that cook, but the women cook all of the other dishes. Many times we will have more than one meat: pig, turkey Cuban style, or guinea hens. We change our traditions because things are different in the United States.[18]

Asley L. Marmol, who emigrated from Cuba in 2001, has experienced the differences in customs between families.

> The families here in the United States kept the traditions from before and cultivated them here. The family in Cuba has traditions that were left which you would say would be the traditional reunion at the end of the year. The only stable custom that we have is getting together at the end of year and celebrating, eating pork, meat, a lot of food and drinking a little bit. Over here, the family kept all the Catholic celebrations of Easter, of Christmas that are rare in Cuba — or are extinguished in Cuba. I was very surprised that I was invited to the Easter reunion. I said, "What's the Easter reunion?" I didn't know. It was the Holy week. Cuba was mostly a Catholic country before, and those traditions were kept by families that came over here.[19]

Language

The place of Spanish in the lives of the Cuban emigrants varies. Some retain Spanish and use it in addition to English. Some of the children of emigrants do not learn Spanish. Pedro Ferreira, Ph.D., Master of Business Administration, child of Operation Peter Pan, is today a licensed psychologist in Wilmington, Delaware. Ferreira has two nieces who "do not speak Spanish. It happens that the power of the dominant language is such that we should never have to worry about making English the official language of the United States."[20]

Ferreira, on the other hand, works diligently to maintain his Spanish.

> I have always had this crazy — I call it crazy because it is crazy — dream that — and I have maintained my Spanish very well; I read every day and I teach it and I tell jokes and I write some things— that if I ever met my grandmother and I had forgotten how to speak to her in Spanish, my soul would be lost. I hope I sound clear enough to you even with an accent, but, at the same time, I have not lost my ability to communicate in that other language because I think of those elders of mine, of those relatives of mine, that I might find them on the road to Heaven. You have this feeling they are not going to speak in English. It is crazy, right?[21]

Conclusions

Cuban Americans maintain many of the customs and values they brought with them from Cuba. Some of the customs change as they become assimilated into the mainstream of American society. Most hold Cuba, or at least its memories, close. But all hold the members of their families dear, whether in Cuba or in the United States.

10

Looking Forward

A sincere man am I
From the land where palm trees grow,
And I want before I die
My soul verses to bestow.
I come from all parts,
towards all parts I go:
Art I am between the arts,
In the mountains, the mountains I am.
— José Martí, *Simple Verses*[1]

"Cuba is a keystone element in world reconstruction," write Donald Bray and Marjorie Bray.[2] Cuba is a standout in what they call a struggle for a new kind of world, a transformation to have more effort put into getting policies of wealthy countries to do more to aid the poorer countries.

Hope

On January 21–25, 1998, Pope John Paul II visited Cuba. He criticized the United States' embargo, stressing that it denied the Cuban people contacts with other peoples necessary for economic, social and cultural development. He asked that the world open to and for Cuba with its "magnificent possibilities" to open, in return, to the world.[3] United States domestic politics began to shift as United States cardinals viewed the pope's visit as the beginning of a campaign for change. The United States House and Senate introduced bills to allow the sale of medicine and medical supplies to Cuba. On March 20, 1998, Clinton restored humanitarian provisions that were in effect when he took office, but suspended in 1994 and 1996. Although Clinton's measures were approved, the United States Department of Defense announced that Cuba constituted no threat to the national security of the United States.[4] The administration under President Clinton relaxed some of the restrictions under Track 2 of the Torricelli Act, which allowed people-to-people contacts and direct mail services. The people-to-people contacts included the transfer of US$300 quarterly by any United States citizen to any Cuban family in addition to the ongoing sending of money by Cuban Americans.[5] Improved relations with Cuba dominated intellectual debates, but it did not translate into the political arena. The Elián González case in 1999 is but one example.[6]

Change

Robert A. Pastor speaks to the Cuban people and their success in the United States. He outlines what he believes needs to change if Cuba is to prosper. He states,

> Ten percent of the Cuban population have moved to the United States since the revolution. They have been extremely productive and effective in the United States. Indeed, they probably create an economy that is larger than the economy in Cuba where ninety percent of the population lives, which shows what individual initiative can do if the government does not prevent the people from pursuing their interests in a way that would serve the whole.... There are two important steps that are needed in the future. One is for the United States to approach Cuba with greater respect and willingness to deal with the Revolution in a straightforward and correct way. The second is that all free peoples in the Americas hope that the people in Cuba will also be permitted to exercise their freedoms fully, just like they do in any other country. The sooner that occurs, the better off all the people of the Americas will be.[7]

Since the Special Period when Cuba was so deeply stressed economically by the collapse of its longtime trading partner, the Soviet Union, the country has made changes by diversifying its agriculture and emphasizing the dollar economy. Cuba is expanding its economy but still struggles with the effects of the United States embargo.

In the United States, efforts to remove the embargo are intensifying. The United States House of Representatives has passed a bill in 2002 that contained provisions to strip away some of the most damaging parts of the embargo. The legislation has not been passed by the Senate and is unlikely to be signed into law by President George W. Bush, but its passage in the House is significant.

In Cuba, the government has lessened the economy's dependence on sugar as the main cash crop and increased the production of food crops.

Castro has also permitted greater expression of religious and political freedom.

Visit of former President Jimmy Carter, May 2002

In May 2002, former President Jimmy Carter visited Cuba by invitation of Fidel Castro. Carter said his purpose was "to establish a dialog
with Castro, to reach out to the Cuban people, and to pursue ways to
improve U.S.-Cuban relations. I wanted to explore with the president and
other Cuban leaders any indication of flexibility in economic or political
policy that might help to ease tensions between our two countries."[8]

Although the Varela Project was defeated, it was the subject of much
debate at the time of Carter's visit. The project called for many of the
same freedoms for the people that President Carter recommended. These
items included "the Varela Project, the right of families to have small businesses and hire neighbors, Cuba's inviting the International Red Cross
and the U.N. High Commissioner on Human Rights to visit the country
and ascertain the status of prisons and human rights, and student
exchanges."[9]

Carter delivered a speech at the University of Havana that was carried live on television and radio. He reported that "all analysts said it was
the first time in 43 years that citizens had heard any public criticism of
the Cuban government."[10]

Carter defined Cuba's history as "complicated" and said there are no
simple answers. He traveled to Cuba, not to interfere in its internal affairs,
"but to extend a hand of friendship to the Cuban people and to offer a
vision of the future for our two countries and for all the Americas."[11]
Carter also expressed hope that the United States would lift travel restrictions, repeal the embargo and resolve property disputes with Cuba. The
future needs to be decided, he said, so that Cubans in the United States
can heal from their families being divided.

Most critically, President Carter said that he was not using a United
States definition of democracy, but the Universal Declaration of Human
Rights' definition. Cuba signed this declaration in 1948. The heart of the
declaration's definition of democracy is that: "all citizens are born with
the right to choose their own leaders, to define their own destiny, to speak
freely, to organize political parties, trade unions and non-governmental
groups, and to have fair and open trials."[12] Carter believes that hope is in
Cuba accepting democracy and in the United States accepting Cuba as its
friend.

United States Policy Progress

Leaders of the world continue work incrementally toward making life better for the Cuban people. Those efforts will automatically help improve family life. But it is the people who hold the real hope. In hope is strength. Alex, a young Cuban, expresses his hope.

> My thought would be for those people who are stopping the possibility of the United States population and the Cuban population to get together as friends. So those people should think that we are all Cubans, no matter where you live, so maybe you live in Miami, I am talking about the people who are in politics in Miami, not the other people, to think that we are all Cubans. So we are shadowed on the finish that I think the most important thing for human beings is life and if you don't live your life as a human being, these people should take into account that in this part of the ocean, in the island live many Cubans as they are. I happen to think they are Cubans too, so stop this policy that is creating a problem to the Cuban population.[13]

Asley Marmol, who came to the United States in 2001 and who spoke firsthand of the difficulties of living in an extended family, also shared his views on the issues of healing within separated families. He responded to my questions: There is a need for a healing process for the people who have emigrated from Cuba to the United States, because of the split in the family. Do you think that there is a need for a healing process and understanding that is in the best interests of these families and future generations? What would you suggest toward the goal of healing for the families?

> A period of healing is necessary, but it is a little bit forced to establish healing as a formal thing. I think that it is going to happen. It is going to happen naturally with the joy of freedom in Cuba, once it comes. If in the 1970s, 1980s when they allowed Cubans to visit, some families put that behind and went to Cuba to visit. At that point that happens when a general change happens, that [healing] is going to flow. It is going to be necessary. There's going to be a lot of forgiveness. Forgiveness, tolerance and a lot of putting behind and passing the page is necessary. I have the faith that it is going to happen naturally. For instance, there are people that keep a lot of hate, not toward the family, but toward some people that they knew that ever crossed them at a point. The government forced Cuban neighbors go against neighbors by going into the streets and breaking windows, throwing animals inside the house because those neighbors wanted to emigrate. Let's say that a month ago, they were playing dominos in the street together. But then suddenly because they were forced to do it, they were fearful of the consequences if they were to stand out and not do it. They joined the crowd. The

crowds were aggressive. There are people that left Cuba with that image
of the person next door. Neighbors going against me did not happen, so
I do not have that image.

The way I dream that day is that I dream those people [with that
image] going back, holding, crying together and saying, "Forgive me, I
had to do it. I was forced to do it. I didn't want to do it. I was afraid."
The other would say, "It's o.k. I understand. I forgive you." Then that's
it. Then they would start playing dominos together. Healing's going to
flow. It's going to happen naturally. We do need healing. We need a lot
of forgiveness to come into place. I know that those wounds are still
bleeding. I know we are by general rule not that type of person that gets
angry. We are the type of people that we have an argument today and
tomorrow we are going out together and having fun.[14]

I believe Asley is right that healing will come about in a natural way.
If the circumstance changes, sometimes (most of the time) it is easier for
people to move ahead and forgive and forget. He responded,

Yes, I know that it is going to happen. In my case, I am not going to
mention the person close to me that did this to me, but I do remember
a close person telling me in my face in the middle of a political argument that if I didn't like how things were in Cuba, that I had to leave.
They told me that I had to leave, just go. I ask them why did I have to
leave? Why couldn't I just enjoy a little bit of what I want in my own
country? They said that, no, if you don't agree, you have to leave. That's
a person I know is missing me right now, but in the middle of circumstances, those things happen. I know that someday when all of this is
behind, I'm going back, I'm going shake hands, [we are going to] hold
each other and that's it.

There's a lot of division and a lot of open wounds that is something
you cannot avoid.[15]

Trends in the Cuban Families

In Cuba, women in general have more educational and occupational
freedom. The state has made efforts to reduce gender discrimination in
the work force. Yet, occupationally, women in the textile mills predominantly remain in lesser positions than men, with less opportunity for
advancement. Single mothers are increasing in number in Cuba. Their
numbers between older and younger are about equal. They receive support from the state. Cuban youth enjoy sexual freedom. They receive educational programs in sexual matters, but while the overall Cuban birthrate
has declined, teen pregnancies have increased. Women are more confident

and have more control over their fertility. Some men do not wish to give up their authority and do not help much with household chores. All of these factors have led to more marital instability in Cuban society. The divorce rate has increased. The severe economic crisis has made the need for women to contribute economically to the household more acute.[16]

Extended families change authority patterns and the division of labor. A single mother in such a household tends to regard her parents as head of the household. The influence of the older generations tends to perpetuate tradition and resist change. The extended family household will have more income, but in so having, the woman's contribution is not as important. If the mother works, support of the family is important, and critical if the mother is single. In general, women identify more closely with family while men identify more closely with their economic role. The state has made efforts to establish gender equity, but a woman's domestic and reproductive roles remain an emphasis.[17]

Cuba as a country faces the challenges of increasing demands for services from its vulnerable population sectors and from those areas damaged during the Special Period. Miren Uriarte, Ph.D. at the University of Massachusetts in Boston, concludes that Cuba will meet these challenges with strength. Cubans have a high level of education and possess a knowhow when it comes to taking care of their own, she says. The most serious problems are not entrenched. Mechanisms in place, experience and adaptable existing services, for example, are also sources of strength. Cuba's social benefits problems are not unlike those that systems face everywhere. But it is the photograph she includes in her report that is most telling concerning sources of strength. The caption reads, "During the crisis, Cuba kept to its priorities of sustaining universal access to a full array of social benefits. Here a mother mixes the daily milk ration for her child in a neighborhood in Central Havana."[18]

Sources of Strength

Cuban Americans find hope in each culture. For Alejandro Concepcion, a Freedom Flight emigrant who prefers to be identified as American, hope rests in life within the United States. He says,

> This country is so great by opening itself up to people whether they are coming to give their professional skills or they are running away from tyranny or they want to get a fresh new start, that's what America is and we should protect that. As citizens, we should constantly participate and keep protecting the democracy that we have.[19]

Hope is can also be described in the actual lives of the people who celebrate having lived part of their experiences in both cultures. Pedro Ferreira, an Operation Peter Pan child and now a licensed psychologist, explains that hope best in a letter to me. The hope is based in the history of Cuba, the lives of its people, and the bonding of its generations as well as in their personal successes in the United States. Ferreira observes,

> Just last night we had a celebration here at my house for the 150th anniversary of the life of Cuban patriot José Martí, who was born on January 28, 1853. We managed to gather a group of 27 people, most of whom had come from Cuba to the U.S. in the early 60s', three of us were Peter Pan children. We had a representative from the Mayor of Wilmington, [Delaware,] Honorable James Baker, a young man whose mother was a Peter Pan child and who came to Wilmington with us in that July 27, 1962, day (a Friday!). I could not recognize her, but she did remember my name. I had not seen her in over 37 years (they separated the boys from the girls, and the younger boys from the older boys— my brother was away in an orphanage in Wilmington for about one year until he was able to join us at the "bigger" house, also in Wilmington). So you see, each of us has tried very hard to be successful and also to maintain a sense of continuity.[20]

Dr. Luis Enrique Vidal Palmer, vice director of the Havana Psychiatric Hospital, reflects Ferreira's assessment when he speaks well of the Cuban family wherever it may find itself. Dr. Vidal Palmer's judgment is an apt description to conclude this book.

> The Cuban family is without comparison, even with the difficulties, I would say that it is made greater and always finds a solution for everything. It maintains a great sense of humor, hospitality and solidarity. Cubans, wherever they may find themselves, conserve their identity, help each other, and, to a certain point, feel they are a unique race. That is how we are in essence, without being humble, I would dare to assure you that we are good people and great friends.[21]

Appendix 1:
Selected Provisions
of the Constitution
of the Republic of Cuba

24 February 1976
Marriage, Dissolution of Marriage, Parent-child
Relations, Filiation, the Right to Education,
Equality and the Right to Health Care

CHAPTER IV
THE FAMILY

ARTICLE 35. The state protects the family, motherhood and matrimony.

The state recognizes the family as the main nucleus of society and attributes to it the important responsibilities and functions in the education and formation of the new generations.

ARTICLE 36. Marriage is the voluntarily established union between a man and a woman, who are legally fit to marry, in order to live together. It is based on full equal of rights and duties for the partners, who must see to the support of the home and the integral education of their children through a joint effort compatible with the social activities of both.

The law regulates the formalization, recognition and dissolution of marriage and the rights and obligations deriving from such acts.

ARTICLE 37. All children have the same rights, regardless of being born in or out of wedlock.

Any qualification concerning the nature of the filiation is abolished.

No statement shall be made either with regard to the difference in birth or the civil status of the parents in the registration of the children's birth or in any other documents that mention parenthood.

The state guarantees, through adequate legal means, the determination and recognition of paternity.

ARTICLE 38. The parents have the duty to provide nourishment for their children; to help them to defend their legitimate interests and in the realization of their just aspirations; and to contribute actively to their education and integral development as useful and well-prepared citizens for life in a socialist society.

It is the children's duty, in turn, to respect and help their parents.

CHAPTER V
EDUCATION AND CULTURE

ARTICLE 39. The state orients, foments and promotes education, culture and science in all their manifestations.

Its educational and cultural policy is based on the following principles:

a) the state bases its educational and cultural policy on the progress made in science and technology, the ideology of Marx and Martí, and universal and Cuban progressive pedagogical tradition;

b) education is a function of the state and is free of charge. It is based on the conclusions and contributions made by science and on the close relationship between study and life, work and production.

The state maintains a broad scholarship system for students and provides the workers with multiple opportunities to study to be able to attain the highest possible levels of knowledge and skills.

The law establishes the integration and structure of the national system of education and the extent of compulsory education and defines the minimum level of general education that every citizen should acquire;

c) the state promotes the patriotic and communist education of the new generations and the training of children, young people and adults for social life.

In order to make this principle a reality, general education and specialized scientific, technical or artistic education are combined with work, development research, physical education, sports, participation in political and social activities and military training;

d) there is freedom of artistic creation as long as its content is not contrary to the Revolution. There is freedom of artistic expression;

e) in order to raise the level of culture of the people, the state foments and develops artistic education, the vocation for creation and the cultivation and appreciation of art;

f) there is freedom of creation and research in science. The state encourages and facilitates research and gives priority to that which is aimed at solving the problems related to the interests of society and the well-being of the people;

g) the state makes it possible for workers to engage in scientific work and to contribute to the development of science;

h) the state promotes, foments and develops all forms of physical education and sports as a means of education and of contribution to the integral development of citizens;

i) the state defends Cuban culture's identity and sees to the conservation of the nation's cultural heritage and artistic and historic wealth. The state protects national monuments and places known for their natural beauty or their artistic or historic values;

j) the state promotes the participation of the citizens, through the country's social and mass organizations, in the development of its educational and cultural policy.

ARTICLE 40. The state and society give special protection to children and young people.

It is the duty of the family, the schools, the state agencies and the social and mass organizations to pay special attention to the integral development of children and young people.

CHAPTER VI
EQUALITY

ARTICLE 41. All citizens have equal rights and are subject to equal duties.

ARTICLE 42. Discrimination because of race, skin color, sex, national origin, religious beliefs and any other form of discrimination harmful to human dignity is forbidden and will be punished by law.

The institutions of the state educate everyone from the earliest possible age in the principle of equality among human beings.

ARTICLE 43. The state consecrates the right achieved by the Revolution that all citizens, regardless of race, skin color, sex, religious belief, national origin and any situation that may be harmful to human dignity:

—have access, in keeping with their merits and abilities, to all state, public administration, and production and services positions and jobs;

—can reach any rank in the Revolutionary Armed Forces and in Security and internal order, in keeping with their merits and abilities;

—be given equal pay for equal work;

—have a right to education at all national educational institutions, ranging from elementary schools to the universities, which are the same for all;

—be given health care in all medical institutions;

—live in any sector, zone or area and stay in any hotel;

—be served at all restaurants and other public service establishments;

—use, without any separations, all means of transportation by sea, land and air;

—enjoy the same resorts, beaches, parks, social centers and other centers of culture, sports, recreation and rest.

ARTICLE 44. Women and men have the same rights in the economic, political, cultural and social fields, as well as in the family.

The state guarantees women the same opportunities and possibilities as men, in order to achieve women's full participation in the development of the country.

The state organizes such institutions as children's day-care centers, semi-boarding schools and boarding schools, homes for the elderly and services to make it easier for the working family to carry out its responsibilities.

The state looks after women's health as well as that of their offspring, giving working women paid maternity leave before and after giving birth and temporary work options compatible with their maternal activities.

The state strives to create all the conditions which help make real the principle of equality.

CHAPTER VII
FUNDAMENTAL RIGHTS, DUTIES AND GUARANTEES

ARTICLE 50. Everyone has the right to health protection and care. The state guarantees this right:

—by providing free medical and hospital care by means of the installations of the rural medical service, network, polyclinics, hospitals, preventative and specialized treatment centers;

—by providing free dental care;

—by promoting the health publicity campaigns, health education, regular medical examinations, general vaccinations and other measures to prevent the out-break of disease. All the population cooperates in these activities and plans through the social and mass organizations.

SOURCE: *Constitution of the Republic of Cuba*. Editions ONBC (Feb. 24, 1976, with Reforms of 1992), 17–21, 24. *Note:* Purchased by the author at the XII International Congress on Family Law, September 22–27, 2002, Havana, Cuba.

Appendix 2:
The Family Code of Cuba

ARTICLE 85

Paternal custody refers to the following rights and responsibilities of the parents:

1. Provide for their children so long as they are under their guard and custody; undertake all efforts to provide for them stable housing and adequate feeding; take care of their health and personal hygiene; provide them with recreation adequate to their ages and within their means; provide adequate protection; watch over their conduct and cooperate with the corresponding authorities in order to overcome any issue or environmental situation that is influencing or that could influence their development unfavorably;

2. Take care of their children's education; instill in them love for learning; make sure they attend the educational institution where they are registered; watch so that their technical, scientific, and cultural development improves adequately, within their aptitude, vocation and the country's needs; collaborate with school authorities in the planning of school activities;

3. Direct their children's social growth; instill in them love for the country, respect for the national symbols and esteem for its values, internationalist spirit, coexistence norms, socialist moral and respect to society's patrimony and to the rights and assets of others; inspire them with their attitude and their treatment of others with the respect owed to them, and teach them to respect authority, to their teachers and other persons;

4. Administer and watch their children's assets with utmost diligence; watch so that their children use and enjoy the assets they own adequately; they cannot jeopardize, exchange, nor relinquish said assets, unless it is for the good of their minor children and in compliance with the requirements established in this Code;

5. Represent their children in all acts and judicial businesses in which the children's interests are part; complement the children's personal participation in those instances in which the children's capacity of action is

required (*may mean, for example, signing of documents accepting an inheritance*); exercise with diligence and in due process those actions which by right correspond to the children in order to defend their interests and assets.

SOURCE: *Codigo De Familia*, "Article 85" (La Habana, Cuba: Ministerio de Justicia), 2002, pp. 23–24. Note: Purchased by the author at the XII International Congress on Family Law, September 22–27, 2002, Havana, Cuba. Translated by Mercedes Ayala (Grand Island, Neb.), Nov. 9, 2002.

Notes

Preface

1. José Martí in Lic. Consuelo León Valle and Lic. Samuel Morales Castro (Pinar del Río), "The One-parent Family: Legal Protection," Commission 2, paper, XII International Congress on Family Law, Havana, Cuba, *Memorias* (CD), Sept. 22–27, 2002.

2. Martin Guggenheim (New York University School of Law, professor of Clinical Law), "How Child-Centered is United States Family Law?" Congerencias Magistrales, XII International Congress on Family Law: Family Law in Front of the Challenges of the New Millennium, International Conference Center, Havana Cuba, Sept. 26, 2002. Translation broadcast by the Congress and transcribed by the author.

3. Announcement, XII International Congress, *Memorias* (CD).

4. Gerald W. Creed, "'Family Values' and Domestic Economies," *Annual Review of Anthropology* 29 (2000): 330.

5. Ruth Pearson, "The Political Economy of Social Reproduction: the Case of Cuba in the 1990s," in Joanne Cook, Jenifer Roberts and Georgina Waylen (eds.), *Towards a Gendered Political Economy*. New York: St. Martin's Press, Inc., 2000, 227–230.

Chapter 1

1. William Wordsworth "Ode, Intimations of Immortality from Recollections of Early Childhood," 1770–1850. Jan. 24, 2003 http://www.daypoems.net/poems/488.html.

2. Dra. Ediltrudis Panadero de la Cruz (Faculty of Law, University of Oriente, Santi-

ago, Cuba), "The Succession and the Protection to the Surviving Spouse of the Family House and Furniture: Tendencies in Comparative Law," Commission 2, paper, XII International Congress on Family Law, Havana, Cuba, *Memorias* (CD), Sept. 22–27, 2002. Translated by James C. Skaine and assisted by SYSTRAN Premium 4.0 translation program, Jan. 7, 2003.

3. CubaGenWeb, "Notes on Cuban Surnames," Jan. 18, 2003. Jan. 26, 2003 http://www.cubagenweb.org/names.htm.

4. Delvis Fernández Levy, Ph.D. (president, Cuban American Alliance Education Fund, Inc.), interview by the author, July 9, 2002.

5. CubaGenWeb.

6. CubaGenWeb.

7. CubaGenWeb.

8. Anton L. Allahar, "Women and the Family in Cuba: A Study Across Time," *Humboldt Journal of Social Relations* (1994): 89.

9. Allahar, 90.

10. Allahar, 91.

11. Allahar, 90–92.

12. Jesús Guanche Pérez, Panel: "Civil Society and Family Diversity," XII International Congress. Translation broadcast by the Congress, recorded by the author and transcribed by Sue Ravn (Cedar Falls, Ia.).

13. Guanche Pérez.

14. Verena Martinez-Alier, *Marriage, Class and Colour in Nineteenth-Century Cuba: A Study of Racial Attitudes and Sexual Values in a Slave Society*. New York, N.Y.: Cambridge University Press, 1974, 133.

15. Martinez-Alier, 122–123.

16. Martinez-Alier, 122.

17. Martinez-Alier, 123.

18. Martinez-Alier, 127–129.

19. Martinez-Alier, 138–139.

20. Martinez-Alier, viii.

21. Martinez-Alier, vii.

22. Martinez-Alier, 140–141.

23. Dra. Ana Vera Estrada, Coordinator, Panel: "Civil Society and Family Diversity," XII International Congress. Translation broadcast by the Congress and transcribed by Sue Ravn (Cedar Falls, Ia.).

24. Fernández Levy interview, July 9, 2002.

25. Guanche Pérez.

26. Guanche Pérez.

27. Guanche Pérez.

28. Guanche Pérez.

29. Katia de Llano Cuesta, "Women in Cuba: Background," St. Paul, Minn., November 2000. May 16, 2002 http://www.canadacuba.ca/05aboutcuba/articleWomen.html.

30. Lic. Xóchitl Aguirre Tamayo (Cuba), "The Legal Protection of the Unions in fact in Cuba," Commission 2, paper, XII International Congress. Translated by James C. Skaine and assisted by SYSTRAN Premium 4.0 translation program, Jan. 16, 2003.

31. Aguirre Tamayo.

32. Aguirre Tamayo.

33. Lic. Rosario Marquetti Pérez and Lic. Lidice Crespo Sosa, "The Legal Protection of Minors Without Family Shelter in Cuba," Commission 1, paper, XII International Congress. Translated by James C. Skaine and assisted by SYSTRAN Premium 4.0 translation program, Jan. 5, 2003.

34. Allahar, 92.

35. Allahar, 92–93.

36. Allahar, 93.

37. Allahar, 93.

38. Allahar, 93.

39. Allahar, 97–101.

40. Helen I. Safa, *The Myth of the Male Breadwinner: Women and Industrialization in the Caribbean*. Boulder, Colo.: Westview Press, 1995, 26.

41. M.G. Rosenthal, "The Problem of Single Motherhood in Cuba," in S. Halebsky and J.M. Kirk (eds.), *Cuba in Transition: Crisis and Transformation*. Boulder, Colo.: Westview Press, 1992, 168, in Allahar, 105–106.

42. Allahar, 107.

43. Germaine Greer, "Women and Politics: Cuba," *Women: A World Report*. New York: Oxford University Press, 1985, 280, in Allahar, 107.

44. Allahar, 109.

45. Allahar, 112.

46. Allahar, 113, 115, 117.

47. Cuban American Alliance Education Fund, Inc. (CAAEF), "Social Work Development and Practice in Cuba and in the U.S.: A Report," Feb. 2002, 16.

48. Allahar, 113, 115, 117.

49. Panadero de la Cruz.

50. Gisela Arandia Covarrubia (researcher at the Center for Studies of the United States, University of Havana), "One Way to Strengthen Nationality," AfroCuba Web, 1997. Jan. 21, 2003 http://www.afrocubaweb.com/arandia-art.htm.

51. Arandia Covarrubia.

52. Arandia Covarrubia.

53. Belkis Caridad Núñez Travieso (lawyer, City of Havana, Cuba), "Theoretical Disquisitions About the Institute of The Mother Country Power in Cuba," 2002, Commission 1, paper, XII International Congress. Translated by James C. Skaine and assisted by SYSTRAN Premium 4.0 translation program, Jan. 7, 2003.

54. Caridad Núñez Travieso.

55. Caridad Núñez Travieso.

56. Caridad Núñez Travieso.

Chapter 2

1. Tom Haines, "Cuba, On and Off Track from East to West, a Sprawling Yet Sporadic Rail System Reveals Lazy Tableaux of a Country Battered by Revolution and a People Left Behind," *The Boston Globe*, Santa Clara, Dec. 29, 2002, 3d ed., Section: Travel, M1.

2. Net for Cuba, "Government, Communist Party" and "Political Organizations," Jan. 30, 2003. Jan. 30, 2003 http://www.netforcuba.org/communistparty.htm and http://www.netforcuba.org/politicalorganizations.htm.

3. Net for Cuba, "Communist Party" and "Political Organizations."

4. The Constitution of the Republic of Cuba, Chapter IV, The Family, Article 38, in Net for Cuba, "Government — Political Organizations."

5. U.S. Department of State, "Cuba, Country Reports on Human Rights Practices—2001," released by the Bureau of Democracy, Human Rights, and Labor, March 4, 2002. May 16, 2002 http://www.state.gov/g/drl/rls/hrrpt/2001/wha/8333.htm.

6. U.S. Department of State.

7. Isabel Garcia-Zarza (Reuters), "Big Brother at 40: Cuba's Revolutionary Neighborhood Watch System," sun-sentinel.com,

Web-posted: Oct. 10, 2000. Nov. 11, 2002, http://xld.com/public/cuba/embargo/cdr.htm.

8. Garcia-Zarza.

9. Garcia-Zarza.

10. Global Exchange Reality Tour, "Cuba: Politics and Government," San Francisco, 2002. Nov. 10, 2002 http://www.globalexchange.org/tours/profile/cuba/politics.html.

11. U.S. Department of State.

12. Garcia-Zarza.

13. U.S. Department of State.

14. The Constitution of the Republic of Cuba, Article 53, in Net for Cuba, "Government, Justice System," May 18, 2002. May 18, 2002 http://www.netforcuba.org/justicesystem.htm; SFBG News, "World View: Inside Cuba's Legal System." Nov. 3, 1999. May 18, 2002 http://www.sfbg.com/News/34/05/5world.html.

15. PRODOS Institute and PRODOS.com, "Inside Cuba, Reports from January 2001," Jan. 2001 Archive. May 18, 2002 http://www.cubacampaign.org/january2001.html.

16. PRODOS Institute and PRODOS.com, "Inside Cuba, Reports from January 2001."

17. PRODOS Institute and PRODOS.com, "Inside Cuba, First-hand Reports from Dissidents and Human Rights Activists Within Cuba," June 2001. July 24, 2002 http://www.cubacampaign.org/June2002.html.

18. Haroldo Dilla and Philip Oxhorn, "The Virtues and Misfortunes of Civil Society in Cuba," Issue 125, Vol. 29, No. 4, *Latin American Perspectives* (July 2002): 21.

19. U.S. Department of State.

20. Robert A. Pastor (vice president of International Affairs and professor of International Relations, American University, Washington, D.C.), interview by the author, June 28, 2002.

21. Pastor, interview, June 28, 2002.

22. Pastor, interview, June 28, 2002.

23. David Gonzalez, "World Briefing Americas: Cuba: Socialism Forever, Assembly Declares," *The New York Times*, June 28, 2002, Late Ed., Final, A11.

24. Net for Cuba, "Government, Electoral System," May 18, 2002. May 18, 2002 http://www.netforcuba.org/electoralsystem.htm.

25. Pastor, interview, June 28, 2002.

26. Pastor, interview, June 28, 2002.

27. Anthony Boadle, "Cubans Vote in Local One-Party Elections," Havana, Reuters.com, Oct. 20, 2002.

28. CIA, "The World Fact Book 2001—Cuba," Jan. 1, 2001. July 4, 2002 http://www.cia.gov/cia/publications/factbook/geos/cu.html.

29. Donald W. Bray and Marjorie Woodford Bray, "Introduction: The Cuban Revolution and World Change," Issue 124, Vol. 29, No. 3, *Latin American Perspectives* (May 2002): 3.

30. CIA.

31. Andrew Yurkovsky, "Cuba Goes Its Own Way: Looking Beyond Elian," *World Press Review*, April 2001, 19.

32. Paul Cullen, "'Third Way' Could Save Revolutionary Gains: Will Fidel Buy Time or Sell Out?" *The Irish Times*, Dublin, Ireland, Jan. 8, 2001, in *World Press Review*, April 2001, 19.

33. Bray and Woodford Bray, 3.

34. Cullen, in *World Press Review*, 19.

35. Bray and Woodford Bray, 3–4, 8.

36. Douglas Hamilton, "Whiter Cuban Socialism? The Changing Political Economy of the Cuban Revolution," Issue 124, Vol. 29, No. 3, *Latin American Perspectives* (May 2002): 23–24.

37. Miren Uriarte, Ph.D., "Cuba Social Policy at the Crossroads: Maintaining Priorities, Transforming Practice," Boston, Mass.: Oxfam America Report, 2002, 16. Jan. 12, 2003 http://www.oxfamamerica.org/pdfs/social_policy.pdf.

38. Uriarte, 16

39. Hamilton, 23–24.

40. Hans-Jürgen Burchardt, "Contours of the Future: The New Social Dynamics in Cuba," Issue 124, Vol. 29, No. 3, *Latin American Perspectives* (May 2002): 63–64.

41. David Strug, Ph.D., and Walter Teague, Master of Social Work, "New Directions in Cuban Social Work Education: What Can We Learn?" Sept. 2, 2002. Jan. 12, 2003 http://users.erols.com/wteague/Cuba/Cuban_Social_Work_Education.htm. (Article also appears in *Social Work Today*, Sept. 2, 2002.)

42. Burchardt, 64.

43. Uriarte, 344-35.

44. Bray and Woodford Bray, 3–4, 8.

45. Bray and Woodford Bray, 4.

46. Bray and Woodford Bray, 4.

47. Uriarte, 28–29.

48. Uriarte, 23–24.

49. Burchardt, 63.

50. Uriarte, 29.

51. Cullen, in *World Press Review*, 19.

52. Uriarte, 29–30.

53. Uriarte, 39.

54. Uriarte, 40.

55. Yurkovsky, 19.

56. Cullen, in *World Press Review*, 19–20.

57. CIA, "The World Fact Book 2001—Cuba."

58. Marelys Valencia, "Dollar Is a Tool, Not the Rule," *Granma Internacional* (Communist Party weekly), Havana, Cuba, Jan. 26, 2001, in *World Press Review*, April 2001, 23.

59. Aldo Mariátegui, "The Revolution Comes Full Circle: Commerce's Fallen Idol Restored," *El Comercio* (centrist), Lima, Peru, Jan. 31, 2001, in *World Press Review*, April 2001, 23.

60. Larry Luxner, "Street Markets Offer Alternative Work Options for Cubans," *Cuba News*, 9, Issue 7 (July 2001): 10.

61. Luxner, 10.

62. Luxner, 10.

63. Alex (young Cuban teacher), interview by the author and James C. Skaine in Havana, Sept. 26, 2002.

64. Alex, interview, Sept. 26. 2002.

65. Constitution of the Republic of Cuba, "Education and Culture," Chapter V, 18–20, Editions ONBC (Feb. 24, 1976, with Reforms of 1992), 1–56. Note: Purchased by the author at the XII International Congress on Family Law.

66. Sheryl L. Lutjens, "Schooling and 'Clean Streets' in Socialist Cuba: Children and the Special Period," in Roslyn Arlin Mickelson, *Children on the Streets of the Americas: Homelessness, Education, and Globalization in the United States, Brazil, and Cuba.* London; New York: Routledge, 2000, 56.

67. Lutjens, in Mickelson, 57.

68. Lutjens, in Mickelson, 57.

69. Lutjens, in Mickelson, 57–58.

70. Lutjens, in Mickelson, 58.

71. Lutjens, in Mickelson, 59.

72. Lutjens, in Mickelson, 60–61.

73. Uriarte, 32-33.

74. Uriarte, 16.

75. Uriarte, 16.

76. Lutjens, in Mickelson, 60.

77. David Strug, Ph.D., and Walter Teague, Master of Social Work, "New Directions in Cuban Social Work Education: What Can We Learn?" Sept. 2, 2002. Jan. 12, 2003 http://users.erols.com/wteague/Cuba/Cuban_Social_Work_Education.htm. (Article also appears in *Social Work Today*, Sept. 2, 2002.)

78. Strug and Teague.

79. Strug and Teague.

80. CIA, "The World Fact Book 2001— Cuba."

81. Constitution of the Republic of Cuba, Article 49, in Michèle Barry, M.D., "Effect of the U.S. Embargo and Economic Decline on Health in Cuba," *Annals of Internal Medicine*, 132, No. 2 (Jan. 18, 2000): 151–152.

82. Michèle Barry, "Effect of the U.S. Embargo and Economic Decline on Health in Cuba," *Annals of Internal Medicine* 132, No. 2 (Jan. 18, 2000): 151–4. Dec. 28, 2002 http://www.annals.org/issues/v132n2/full/200001180-00010.html.

83. Howard Waitzkin, M.D., Ph.D., Karen Wald, Romina Kee, M.D., Ross Danielson, Ph.D., and Lisa Robinson, Registered Nurse, ARNP, "Primary Care in Cuba: Family Medicine Paper, Low- and High-technology Developments Pertinent to Family Medicine," April 1997. Dec. 28, 2002 http://www.cubasolidarity.net/waitzkin.html.

84. Dr. Luis Enrique Vidal Palmer (Degree Specialist First Class in Psychiatry, Professor and Vicedirector for the Psychiatry, Forensic and Legal Medicine, Psychiatric Hospital of Havana-Cuba), email interview, Dec. 17, 2002. Translated by Mercedes Ayala (Grand Island, Neb.), Dec. 18, 2002.

85. XII International Congress on Family Law: Family Law in Front of the Challenges of the New Millennium, International Conference Center, Havana, Cuba, and New York City Bar Association, Hospital Psiquiatrico de la Habana-Cuba Tour, September 24, 2002.

86. Vidal Palmer, email interview, Dec. 17, 2002.

87. Vidal Palmer, email interview, Dec. 17, 2002.

88. Vidal Palmer, email interview, Dec. 17, 2002.

89. Vidal Palmer, email interview, Dec. 17, 2002.

90. Vidal Palmer, email interview, Dec. 17, 2002.

91. Vidal Palmer, email interview, Dec. 17, 2002.

92. Vidal Palmer, email interview, Dec. 17, 2002.

93. Vidal Palmer, email interview, Dec. 17, 2002.

94. Barry, 152.

95. Barry, 153.

96. Barry, 151–4.

97. Uriarte, 21.

98. Alex, interview, Sept. 26, 2002.

99. Alex, interview, Sept. 26, 2002.

100. Ruth Pearson, "The Political Economy of Social Reproduction: the Case of Cuba in the 1990s," in Joanne Cook, Jennifer Roberts and Georgina Waylen (eds.), *Towards a Gendered Political Economy*. New York: St. Martin's Press, Inc., 2000, 230–231.

101. Pearson, in Cook, *et al.* (eds.), 231.

102. Uriarte, 16.

103. Pearson, in Cook, *et al.* (eds.), 232.

104. "Transportation — Culture," 1998. November 24, 2002 http://library.thinkquest. org/18355/transportation_-_culture.html.

105. Dilla and Oxhorn, 18.

106. Dilla and Oxhorn, 18–19.

107. Dilla and Oxhorn, 19.

108. Ron Howell (reporter, *Newsday*), email interview by the author, Nov. 16, 2002.

109. Howell, email interview by the author, Nov. 16, 2002.

110. Brett Kelliher, Religion, "Santeria." May 16, 2002 http://www.intl.pdx.edu/latin/ religion/santeria2.html.

111. Keith Aoki, "Panel: Races, Nationalities, Ethnicities: Mapping Latcrit (Dis)continuities: Representing Representation," 2 *Harvard Latino Law Review* 247, n6 (Fall 1997).

112. Kelliher.

113. Tom Masland and Brook Larmer, "Cuba's Real Religion," *Newsweek*, Jan. 19, 1998, p. 42.

114. Masland and Larmer, 42.

115. Nazia Shaikh, "Cuban Women: Before and After the Revolution," May 19, 2000. May 16, 2002 http://www.saxakali.com/caribbean/ nshaikh.htm.

116. Shaikh; themilitant.com, Sept. 29, 2003.

117. Shaikh.

118. George McGovern, *The Third Freedom: Ending Hunger in Our Time.* Lanham, Maryland: Rowman and Littlefield Publishers, Inc., 2001, 107.

119. Alex, interview, Sept. 26, 2002.

120. Delvis Fernández Levy (president, Cuban American Alliance Education Fund, Inc.), interview by the author, July 9, 2002.

121. Hamilton, 28.

122. Hamilton, 28.

123. Pastor, interview, June 28, 2002.

124. Pastor, interview, June 28, 2002.

125. Pastor, interview, June 28, 2002.

126. Pastor, interview, June 28, 2002.

127. Pastor, interview, June 28, 2002.

128. Pastor, interview, June 28, 2002.

129. Sorya M. Castro Mariño, "U.S.-Cuban Relations During the Clinton Administration," Issue 125, Vol. 29, No. 4, *Latin American Perspectives* (July 2002): 57–59.

130. MATP, "Iran Top of Terror List — War on Terror: Target — New York," *The Daily Telegraph* (Sydney), May 23, 2002, 33, Sec. World.

131. Phillip T. Reeker, acting spokesman; Edmund J. Hull, acting coordinator for counterterrorism, Briefing Upon the Release of the U.S. Department of State Report "Patterns of Global Terrorism 2000," Washington, D.C., April 30, 2001. July 23, 2002 http://www.state. gov/s/ct/rls/rm/2001/2571.htm.

132. Jim Abrams, "House Votes in Favor of Lifting Sanctions on Cuba," AP, Washington Dateline, July 24, 2002.

133. Abrams.

134. Abrams; Ted Barrett, Washington Bureau Cnn.com/Inside Politics, White House Loses Key House Votes on Cuba, Bush Expected to Veto Effort to Lift Travel Ban," July 24, 2002. July 24, 2002 http://www.cnn.com/2002/ALL POLITICS/07/24/congress.cuba/index.html.

135. Pastor, interview, June 28, 2002.

136. Cuban American Alliance Education Fund, Inc., "What is CAAEF," flyer provided to the author by Delvis Fernández Levy, president, Aug. 4, 2002.

137. CIA.

138. Bray and Woodford Bray, 4.

139. Aldo Mariátegui, "The Revolution Comes Full Circle: Commerce's Fallen Idol Restored," *El Comercio* (centrist), Lima, Peru, Jan. 31, 2001, in *World Press Review*, April 2001, 23.

140. Bray and Woodford Bray, 4.

141. Uriarte, 5.

142. Uriarte, 5.

Chapter 3

1. Rosemarie Skaine, "A Study of Perceptions of Inequity Among Merit System Employees at the University of Northern Iowa," A Thesis, University of Northern Iowa, August 1977, 17.

2. Ruth Pearson, "The Political Economy of Social Reproduction: the Case of Cuba in the 1990s," in Joanne Cook, Jennifer Roberts and Georgina Waylen (eds.), *Towards a Gendered Political Economy.* New York: St. Martin's Press, Inc., 2000, 238.

3. XII International Congress on Family Law, Havana, Cuba, Sept. 22–27, 2002.

4. Douglas Hamilton, "Whiter Cuban Socialism? The Changing Political Economy of the Cuban Revolution," Issue 124, Vol. 29, No. 3, *Latin American Perspectives* (May 2002): 27.

5. Pearson, "The Political Economy of Social Reproduction...," in Cook *et al.*, 239.

6. Pearson, "The Political Economy of Social Reproduction...," in Cook *et al.*, 241.

7. Ron Howell (reporter, *Newsday*), email interview by the author, Nov. 16, 2002.

8. Howell, email interview, Nov. 16, 2002.

9. Joanne P. Cavanaugh, "Cuba's Marry-go-round," Special Report, *Johns Hopkins Magazine*, April 1998. May 16, 2002 http://www.jhu.edu/~jhumag/0498web/wedding.html.

10. Miren Uriarte, Ph.D., "Cuba Social Policy at the Crossroads: Maintaining Priorities, Transforming Practice," Boston, Mass.: Oxfam America Report, 2002, 4. Jan. 12, 2003 http://www.oxfamamerica.org/pdfs/social_pol icy.pd.

11. Archibald R.M. Ritter, "Cuba in the 1990s: Economic Reorientation and International Reintegration," in Sandor Halebsky and John M. Kirk with Carollee Bengelsdorf, Richard L. Harris, Jean Stubbs and Andrew Zimbalist (eds.), *Cuba in Transition: Crisis and Transformation*. Boulder, Colo: Westview Press, 1992, 128.

12. Asley L. Marmol (Miami, Fla.), interview by the author, Oct. 17, 2002.

13. Uriarte, 21.

14. Ritter, "Cuba in the 1990s...," in Halebsky *et. al.*, 128.

15. Alex (young Cuban teacher), interview by the author and James C. Skaine in Havana, Sept. 26, 2002.

16. Alex, interview, Sept. 26, 2002.

17. Alex, interview, Sept. 26, 2002.

18. Alex, interview, Sept. 26, 2002.

19. Katia de Llano Cuesta, "Women in Cuba: Background," St. Paul, Minnesota, November 2000. May 16, 2002 http://www.can adacuba.ca/05aboutcuba/articleWomen.html.

20. Smith, "Sexuality and Socialism," in Halebsky *et al.*, 179.

21. Smith, "Sexuality and Socialism," in Halebsky *et al.*, 188.

22. Anton L. Allahar, "Women and The Family in Cuba: A Study Across Time," *Humboldt Journal of Social Relations* (1994): 103–105.

23. Allahar, 103–105.

24. Pearson, "The Political Economy of Social Reproduction...," in Cook *et al.*, 234.

25. Allahar, 105.

26. Pearson, "The Political Economy of Social Reproduction...," in Cook *et al.*, 232–233.

27. Allahar, 105.

28. Carollee Bengelsdorf and Jean Stubbs, "Introduction to Part 3," in Halebsky *et al.*, 155.

29. The Cultural Orientation Project: Cubans—Their History and Culture, Refugee Fact Sheet No. 12, "Political, Religious and Family Life," Washington, D.C.: Cultural Orientation Resource Center, March 24, 2000. Nov. 12, 2002 http://www.culturalorientation.net/cubans/life.htm.

30. Uriarte, 16.

31. The Cultural Orientation Project, Refugee Fact Sheet No. 12.

32. Dr. Luis Enrique Vidal Palmer (Degree Specialist First Class in Psychiatry, Professor and Vicedirector for the Psychiatry, Forensic and Legal Medicine, Psychiatric Hospital of Havana-Cuba), email interview, Dec. 17, 2002. Translated by Mercedes Ayala (Grand Island, Neb.), Dec. 18, 2002.

33. Vidal Palmer, email interview, Dec. 17, 2002.

34. Vidal Palmer, email interview, Dec. 17, 2002.

35. Vidal Palmer, email interview, Dec. 17, 2002.

36. Vidal Palmer, email interview, Dec. 17, 2002.

37. Vidal Palmer, email interview, Dec. 17, 2002.

38. Delvis Fernández Levy (president, Cuban American Alliance Education Fund, Inc.), interview by the author, July 9, 2002.

39. Alex, interview, Sept. 26, 2002.

40. Alex, interview, Sept. 26, 2002.

41. Asley L. Marmol, interview, Oct. 17, 2002.

42. Leonardo M. Marmol, Ph.D., ABPP (professor and chair, Dept. of Graduate Psychology, Seattle Pacific University), interview by the author, July 30, 2002.

Chapter 4

1. Cuban American Alliance Education Fund, Inc. (CAAEF), "Social Work Development and Practice in Cuba and in the U.S.: A Report," February 2002, 16.

2. "Program." "Call," XII International Congress on Family Law: Family Law in Front of the Challenges of the New Millennium, International Conference Center. Havana, Cuba, *Memorias* (CD), Sept. 22–27, 2002, p. 4.

3. Reporter's Report of Commission 1B: "Family Law and Fundamental Rights: Institutions to Means of Protection," Closing Ceremony, XII International Congress. Broadcast

translation by the Congress and transcribed by James C. Skaine.

4. Constitution of the Republic of Cuba, Editions ONBC (Feb. 24, 1976, with Reforms of 1992), 2, 3. Note: Copy of Constitution purchased by the author at XII International Congress.

5. Constitution, "Chapter IV, The Family," Articles 35–38, 17–18; The Family Code, Ley 1289, Ministerio de Justicia: No. 216, Vedado, La Habana, Cuba, 2002. Note: Copy of Family Code purchased by the author at XII International Congress.

6. Constitution, Article 35, 17.

7. Constitution, Article 36, 17–18.

8. Dr. Ruth Juarez Fontanet, Dr. Lazara Valdes Career and Dr. Sigrid Isabel Pou Salvi (Institute of Medical Sciences of Havana, Faculty "General Calixto Garcia" Institute of Legal Medicine), "Biological Forensic Investigation Report in the Processes of Filiation. Juridical Signification," Commission 4, paper, XII International Congress, *Memorias* (CD). Translated by Marco Poblete (Dept. of Modern Languages, Univ. of Northern Iowa, Cedar Falls).

9. Constitution of the Republic of Cuba of 24-02-1976, Articles 35 to 38 on the family, Editions ENPES, 59 pages, 1976 in Fontanet *et al.*

10. Constitution, Articles 35 to 38, in Fontanet *et al.*

11. Constitution, Articles 35 to 38, Civil Code, Articles 492 to 495, Code of the Childhood and the Youth, Law 76|84, Law of Civil, Administrative and Labor Procedure, Articles 261-263, 301–315, *Family Code*, Law of the Civil Record of the Inscription of Birth, in Fontanet *et al.*

12. Constitution, Articles 35 to 38, in Fontanet *et al.*

13. Lic. Zoraida Puentes Hernández, Lic. Ana Margarita Hoyo Pérez and Lic. Issel María Veitia Cabezas (lawyers, Villa Clara, Cuba), "Finding Options for Legal Considerations on the Biological Expert Testing for Determination of Paternity and Maternity," Commission 4, paper, XII International Congress. Translated by Mercedes Ayala (Grand Island, Neb.).

14. Constitution, Art. 38, 18.

15. Constitution, "Equality," Chapter VI, Articles 41–44, 21–22.

16. The Family Code, "Objectives of the Code," Article 1, Ley 1289, Ministerio de Justicia: O No. 216, Vedado, La Habana, Cuba,

2002, 5. Translated by Rosemarie Skaine and James Skaine and assisted by SYSTRAN Premium 4.0 translation program, Feb. 5, 2003.

17. Helen I. Safa, *The Myth of the Male Breadwinner: Women and Industrialization in the Caribbean.* Boulder, Colo.: Westview Press, 1995, 26–28.

18. Safa, 26.

19. Safa, 34–5.

20. Safa, 162–163.

21. "Civil Society and Family Diversity," International Panel, question and answer period, XII International Congress. Broadcast translation by the Congress and transcribed by the author.

22. Safa, 166.

23. Safa, 165–166.

24. Cuba: Culture, "Marriage Rate: Do Cubans get married?" Dec. 2, 2002 http://www.cuba.ru/view/docs/doc_read.php3?id_object=11&id_rubr=1238.

25. Cuba: Culture, "Marriage Rate."

26. Alex (Cuban resident, Havana), interview by the author and James C. Skaine, Sept. 26, 2002.

27. Alex, interview, Sept. 26, 2002.

28. Joanne P. Cavanaugh, "Cuba's Marry-go-round," Special Report, *Johns Hopkins Magazine,* April 1998. May 16, 2002 http://www.jhu.edu/~jhumag/0498web/wedding.html.

29. Gulnar Nugman, "World Divorce Rates," Heritage Foundation, 2002. Dec. 2, 2002 http://www.divorcereform.org/gul.html.

30. Cuba: Culture, "Divorce." Dec. 2, 2002 http://www.cuba.ru/view/docs/doc_read.php3?id_object=12&id_r ubr=1238.

31. Reporter's Report of Commission 1B: "Family Law and Fundamental Rights."

32. Ron Howell (reporter, *Newsday*), email interview by the author, Nov. 16, 2002.

33. Safa, 163–165.

34. Carollee Bengelsdorf and Jean Stubbs, "Introduction to Part 3," in Sandor Halebsky and John M. Kirk with Carollee Bengelsdorf, Richard L. Harris, Jean Stubbs and Andrew Zimbalist (eds.), *Cuba in Transition: Crisis and Transformation.* Boulder, Colo.: Westview Press, 1992, 157.

35. Marguerite G. Rosenthal, "Problems of Single Motherhood," in Halebsky *et al.*, 166.

36. Lic. Consuelo León Valle and Lic. Samuel Morales Castro (Pinar Del Río), "The One-parent Family. Legal Protection," Commission 2, paper, XII International Congress, *Memorias* (CD). Translated by Mercedes Ayala (Grand Island, Neb.).

37. Safa, 163–165.

38. Safa, 165.

39. Rosenthal, "Problems of Single Motherhood," in Halebsky et al., 1992, 166–167.

40. Rosenthal, "Problems of Single Motherhood," in Halebsky et al., 172–173.

41. Constitution, Article 37, 18.

42. Gaceta Oficial de la República de Cuba, No. 50, Aug. 22, 1985, Act No. 51, July 1985, p. 844, in "Cuba," 13 Annual Review of Population Law (1986), 256. See also Constitution, Article 37, 18.

43. León Valle and Morales Castro, "The One-parent Family."

44. León Valle and Morales Castro, "The One-parent Family."

45. León Valle and Morales Castro, "The One-parent Family."

46. León Valle and Morales Castro, "The One-parent Family."

47. Miren Uriarte, Ph.D., "Cuba Social Policy at the Crossroads: Maintaining Priorities, Transforming Practice," Boston, Mass.: Oxfam America Report, 2002, 40. Jan. 12, 2003 http://www.oxfamamerica.org/pdfs/social_pol icy.pdf.

48. Lic. Rosario Marquetti Perez and Lic. Lidice Crespo Sosa, "The Legal Protection of Minors Without Family Shelter in Cuba," Commission 1, paper, XII International Congress on Family Law, Havana, Cuba, Memorias (CD), Sept. 22–27, 2002. Translated by James C. Skaine and assisted by SYSTRAN Premium 4.0 translation program, Jan. 5, 2003.

49. Marquetti Perez and Crespo Sosa, "The Legal Protection of Minors."

50. Marquetti Perez and Crespo Sosa, "The Legal Protection of Minors."

51. Marquetti Perez and Crespo Sosa, "The Legal Protection of Minors."

52. Marquetti Perez and Crespo Sosa, "The Legal Protection of Minors."

53. Marquetti Perez and Crespo Sosa, "The Legal Protection of Minors."

54. Marquetti Perez and Crespo Sosa, "The Legal Protection of Minors."

55. M.Sc. Irma Renee Fernández Guerra and M.Sc. Luís Palenzuela Paéz (Havana, Cuba), "Considerations on Extraterritorial Adoption of Cuban Children," Commission 1, paper, XII International Congress. Translated by Mercedes Ayala (Grand Island, Neb.).

56. Family Code, Articles 85, 100, 101, and 102, in Fernández Guerra and Palenzuela Paéz.

57. Family Code, Articles 85, 100, 101, and 102, in Fernández Guerra and Palenzuela Paéz.

58. Fernández Guerra and Palenzuela Paéz, "Considerations on Extraterritorial Adoption."

59. Fernández Guerra and Palenzuela Paéz, "Considerations on Extraterritorial Adoption."

60. Fernández Guerra and Palenzuela Paéz, "Considerations on Extraterritorial Adoption."

61. Fernández Guerra and Palenzuela Paéz, "Considerations on Extraterritorial Adoption."

62. Lic. Xóchitl Aguirre Tamayo (Cuba), "The Legal Protection of the Unions in Fact in Cuba," Commission 2, paper, XII International Congress on Family Law, Havana, Cuba, Memorias (CD), Sept. 22–27, 2002. Translated by James C. Skaine and assisted by SYSTRAN Premium 4.0 translation program, Jan. 16, 2003.

63. Aguirre Tamayo, "The Legal Protection of the Unions."

64. Aguirre Tamayo, "The Legal Protection of the Unions."

65. Aguirre Tamayo, "The Legal Protection of the Unions."

66. Aguirre Tamayo, "The Legal Protection of the Unions."

67. Aguirre Tamayo, "The Legal Protection of the Unions."

68. Aguirre Tamayo, "The Legal Protection of the Unions."

69. Aguirre Tamayo, "The Legal Protection of the Unions."

70. Aguirre Tamayo, "The Legal Protection of the Unions."

71. Aguirre Tamayo, "The Legal Protection of the Unions."

72. Aguirre Tamayo, "The Legal Protection of the Unions."

73. Dra. Olga Mesa Castillo, Family Law, in Aguirre Tamayo, "The Legal Protection of the Unions."

74. Aguirre Tamayo, "The Legal Protection of the Unions."

75. Aguirre Tamayo, "The Legal Protection of the Unions."

76. Roslyn Arlin Mickelson, Children on the Streets of the Americas: Homelessness, Education, and Globalization in the United States, Brazil, and Cuba. London, New York: Routledge, 2000, 26–27.

77. Sheryl L. Lutjens, "Schooling and 'Clean Streets' in Socialist Cuba: Children and the Special Period," in Mickelson, 59–63.

78. Lutjens, "Schooling and 'Clean Streets'," in Mickelson, 63.

79. Naomi Koppel, "U.S. Sanctions May Be Robbing Cuban Women of Rights, U.N. Expert Says," Geneva, NandoMedia/Associated Press, March 24, 2000. July 4, 2002 http://www.globalpolicy.org/security/sanction/cuba/cuba18.htm.

80. Asley L. Marmol (Miami, Fla.), interview by the author, Oct. 17, 2002.

81. Reporter's Report of Commission 1B, "Family Law and Fundamental Rights."

Chapter 5

1. Delvis Fernández Levy (president, Cuban American Alliance Education Fund, Inc.), "But Who Am I?" *La Alborada* (Hayward, Calif.: Cuban American Alliance Education Fund, Inc.), Vol. 1, No. 4, Winter 1997, p. 2.

2. Delvis Fernández Levy (president, Cuban American Alliance Education Fund, Inc.), interview by the author, July 9, 2002.

3. Fernández Levy, interview, July 9, 2002.

4. Sarah Left and Agencies, "Bush Sets Tough Conditions for Easing Cuban Embargo," *Guardian Unlimited*, May 20, 2002. Dec. 18, 2002 http://www.guardian.co.uk/cuba/story/0,11983,719086,00.html; Mark P. Sullivan and Maureen Taft-Morales, "Cuba: Issues for Congress," "Summary," *Report for Congress*, Congressional Research Service (CRS) RL30806, the Library of Congress, Nov. 29, 2002. Dec. 20, 2002 http://fpc.state.gov/c4763.htm.

5. Sullivan and Taft-Morales, "Cuba: Issues for Congress," "Summary."

6. Fernández Levy, interview, July 9, 2002.

7. Fernández Levy, interview, July 9, 2002.

8. Fernández Levy, interview, July 9, 2002.

9. Sullivan and Taft-Morales, "Cuba: Issues for Congress," "Summary."

10. Cuban American Alliance, "Essential Components of the U.S./Cuba Policy," *La Alborada*, n.d. Dec. 20, 2002 http://www.cubamer.org/alb3.htm.

11. Fernández Levy, interview, July 9, 2002.

12. Nicanor León Cotayo, "Mixed Signals to an Isolated Nation: 'Adjust' Hostile Citizenship Act," *Bohemia* (weekly newsmagazine), Havana, Cuba, Jan. 26, 2001, in *World Press Review*, April 2001, 20.

13. Law Offices of James G. Beirne, "Cuban Nationals or Citizens Seeking Lawful Permanent Resident Status," May 16, 2002. May 16, 2002 http://www.lawcenterca.com/immi_CAA.asp.

14. Ruth Ellen Wasem, *Cuban Migration Policy and Issues*, CRS Report RS20468, Feb. 14, 2000.

15. Wasem, *Cuban Migration Policy and Issues*.

16. Beirne, "Cuban Nationals."

17. Beirne, "Cuban Nationals."

18. Beirne, "Cuban Nationals."

19. Beirne, "Cuban Nationals."

20. Beirne, "Cuban Nationals."

21. Emily H. Skop, "Race and Place in the Adaptation of Mariel Exiles," *International Migration Review* 35, I. 2 (Summer 2001), 449.

22. Skop, 449.

23. Wasem, *Cuban Migration Policy and Issues*.

24. Mark P. Sullivan and Maureen Taft-Morales, "Cuba: Issues for Congress," "U.S. Policy Toward Cuba," *Report for Congress*, Congressional Research Service (CRS) RL30806, the Library of Congress, Nov. 29, 2002. Dec. 20, 2002 http://fpc.state.gov/c4763.htm.

25. Sorya M. Castro Mariño, "U.S.-Cuban Relations During the Clinton Administration," Issue 125, *Latin American Perspectives* 29, No. 4 (July 2002): 48.

26. Castro Mariño, 53.

27. Sullivan and Maureen Taft-Morales, "Cuba: Issues for Congress," "U.S. Policy Toward Cuba."

28. Castro Mariño, 53.

29. Wasem, *Cuban Migration Policy and Issues*.

30. Wasem, *Cuban Migration Policy and Issues*.

31. Wasem, *Cuban Migration Policy and Issues*.

32. Beirne, "Cuban Nationals or Citizens Seeking Lawful Permanent Resident Status."

33. Brice M. Clagett, "Agora: the Cuban Liberty and Democratic Solidarity (Libertad) Act: Title III of The Helms-Burton Act Is Consistent with International Law," 90 *The American Journal of International Law* 434 (July 1996).

34. Clagett, 434.

35. Sullivan and Taft-Morales, "Cuba: Issues for Congress," "U.S. Policy Toward Cuba."

36. "Castro Opens the Gates: Closing the Door, 09 World Views, Nov. 1994, 78. Jan. 31, 2003 http://www.worldandi.com/public/1994/november/ci3.cfm.

37. Juan O. Tamayo, "Cuba Toughens Policy on Refugees: Illegal Emigrants Barred from Return," Miami Herald, Sept. 1, 1999. Jan. 31, 2003 http://www.fiu.edu/~fcf/cub toughens.html.

38. Doyle McManus, "Christopher Indicates U.S. May Strike Deal on Cuba," Los Angeles Times (Washington), August 29, 1994, 2. Jan. 31, 2003 http://www-tech.mit.edu/V114/N34/cuba.34w.html.

39. Tamayo, "Cuba Toughens Policy on Refugees: Illegal Emigrants Barred from Return."

40. "Cuba, Overview," Freedom House, Inc., July 22, 2002. Jan. 31, 2003. http://www.freedomhouse.org/research/freeworld/2002/countryratings/cuba.htm.

41. Castro Mariño, 55.

42. Castro Mariño, 55.

43. Kathlyn Gay, Leaving Cuba: From Operation Pedro Pan to Elian. Brookfield, Conn.: Twenty-First Century Books, 2000, 111.

44. Ann Louise Bardach, Cuba Confidential: Love and Vengeance in Miami and Havana. New York, N.Y.: Random House, 2002, 72.

45. Bardach, 74.

46. Bardach, 74.

47. Bardach, 74.

48. Gay, 113.

49. Bardach, 85.

50. Bardach, 87.

51. Bardach, 99-100; Gay, 116-118.

52. Andrew E. Taslitz, "Article: Stories of Fourth Amendment Disrespect: from Elian to the Internment," 70 Fordham Law Review 2347 (2002).

53. Taslitz, 2349.

54. Taslitz, 2352.

55. Geri Díaz (Miami, Fla.), interview by the author, Sept. 12, 2002.

56. Christopher G. Blood, "Article: The 'True' Source of the Immigration Power and its Proper Consideration in the Elián Gonzalez Matter," 18 Boston University International Law Journal 215 (2000).

57. Roger Fontaine, "Let the Courts Decide," World and I, July 2000, Vol. 15, Issue 7, p. 48.

58. Ron Howell (reporter, Newsday), email interview by the author, Nov. 16, 2002.

59. Howell, email interview, Nov. 16, 2002.

60. Cuban American Alliance Education Fund, Inc., "A Year After Elián's Homecoming U.S. Policy Still Fosters Family Divisions," Press Release, June 28, 2001.

61. Blood, 215.

62. Hans-Jürgen Burchardt, "Contours of the Future: The New Social Dynamics in Cuba," Issue 124, Latin American Perspectives 29, No. 3 (May 2002): 66.

63. Burchardt, 66.

64. Jim Burns, "Castro Regime Blocks Father-Child Reunion," CNSNews.com, June 22, 2001. Dec. 16, 2002 http://www.newsmax.com/archives/articles/2001/6/21/163050.shtml; CubaNet — CubaNews, "Daughter, Stepson of Cuban Doctor to Arrive in Miami," The Miami Herald, AP (Miami), posted July 3, 2001. December 16, 2002 http://www.cubanet.org/CNews/y01/jul01/03e4.htm.

65. Albor Ruiz, "2 Cuban Kids Immigrating, Thanks to Elián," Daily News (New York), Sports Final Ed., July 2, 2001, Suburban, p. 2.

66. Jim Abrams, "House Votes in Favor of Lifting Sanctions on Cuba," AP, Washington Dateline, July 24, 2002; Mark P. Sullivan and Maureen Taft-Morales, "Cuba: Issues for Congress," "Most Recent Developments," Report for Congress, Congressional Research Service (CRS) RL30806, the Library of Congress, Nov. 29, 2002. Dec. 20, 2002 http://fpc.state.gov/c4763.htm.

67. Universalist Service Committee, "Votes in House of Representatives Send Strong Signal on Need for Cuba Policy Change," July 23, 2002. Dec. 18, 2002 http://www.uusc.org/index.html.

68. Sarah Left and Agencies, "Bush Sets Tough Conditions for Easing Cuban Embargo."

69. Reuters (Havana, Cuba), "'Critical Mass' Favors Normalizing Relations with Cuba," Dec. 14, 2002. Dec. 19, 2002 http://www.cnn.com/2002/WORLD/americas/12/14/cuba.usa.reut/index.html.

70. Michael Peltier, "Brother's Keeper," CNN.com/Inside Politics, June 10, 2002. Dec. 19, 2002 http://www.cnn.com/2002/ALLPOLITICS/06/10/time.keeper/index.html.

71. Alejandro Concepcion (Waterloo, Iowa), interview by the author and James C. Skaine, July 15, 2002.

72. Cuban American Alliance Education Fund, Inc., "The U.S. Policy of Isolating Cuba is an Anomaly," and "The Travel Restrictions are Unconstitutional," Flyer given to author by Delvis Fernández Levy, president, July 2002.

73. Cuban American Alliance Education Fund, Inc., "The U.S. Policy of Isolating Cuba Is an Anomaly," and "The Travel Restrictions are Unconstitutional," Flyer.

74. Fernández Levy, interview, July 9, 2002.

75. Fernández Levy, interview, July 9, 2002.

76. Sullivan and Taft-Morales, "Cuba: Issues for Congress," "Most Recent Developments."

77. Sullivan and Taft-Morales, "Cuba: Issues for Congress," "Most Recent Developments."

78. Fernández Levy, interview, July 9, 2002.

79. Leonardo M. Marmol, Ph.D., ABPP (professor and chair, Dept. of Graduate Psychology, Seattle Pacific University), interview by the author, July 30, 2002.

80. Betsy Campisi (anthropologist, SUNY-Albany), "Project Summary," email to author, Jan. 1, 2003.

81. Campisi, "Project Summary."

82. Betsy Campisi (anthropologist, SUNY-Albany), interview by the author, Jan. 10, 2003.

83. Campisi, interview, Jan. 10, 2003.

84. Campisi, interview, Jan. 10, 2003.

85. Campisi, interview, Jan. 10, 2003.

86. Campisi, interview, Jan. 10, 2003.

87. Campisi, interview, Jan. 10, 2003.

88. Cuban American Alliance Education Fund, Inc., "Actions by Congress, the President and Ordinary Americans Point to Irreversible Erosion of Embargo," *La Alborada*, n.d. Dec. 20, 2002 http://www.cubamer.org/alb2.htm.

89. Cuban American Alliance Education Fund, Inc., "Actions by Congress, the President and Ordinary Americans Point to Irreversible Erosion of Embargo."

Chapter 6

1. George Santayana, "We Needs Must Be Divided in the Tomb," 1863–1952. Jan. 24, 2003 http://www.daypoems.net/poems/1251.html.

2. Delvis Fernández Levy (president, Cuban American Alliance Education Fund, Inc.), interview by the author, July 9, 2002.

3. Lisandro Pérez, "Cuban American Families," in Ronald L. Taylor (ed.), *Minority Families in the United States: A Multicultural Perspective*, 2d ed., Upper Saddle River, N.J.: Prentice Hall, 1998, 108.

4. U.S. Immigration and Naturalization Service, "Immigration by Region and Selected Country of Last Residence, Fiscal Years 1820–2000," Table 2, *Immigrants, Fiscal Year 2000*, A Report to appear as a chapter in forthcoming *Statistical Yearbook of the Immigration and Naturalization Service*, 2000, 7–10.

5. U.S. Immigration and Naturalization Service, "Immigrants Admitted by Region and Country of Birth," Table 3, *Immigrants, Fiscal Year 2000*, 14.

6. "Cuban Missile Crisis and Aftermath," *Foreign Relations of the United States* 11, No. 10 (1961–63). Dec. 22, 2002 http://www.marxists.org/history/usa/government/kennedy/1961/04/18.htm#a1.

7. Aldo Mariátegui, "The Revolution Comes Full Circle: Commerce's Fallen Idol Restored," *El Comercio* (centrist), Lima, Peru, Jan. 31, 2001, in *World Press Review*, April 2001, 23.

8. Dalia Acosta, "Life Is Elsewhere: Siren's Promise Often Fatal," *Inter Press Service* (international news agency), Jan. 17, 2001, in *World Press Review*, April 2001, 22.

9. Acosta, in *World Press Review*, 22.

10. Sorya M. Castro Mariño, "U.S.-Cuban Relations During the Clinton Administration," Issue 125, *Latin American Perspectives* 29, No. 4 (July 2002): 52.

11. Pérez, "Cuban American Families," in Taylor, 108–110.

12. Pérez, "Cuban American Families," in Taylor, 111.

13. Pérez, "Cuban American Families," in Taylor, 110–111.

14. Lisandro Pérez, "Immigrant Economic Adjustment and Family Organization: The Cuban Success Story Reexamined," *International Migration Review* 20, 1 (Spring 1986), 6.

15. Robert A. Pastor, "Introduction: The Policy Challenge," in Robert A. Pastor (ed.), *Migration and Development in the Caribbean: The Unexplored Connection*. Boulder. Colo.: Westview Press, 1985, 4.

16. Delvis Fernández Levy, interview, July 9, 2002.

17. Kathlyn Gay, *Leaving Cuba: From Operation Pedro Pan to Elian*. Brookfield, Conn.: Twenty-First Century Books, 2000, 10.

18. Nicanor León Cotayo, "Mixed Signals to an Isolated Nation: 'Adjust' Hostile Citizenship Act," *Bohemia* (weekly newsmagazine), Havana, Cuba, Jan. 26, 2001, in *World Press Review*, April 2001, 20.

19. Acosta, in *World Press Review*, 21.

20. Gay, 20–21; Operation Pedro Pan Group, "History," 2001. December 8, 2002 http://www.pedropan.org/html/history.html.

21. Gay, 32.

22. Gay, 34.

23. Gay, 5–6.

24. Gay, 15–16.

25. Gay, 26–27.

26. Gay, 19.

27. Geri Díaz (Miami, Fla.), interview by the author, Sept. 12, 2002.

28. Díaz, interview, Sept. 12, 2002.

29. Díaz, interview, Sept. 12, 2002.

30. Díaz, interview, Sept. 12, 2002.

31. Victor Andres Triay, *Fleeing Castro: Operation Pedro Pan and the Cuban Children's Program.* Gainesville, Fla.: University Press of Florida, 1998, 69–70.

32. Triay, 72, 75.

33. Triay, 93.

34. Pedro Ferreira, Ph.D., M.B.A. (Licensed Psychologist, Pennsylvania, Delaware, Wilmington, Del.), interview by the author, July 15, 2002.

35. Ferreira, interview, July 15, 2002.

36. Ferreira, interview, July 15, 2002.

37. Ferreira, interview, July 15, 2002.

38. Ferreira, interview, July 15, 2002.

39. Ferreira, interview, July 15, 2002.

40. Leonardo M. Marmol, Ph.D., ABPP (professor and chair, Dept. of Graduate Psychology, Seattle Pacific University), interview by the author, July 30, 2002.

41. Gay, 36.

42. Gay, 41.

43. Triay, 100.

44. Gay, 67–68.

45. Gay, 100–101.

46. Adelfa Fernández (Miami, Fla.), interview by the author, Sept. 10, 2002.

47. Adelfa Fernández, interview, Sept. 10, 2002.

48. Triay, 100; Gay, 64, 69.

49. Gay, 70.

50. Alejandro Concepcion (Waterloo, Iowa), interview by the author and James C. Skaine, July 15, 2002.

51. Concepcion, interview, July 15, 2002.

52. Concepcion, interview, July 15, 2002.

53. Concepcion, interview, July 15, 2002.

54. Concepcion, interview, July 15, 2002.

55. Concepcion, interview, July 15, 2002.

56. Concepcion, interview, July 15, 2002.

57. Concepcion, interview, July 15, 2002.

58. Emily H. Skop, "Race and Place in the Adaptation of Mariel Exiles," *International Migration Review* 35, Issue 2 (Summer 2001), 449.

59. Harris N. Miller, "U.S. Immigration Policy and Caribbean Economic Development," in Pastor, 354.

60. Skop, 449.

61. Gay, 80–81, 85.

62. Ruth Ellen Wasem, *Cuban Migration Policy and Issues,* CRS Report RS20468, Feb. 14, 2000.

63. Gay, 77–79.

64. Wasem, *Cuban Migration Policy and Issues.*

65. Saul Landau, "The Day the Counter-revolutionaries Had Waited for Arrived, y en eso Ilgó Fidel," Issue 125, *Latin American Perspectives* 29, No. 4, (July 2002): 77.

66. Landau, 78.

67. Landau, 78.

68. Landau, 78–79.

69. Landau, 79.

70. Acosta, in *World Press Review*, 21.

71. Gay, 8.

72. Catherine Moses, *Real Life in Castro's Cuba.* Wilmington, Del.: Scholarly Resources, Inc., 2000, 100.

73. Moses, 100.

74. Moses, 101–102.

75. Acosta, in *World Press Review*, 21.

76. Mark P. Sullivan (specialist in Latin American Affairs, Foreign Affairs, Defense, and Trade Division) and Maureen Taft-Morales (analyst in Latin American Affairs, Foreign Affairs, Defense, and Trade Division), "Cuba: Background and Current Issues for Congress," Congressional Research Service, RL30806, Jan. 17, 2001. May 16, 2002 http://usinfo.state.gov/regional/ar/us-cuba/crscub1.htm.

77. Moses, 105–107.

78. Gay, 97–98.

79. Betsy Campisi (anthropologist, SUNY-Albany), "Project Summary," email to author, Jan. 1, 2003.

80. Betsy Campisi (anthropologist, SUNY-Albany), interview by the author, Jan. 10, 2003.

81. Campisi, interview, Jan. 10, 2003.

82. Campisi, interview, Jan. 10, 2003.

83. Campisi, interview, Jan. 10, 2003.

84. Campisi, interview, Jan. 10, 2003.

85. Campisi, interview, Jan. 10, 2003.

86. Campisi, interview, Jan. 10, 2003.

87. Campisi, interview, Jan. 10, 2003.

88. Campisi, interview, Jan. 10, 2003.

89. Campisi, interview, Jan. 10, 2003.

90. Acosta, in *World Press Review*, 21.

91. Acosta, in *World Press Review*, 21.

92. Adelfa Fernández, interview, Sept. 10, 2002.

93. Asley L. Marmol (Miami, Fla.), interview by the author, Oct. 17, 2002.

94. Asley L. Marmol, interview, Oct. 17, 2002.

95. Asley L. Marmol, interview, Oct. 17, 2002.

96. Asley L. Marmol, interview, Oct. 17, 2002.

97. Asley L. Marmol, interview, Oct. 17, 2002.

98. Asley L. Marmol, interview, Oct. 17, 2002.

99. Asley L. Marmol, interview, Oct. 17, 2002.

Chapter 7

1. Ronald L. Taylor, "Minority Families in America: An Introduction," Ronald L. Taylor (ed.), *Minority Families in the United States: A Multicultural Perspective*, 2d ed. Upper Saddle River, N.J.: Prentice Hall, 1998, 1.

2. "Latinos Become Main Minority Group in US: Shift is a 'turning point in the nation's history.'" *Guardian Newspapers*, Jan. 22, 2003. Jan. 27, 2003 http://www.buzzle.com/editorials/1-22-2003-34144.asp.

3. Vonnie C. McLoyd, Ana Mari Cauce, David Takeuchi, and Leon Wilson, "Marital Process and Parental Socialization in Families of Color: A Decade Review of Research," Robert M. Milardo (ed.), *Understanding Families Into the New Millennium: A Decade in Review*. Minneapolis, Minn.: National Council on Family Relations, 2001, 289–290.

4. Roberto Suro, "Counting the 'Other Hispanics': How Many Colombians, Dominicans, Ecuadorians, Guatemalans and Salvadorans Are There in the United States?" Washington, D.C.: Pew Hispanic Center, May 9, 2002, 2, 13.

5. U.S. Census Bureau, Profile of General Demographic Characteristics: 2000, "Geographic Area: United States," 2.

6. Lisandro Pérez, "Cuban American Families," in Taylor, 108.

7. Pérez, "Cuban American Families," in Taylor, 112.

8. Melisa Therrien and Roberto R. Ramirez, *The Hispanic Population in the United States: March 2000*, Current Population Reports, P20-535, Washington, D.C.: U.S. Census Bureau, 2000, 2.

9. U.S. Census Bureau, Census 2000 Summary File 1 (SF 1) 100-Percent Data, "Percent of Persons Who Are Cuban," American Factfinder, 2000. Dec. 15, 2002 http://factfinder.census.gov/serverlet/Thematic.

10. Pew Hispanic Center/Kaiser Family Foundation, *Chartpack, 2002 National Survey of Latinos*, "Methodology," Washington, D.C.: December 2002. Dec. 18, 2002 www.pewhispanic.org.

11. Suro, "Counting the 'Other Hispanics'," 39.

12. Suro, "Counting the 'Other Hispanics'," 33.

13. Suro, "Counting the 'Other Hispanics'," 34.

14. Pew Hispanic Center/Kaiser Family Foundation, *Chartpack, 2002 National Survey of Latinos*, "Methodology."

15. Pew Hispanic Center/Kaiser Family Foundation, *Chartpack, 2002 National Survey of Latinos*, Chart 1.

16. Pew Hispanic Center/Kaiser Family Foundation, *Chartpack, 2002 National Survey of Latinos*, Chart 3.

17. Pew Hispanic Center/Kaiser Family Foundation, *Chartpack, 2002 National Survey of Latinos*, Chart 8.

18. Pew Hispanic Center/Kaiser Family Foundation, *Chartpack, 2002 National Survey of Latinos*, Chart 23.

19. Pew Hispanic Center/Kaiser Family Foundation, *Chartpack, 2002 National Survey of Latinos*, Chart 24.

20. Pew Hispanic Center/Kaiser Family Foundation, *Chartpack, 2002 National Survey of Latinos*, Chart 36.

21. Delvis Fernández Levy (president, Cuban American Alliance Education Fund, Inc.), interview by the author, July 9, 2002.

22. Taylor, "Minority Families in America," in Taylor, 13.

23. Robert A. Pastor, "Relating Migration and Development Policies: Summary and Conclusions," Robert A. Pastor (ed.), *Migration and Development in the Caribbean: The Unexplored Connection*. Boulder, Colo.: Westview Press, 1985, 409.

24. Pérez, "Cuban American Families," in Taylor, 111.

25. Lisandro Pérez, "Immigrant Economic Adjustment and Family Organization: The

Cuban Success Story Reexamined," *International Migration Review* 20, 1 (Spring 1986), 4.

26. Emily H. Skop, "Race and Place in the Adaptation of Mariel Exiles," *International Migration Review* 35, Issue 2 (Summer 2001), 449.

27. Skop, 449.

28. Birgit Leyendecker and Michael E. Lamb, "Latino Families," Michael E. Lamb (ed.), *Parenting and Child Development in 'Nontraditional' Families*. Mahwah, N.J.: Lawrence Erlbaum Associates, Publishers, 1999, 249.

29. Leyendecker and Lamb, "Latino Families," in Lamb, 249–255.

30. Leonardo M. Marmol, Ph.D., ABPP (professor and chair, Dept. of Graduate Psychology, Seattle Pacific University), interview by the author, July 30, 2002.

31. Therrien and Ramirez, The Hispanic Population in the United States: March 2000, 3, 4.

32. Therrien and Ramirez, The Hispanic Population in the United States: March 2000, 4.

33. Daniel T. Lichter and Nancy S. Landale, "Parental Work, Family Structure, and Poverty Among Latino Children," *Journal of Marriage and the Family* 57 (May 1995): 347, 349, 351.

34. Sandra L. Hofferth, "Receipt of Public Assistance by Mexican American and Cuban American Children in Native and Immigrant Families," Donald J. Hernandez (ed.), Children of Immigrants: Health, Adjustment, and Public Assistance, Washington, D.C.: National Academy Press, 1999, 576–578.

35. Helen Rose Ebaugh and Mary Curry, "Fictive Kin As Social Capital In New Immigrant Communities," *Sociological Perspectives* 43, No. 2 (2000): 189.

36. Ebaugh and Curry, 190–191.

37. Ebaugh and Curry, 203.

38. Dr. Consuelo Martín Fernández (Training Center of International Migrations, University of Havana), "Communication: Duties and Law Assigned to the Emigrated Cuban Family in the Thought," Commission 1, paper, XII International Congress on Family Law, Havana, Cuba, *Memorias* (CD), Sept. 22–27, 2002. Translated by James C. Skaine and assisted by SYSTRAN Premium 4.0 translation program, Dec. 14, 2002.

39. Ebaugh and Curry, 204.

40. Adelfa Fernández (Miami, Fla.), interview by the author, Sept. 10, 2002.

41. Pérez, "Immigrant Economic Adjustment and Family Organization," 5–6.

42. Pérez, "Immigrant Economic Adjustment and Family Organization," 6.

43. Pérez, "Immigrant Economic Adjustment and Family Organization," 7.

44. Pérez, "Immigrant Economic Adjustment and Family Organization," 8, 10.

45. Pérez, "Immigrant Economic Adjustment and Family Organization," 11.

46. Pérez, "Immigrant Economic Adjustment and Family Organization," 10, 17.

47. Robert Suro, "Explaining Cuban Americans' Success," Nijole V. Benokraitis (ed.), *Contemporary Ethnic Families in the United States: Characteristics, Variation, Dynamics*. Upper Saddle River, N.J.: Prentice Hall, 2002, 226, 230.

48. Suro, "Explaining Cuban Americans' Success," in Benokraitis, 227, 228.

49. Suro, "Explaining Cuban Americans' Success," in Benokraitis, 227.

50. Suro, "Explaining Cuban Americans' Success," in Benokraitis, 227, 228, 229.

51. Suro, "Explaining Cuban Americans' Success," in Benokraitis, 230.

52. Zulema E. Suárez, "Cuban Americans in Exile: Myths and Reality," Harriette Pipes McAdoo (ed.), *Family Ethnicity: Strength in Diversity*, 2d ed., Thousand Oaks, Calif.: Sage Publications, 1999, 152.

53. Betsy Campisi (anthropologist, SUNY-Albany), interview by the author, Jan. 10, 2003.

54. Campisi, interview, Jan. 10, 2003.

55. Campisi, interview, Jan. 10, 2003.

56. Suro, "Explaining Cuban Americans' Success," in Benokraitis, 230, 231.

57. Suárez, "Cuban Americans in Exile: Myths and Reality," in McAdoo, 149.

58. Cuban American Alliance Education Fund, Inc., Sept. 2002. Oct. 15, 2002 http://www.cubamer.org.

59. Reuters AlertNet, "Famed Cuban Exile Rescue Group Grounded," Feb. 5, 2003. Feb. 7, 2003 http://www.alertnet.org/thenews/newsdesk/NAJL20406.

60. Suárez, "Cuban Americans in Exile: Myths and Reality," in McAdoo, 149.

61. Delvis Fernández Levy, interview, July 9, 2002.

62. Adelfa Fernández (Miami, Fla.), interview by Rosemarie Skaine, Sept. 10, 2002.

63. Asley L. Marmol (Miami, Fla.), interview by the author, Oct. 17, 2002.

64. Asley L. Marmol, interview, Oct. 17, 2002.

65. Asley L. Marmol, interview, Oct. 17, 2002.

66. Adelfa Fernández, interview, Sept. 10, 2002.

67. McLoyd *et al.*, "Marital Process and Parental Socialization in Families of Color," 306.

68. Harriette Pipes McAdoo, "The Social Cultural Contexts of Ecological Developmental Family Models," *Sourcebook of Family Theories and Methods*. New York: Plenum Press, 1993, 300.

69. McAdoo, "The Social Cultural Contexts of Ecological Developmental Family Models," 301.

70. Elizabeth Arias, "Change in Nuptiality Patterns Among Cuban Americans: Evidence of Cultural and Structural Assimilation?" *International Migration Review* 35, Issue 2 (Summer 2001): 525–556.

71. Arias, 525–556.

72. Arias, 525–556.

73. Arias, 525–556.

74. Arias, 525–556.

75. Arias, 525–556.

76. Sean M. Bolks, Diana Evans, J. L. Polinard and Robert D. Wrinkle, "Core Beliefs and Abortion Attitudes: a Look at Latinos," *Social Science Quarterly* 81, No. 1 (2000): 253–260.

77. McAdoo, "The Social Cultural Contexts of Ecological Developmental Family Models," 298.

78. McAdoo, "The Social Cultural Contexts of Ecological Developmental Family Models," 299.

79. Leyendecker and Lamb, "Latino Families" in Lamb, 256.

80. McAdoo, "The Social Cultural Contexts of Ecological Developmental Family Models," 300.

81. Teresa W. Julian, Patrick C. McKenry and Mary W. McKelvey, "Cultural Variations in Parenting: Perceptions of Caucasian, African-American, Hispanic, and Asian-American Parents," *Family Relations* 43, No. 1 (Jan. 1994): 30, 31, 36.

82. Julian, *et al.*, 30.

83. Julian, *et al.*, 31.

84. Julian, *et al.*, 36, 37.

85. Leyendecker and Lamb, "Latino Families," in Lamb, 255.

86. Leyendecker and Lamb, "Latino Families," in Lamb, 255–256.

87. McLoyd, *et al.*, "Marital Process and Parental Socialization in Families of Color," in Milardo, 306.

88. McLoyd, *et al.*, "Marital Process and Parental Socialization in Families of Color," in Milardo, 304.

89. Concepcion, interview, July 15, 2002.

90. Gretchen Concepcion (Waterloo, Iowa), interview by the author and James C. Skaine, July 15, 2002.

91. Concepcion, interview, July 15, 2002.

92. Trinidad Arguelles, "The Immigrant Experience," *National Forum* 74, No. 3 (Summer 1994):41(1).

93. Arguelles, 41(1).

94. Arguelles, 41(1).

95. Arguelles, 41(1).

96. Adelfa Fernández, interview, Sept. 10, 2002.

97. Adelfa Fernández, interview, Sept. 10, 2002.

98. Asley L. Marmol, interview, Oct. 17, 2002.

99. Asley L. Marmol, interview, Oct. 17, 2002.

100. Leyendecker and Lamb, "Latino Families," in Lamb, 251.

101. Leyendecker and Lamb, "Latino Families," in Lamb, 255.

102. Leyendecker and Lamb, "Latino Families," in Lamb, 251.

103. Leyendecker and Lamb, "Latino Families," in Lamb, 259–260.

Chapter 8

1. Coventry Patmore, "A Farewell," 1823–1896. Jan. 24, 2003 http://www.daypoems.net/poems/713.html.

2. Alejandro Concepcion (Waterloo, Iowa) interview by the author and James C. Skaine, July 15, 2002.

3. Geri Díaz (Miami, Fla.), interview by the author, Sept. 12, 2002.

4. Asley L. Marmol (Miami, Florida), interview by the author, Oct. 17, 2002.

5. Fabiola Santiago, "Mami, I'm Going to Harvard," *Miami Herald*, May 7, 2002, E1.

6. Miguel Arguelles, "College Essay Excerpt," in Santiago, E2.

7. Dr. Alberto N. Jones, "A Cuba in Diaz-Balart's Image or That of Today's Miami," *La Alborada*, Summer 1998, 10–11.

8. Adelfa Fernández (Miami, Fla.), interview by Rosemarie Skaine, Sept. 10, 2002.

9. Adelfa Fernández, interview, Sept. 10, 2002.

10. Leonardo M. Marmol, Ph.D., ABPP (professor and chair, Dept. of Graduate Psychology, Seattle Pacific University), interview by the author, July 30, 2002.

11. Díaz, interview, Sept. 12, 2002.

12. Asley L. Marmol, interview, Oct. 17, 2002.

13. Alex (young Cuban teacher), interview by the author and James C. Skaine in Havana, Sept. 26, 2002.

14. Alex, interview, Sept. 26, 2002.

15. Asley L. Marmol, interview, Oct. 17, 2002.

16. Asley L. Marmol, interview, Oct. 17, 2002.

17. Asley L. Marmol, interview, Oct. 17, 2002.

18. Asley L. Marmol, interview, Oct. 17, 2002.

19. Alex, interview, Sept. 26, 2002.

20. Adelfa Fernández, interview, Sept. 10, 2002.

Chapter 9

1. Pedro Ferreira Ph.D., Master of Business Administration (licensed psychologist, Pennsylvania, Delaware, Wilmington, Delaware), interview by the author, July 15, 2002.

2. Leonardo M. Marmol, Ph.D., ABPP (professor and chair, Dept. of Graduate Psychology, Seattle Pacific University), interview by the author, July 30, 2002.

3. Leonardo M. Marmol, interview, July 30, 2002.

4. Leonardo M. Marmol, interview, July 30, 2002.

5. Delvis Fernández Levy, "To Cuba with Love," *La Alborada* (Hayward, Calif.: Cuban American Alliance Education Fund, Inc.), June 1996, p. 9.

6. Leonardo M. Marmol, interview, July 30, 2002.

7. Leonardo M. Marmol, interview, July 30, 2002.

8. Asley L. Marmol (Miami, Fla.), interview by the author, Oct. 17, 2002.

9. Asley L. Marmol, interview, Oct. 17, 2002.

10. "Cuban Rafters Meet Reality — Not Paradise," *La Alborada*, Oct. 1996, p. 7.

11. Orestes Lorenzo, "In Cuba, Family Isn't Everything," *New York Times*, Feb. 5, 2000, p.

A27(N) p. A15(L). Dec. 28, 2002 http://www.nocastro.com/archives/elian36.htm.

12. Lorenzo, p. A27(N) p. A15(L).

13. Lorenzo, p. A27(N) p. A15(L).

14. Geri Díaz (Miami, Fla.), interview by the author, Sept. 12, 2002.

15. Alejandro Concepcion (Waterloo, Iowa), interview by the author and James C. Skaine, July 15, 2002.

16. Concepcion, interview, July 15, 2002.

17. Leonardo M. Marmol, interview, July 30, 2002.

18. Geri Díaz (Miami, Fla.), interview by the author, Sept. 12, 2002.

19. Asley L. Marmol, interview, Oct. 17, 2002.

20. Ferreira, interview, July 15, 2002.

21. Ferreira, interview, July 15, 2002.

Chapter 10

1. José Martí, *Simple Verses*, Translated by James C. Skaine and assisted by SYSTRAN Premium 4.0 translation program, Feb. 8, 2003. http://www.liceocubano.com/Spn/Marti/Marti.asp; and http://www.boondocksnet.com/cgi-perl/apfh-item_id-1875284125-search_type-AsinSearch-locale-us.html.

2. Donald W. Bray and Marjorie Woodford Bray, "Introduction: The Cuban Revolution and World Change," Issue 124, *Latin American Perspectives* 29, No. 3 (May 2002): 8.

3. Sorya M. Castro Mariño, "U.S.-Cuban Relations During the Clinton Administration," Issue 125, *Latin American Perspectives* 29, No. 4 (July 2002):65.

4. Castro Mariño, 65–68.

5. Castro Mariño, 70.

6. Castro Mariño, 71.

7. Robert A. Pastor (vice president of International Affairs and professor of International Relations, American University, Washington, D.C.), interview by the author, June 28, 2002.

8. Jimmy Carter, "President Carter's Cuba Trip Report," Carter Center, May 21 2002. June 27, 2002 http://www.carter-center.org/viewdoc.asp?docID=528&sub-menu=ne ws.

9. Carter, "President Carter's Cuba Trip Report."

10. Carter, "President Carter's Cuba Trip Report."

11. Jimmy Carter, "The United States and

Cuba: A Vision for the 21st Century: Remarks by Former U.S. President Jimmy Carter at the University of Havana, Cuba," May 14, 2002. June 27, 2002 http://www.cartercenter.org/viewdoc.asp?docID=528&submenu=news.

12. Carter, "The United States and Cuba."

13. Alex (young cuban teacher), interview by the author and James C. Skaine in Havana, Sept. 26, 2002.

14. Asley L. Marmol (Miami, Fla.), interview by the author, Oct. 17, 2002.

15. Asley L. Marmol, interview, Oct. 17, 2002.

16. Helen I. Safa, *The Myth of the Male Breadwinner: Women and Industrialization in the Caribbean*. Boulder, Colo.: Westview Press, 1995, 166, 177, 180.

17. Safa, 181, 184.

18. Miren Uriarte, Ph.D., "Cuba Social Policy at the Crossroads: Maintaining Priorities, Transforming Practice," Boston, Mass.: Oxfam America Report, 2002, 58. Jan. 12, 2003 http://www.oxfamamerica.org/pdfs/social_policy.pdf.

19. Alejandro Concepcion (Waterloo, Iowa), interview by the author and James C. Skaine, July 15, 2002.

20. Pedro M. Ferreira, Ph.D., M.B.A. (licensed psychologist, Pennsylvania, Delaware, Wilmington, Delaware), fax to the author, Jan. 26, 2003.

21. Dr. Luis Enrique Vidal Palmer (vicedirector of the Havana Psychiatric Hospital), email interview, Dec. 17, 2002. Translated by Mercedes Ayala (Grand Island, Neb.), Dec. 18, 2002.

Bibliography

Abraham, Spencer. "United States Senator Spencer Abraham (R): Immigrants Enrich America," *Miami Herald*, Oct. 24, 1997.

Abrams, Jim. "House Votes in Favor of Lifting Sanctions on Cuba," AP, Washington Dateline, July 24, 2002.

Acosta, Dalia. "Life Is Elsewhere: Siren's Promise Often Fatal," Inter Press Service (international news agency), Jan. 17, 2001, in *World Press Review*, April 2001, 21–22.

Aguirre Tamayo, Lic. Xóchitl (Cuba). "The Legal Protection of the Unions in Fact in Cuba," Commission 2, paper, XII International Congress of Family Law, Havana, Cuba, *Memorias* (CD), Sept. 22–27, 2002. Translated by James C. Skaine and assisted by SYSTRAN Premium 4.0 translation program, Jan. 16, 2003.

Albright, Madeleine K. "Economic Sanctions and Public Health: A View from the Department of State" [editorial], *Annals of Internal Medicine* 132, No. 2 (Jan. 18, 2000): 155–7. Dec. 28, 2002 http://www.annals.org/issues/v132n2/full/200001180-00012.html.

Alex (Cuban resident, Havana). Interview by the author and James C. Skaine, Sept. 26, 2002.

Allahar, Anton L. "Women and the Family in Cuba: A Study Across Time," *Humboldt Journal of Social Relations* (1994): 87–120.

Aoki, Keith. "Panel: Races, Nationalities, Ethnicities: Mapping Latcrit (Dis)continuities: Representing Representation," 2 *Harvard Latino Law Review* 247 (Fall 1997).

Arandia Covarrubia, Gisela (researcher at the Centro de Estudios de los Estados Unidos, Universidad de la Habana). "One Way to Strengthen Nationality," AfroCuba Web, 1997. Jan. 21, 2003 http://www.afrocubaweb.com/arandia-art.htm.

Arguelles, Trinidad. "The Immigrant Experience," *National Forum* 74, No. 3 (Summer 1994): 41 (1).

Arias, Elizabeth. "Change in Nuptiality Patterns Among Cuban Americans: Evidence of Cultural and Structural Assimilation?" *International Migration Review* 35, I. 2 (Summer 2001): 525–556.

Bardach, Ann Louise. *Cuba Confidential: Love and Vengeance in Miami and Havana*. New York, N.Y.: Random House, 2002.

Barrett, Ted. Washington Bureau, Cnn.com/Inside Politics, "White House Loses

Key House Votes on Cuba, Bush Expected to Veto Effort to Lift Travel Ban," July 24, 2002. July 24, 2002 http://www.cnn.com/2002/ALLPOLITICS/07/24/congress.cuba/index.html.

Barry, Dr. Michèle. "Effect of the U.S. Embargo and Economic Decline on Health in Cuba," *Annals of Internal Medicine* 132, No. 2 (Jan. 18, 2000): 151–4. Dec. 28, 2002 http://www.annals.org/issues/v132n2/full/200001180-00010.html.

Beirne, James G. Law Offices. "Cuban Nationals or Citizens Seeking Lawful Permanent Resident Status," May 16, 2002. May 16, 2002 http://www.lawcenter ca.com/immi_CAA.asp.

Bengelsdorf, Carollee, and Jean Stubbs. "Introduction to Part 3," in Sandor Halebsky and John M. Kirk with Carollee Bengelsdorf, Richard L. Harris, Jean Stubbs and Andrew Zimbalist (eds.), *Cuba in Transition: Crisis and Transformation.* Boulder, Colo.: Westview Press, 1992, 155–159.

Blood, Christopher G. "Article: The 'True' Source of the Immigration Power and its Proper Consideration in the Elian Gonzalez Matter," 18 *Boston University International Law Journal* 215 (2000).

Boadle, Anthony. "Cubans Vote in Local One-Party Elections," Havana, Reuters.com, Oct. 20, 2002.

Bolks, Sean M., Diana Evans, J.L. Polinard, and Robert D. Wrinkle. "Core Beliefs and Abortion Attitudes: A Look at Latinos," *Social Science Quarterly* 81, No. 1 (2000): 253–260.

Bray, Donald W., and Marjorie Woodford Bray. "Introduction: The Cuban Revolution and World Change," Issue 124, *Latin American Perspectives* 29, No. 3 (May 2002): 3–17.

Burchardt, Hans-Jürgen. "Contours of the Future: The New Social Dynamics in Cuba," Issue 124, *Latin American Perspectives* 29, No. 3 (May 2002): 57–74.

Burns, Jim. "Castro Regime Blocks Father-Child Reunion," CNSNews.com, June 22, 2001. Dec. 16, 2002 http://www.newsmax.com/archives/articles/2001/6/21/163050.shtml.

Campisi, Betsy (anthropologist, State University of New York–Albany). Interview by the author, Jan. 10, 2003.

_____. "Project Summary," email to author, Jan. 1, 2003.

Caridad Núñez Travieso, Belkis (lawyer, City of Havana, Cuba). "Theoretical Disquisitions about the Institute of the Mother Country Power in Cuba," 2002, Commission 1, paper, XII International Congress of Family Law, Havana, Cuba, *Memorias* (CD), Sept. 22–27, 2002. Translated by James C. Skaine and assisted by SYSTRAN Premium 4.0 translation program, Jan. 7, 2003.

Carter, Jimmy. "President Carter's Cuba Trip Report," Carter Center, May 21 2002. June 27, 2002 http://www.cartercenter.org/viewdoc.asp?docID=528&submenu=news.

_____. "The United States and Cuba: A Vision for the 21st Century; Remarks by Former U.S. President Jimmy Carter at the University of Havana, Cuba," May 14, 2002. June 27, 2002 http://www.cartercenter.org/viewdoc.asp?doc ID=528&submenu=news.

Castro Mariño, Sorya M. "U.S.-Cuban Relations During the Clinton Administration," Issue 125, *Latin American Perspectives* 29, No. 4 (July 2002): 47–76.

"Castro Opens the Gates: Closing the Door," 09 *World Views*, Nov. 1994, 78. Jan. 31, 2003 http://www.worldandi.com/public/1994/november/ci3.cfm.

Cavanaugh, Joanne P. "Cuba's Marry-go-round," Special Report, *Johns Hopkins Magazine*, April 1998. May 16, 2002 http://www.jhu.edu/~jhumag/0498web/wedding.html.

CIA. "The World Factbook 2001—Cuba," Jan. 1, 2002. Jan. 5, 2003 http://www.cia.gov/cia/publications/factbook/geos/cu.html#People.

Citizenship and Immigration Canada. "Cuba—A Cultural Profile Project," "Cuba to Canada," Oct. 31, 2002. Nov. 30, 2002 http://cwr.utoronto.ca/cultural/english/cuba/index.html.

"Civil Society and Family Diversity." International Panel, question and answer period, XII International Congress on Family Law: Family Law in Front of the Challenges of the New Millennium, International Conference Center, Havana, Cuba, Sept. 26, 2002. Translation broadcast by the Congress and transcribed by the author.

Clagett, Brice M. "Agora: the Cuban Liberty and Democratic Solidarity (Libertad) Act: Title III of the Helms-Burton Act Is Consistent with International Law," 90 *The American Journal of International Law* 434 (July 1996).

Codigo De Familia. "Article 85" (La Habana, Cuba: Ministerio de Justicia), 2002, pp. 23–24. Translated by Mercedes Ayala (Grand Island, Neb.), Nov. 9, 2002.

Concepcion, Alejandro (Waterloo, Iowa). Interview by the author and James C. Skaine, July 15, 2002.

Concepcion, Gretchen (Waterloo, Iowa). Interview by the author and James C. Skaine, July 15, 2002.

Constitution of the Republic of Cuba. Editions ONBC (Feb. 24, 1976, with Reforms of 1992) 1–56.

_____. Feb. 24, 1976, Art. 35, in "Cuba," "Rights of Spouses Established in New Constitution," 3 *Annual Review of Population Law* (1976), 77.

_____. Feb. 24, 1976, Art. 36, in "Cuba," "Abolishment of 'Illegitimacy' in New Constitution," 3 *Annual Review of Population Law* (1976), 105.

_____. Feb. 24, 1976, Art. 37, in "Cuba," "Provisions for Parental Protection of Children in New Constitution," 3 *Annual Review of Population Law* (1976), 90.

_____. Feb. 24, 1976, Art. 40, 41, 43, in "Cuba," "Promotion of Equality in New Constitution," 3 *Annual Review of Population Law* (1976), 145–146.

_____. Feb. 24, 1976, Art. 49, in "Cuba," "Health Provision in New Constitution," 3 *Annual Review of Population Law* (1976), 150–151.

_____. Feb. 24, 1976, Art. 50, in "Cuba," "Educational Guarantees in New Constitution," 3 *Annual Review of Population Law* (1976), 160.

Cotayo, Nicanor León. "Mixed Signals to an Isolated Nation: 'Adjust' Hostile Citizenship Act," *Bohemia* (weekly newsmagazine), Havana, Cuba, Jan. 26, 2001, in *World Press Review*, April 2001, 20.

Creed, Gerald W. "'Family Values' and Domestic Economies," *Annual Review of Anthropology* 29 (2000): 329–55.

Cuba: Culture. "Divorce." Dec. 2, 2002 http://www.cuba.ru/view/docs/doc_read.php3?id_object=12&id_r ubr=1238.

_____. "Marriage Rate: Do Cubans Get married?" Dec. 2, 2002 http://www.cuba.ru/view/docs/doc_read.php3?id_object=11&id_rubr=1238.

"Cuba, Overview." Freedom House, Inc., July 22, 2002. Jan. 31, 2003. http://
    www.freedomhouse.org/research/freeworld/2002/countryratings/cuba.htm.
Cuban American Alliance Education Fund, Inc. (CAAEF). Sept. 2002. Oct. 15,
    2002 http://www.cubamer.org.
_____. "Actions by Congress, the President and Ordinary Americans Point to Irre-
    versible Erosion of Embargo," La Alborada, n.d. Dec. 20, 2002 http://www.
    cubamer.org/alb2.htm.
_____. "Essential Components of the U.S./Cuba Policy," La Alborada, n.d. Dec.
    20, 2002 http://www.cubamer.org/alb3.htm.
_____. "Social Work Development and Practice in Cuba and in the U.S.: A Report,"
    Feb. 2002, 16.
_____. "The U.S. Policy of Isolating Cuba Is an Anomaly," and "The Travel Restric-
    tions are Unconstitutional," flyer given to author by Delvis Fernández Levy,
    Ph.D., CAAEF President, July 2002.
_____. "What Is CAAEF," flyer provided to the author by Delvis Fernández Levy,
    Ph.D., CAAEF President, Aug. 4, 2002.
"Cuban Missile Crisis and Aftermath." Foreign Relations of the United States 11, No.
    10 (1961–63). Dec. 22, 2002 http://www.marxists.org/history/usa/government/
    kennedy/1961 /04/18.htm#a1.
"Cuban Rafters Meet Reality — Not Paradise." La Alborada (Hayward, Calif.:
    Cuban American Alliance Education Fund, Inc.), October 1996, p. 7.
CubaNet — CubaNews. "Daughter, Stepson of Cuban Doctor to Arrive in Miami,"
    The Miami Herald, AP (Miami), posted July 3, 2001. December 16, 2002
    http://www.cubanet.org/CNews/y01/jul01/03e4.htm.
Cullen, Paul. "'Third Way' Could Save Revolutionary Gains: Will Fidel Buy Time
    or Sell Out?" The Irish Times, Dublin, Ireland, Jan. 8, 2001, in World Press
    Review, April 2001, 19–20.
Cultural Orientation Project. Cubans— Their History and Culture, Refugee Fact
    Sheet No.12, "Political, Religious and Family Life," Washington, D.C.: Cul-
    tural Orientation Resource Center, March 24, 2000. Nov. 12, 2002 http://
    www.culturalorientation.net/cubans/life.htm.
Díaz, Geri (Miami, Fla.). Interview by the author, Sept. 12, 2002.
Dilla, Haroldo, and Philip Oxhorn. "The Virtues and Misfortunes of Civil Society
    in Cuba," Issue 125, Latin American Perspectives 29, No. 4,(July 2002): 11–30.
Ebaugh, Helen Rose, and Mary Curry. "Fictive Kin as Social Capital in New Immi-
    grant Communities," Sociological Perspectives 43, No. 2 (2000): 189–209.
Emory Report. "Coca-Cola CEO Roberto Goizueta Left His Mark on Emory,
    Atlanta and the World," Vol. 50, No. 10, Oct. 27, 1997.
Fernández, Adelfa (Miami, Fla.). Interview by the author, Sept. 10, 2002.
Fernández Levy, Delvis (Ph.D.; president, Cuban American Alliance Education
    Fund, Inc.). "But Who Am I?" La Alborada (Hayward, Calif.: Cuban Amer-
    ican Alliance Education Fund, Inc.), Vol. 1, No. 4, Winter 1997, p. 2.
_____. Interview by the author, July 9, 2002.
_____. "To Cuba with Love," La Alborada (Hayward, Calif.: Cuban American
    Alliance Education Fund, Inc.), June 1996, p. 9.
Ferreira, Pedro (Ph.D., MBA; licensed psychologist; Pennsylvania; Delaware;
    Wilmington, Delaware). Interview by the author, July 15, 2002.

Fontaine, Roger. "Let the Courts Decide," *World and I*, July 2000, Vol. 15, No. 7, p. 48.

Gaceta Oficial de la República de Cuba. No. 50, Aug. 22, 1985, Act No. 51, July 1985, p. 844, in "Cuba," 13 *Annual Review of Population Law* (1986), 256.

Garcia-Zarza, Isabel (Reuters). "Big Brother at 40: Cuba's Revolutionary Neighborhood Watch System," sun-sentinel.com,Web-posted: Oct. 10, 2000. Nov. 11, 2002 http://xld.com/public/cuba/embargo/cdr.htm.

Gay, Kathlyn. *Leaving Cuba: From Operation Pedro Pan to Elian*, Brookfield, Conn.: Twenty-First Century Books, 2000.

Global Exchange Reality Tour. "Cuba: Politics and Government," San Francisco, 2002. Nov. 10, 2002 http://www.globalexchange.org/tours/profile/cuba/politics.html.

Gonzalez, David. "World Briefing Americas: Cuba: Socialism Forever, Assembly Declares," *The New York Times*, June 28, 2002, Late Ed., Final, A11.

Granma Internacional. Nov. 10, 2002. Nov. 11, 1999 http://www.granma.cu/ingles/; in Spanish, http://www.granma.cu/.

Greer, Germaine. "Women and Politics: Cuba," *Women: A World Report*, New York: Oxford University Press, 1985, 280.

Guanche Pérez, Jesús. Panel: "Civil Society and Family Diversity," XII International Congress on Family Law: Family Law in Front of the Challenges of the New Millennium, International Conference Center, Havana, Cuba, Sept. 23, 2002. Translation broadcast by the Congress, recorded by the author and transcribed by Sue Ravn (Cedar Falls, Ia.).

Guerra, M.Sc. Irma Renee Fernández, and M.Sc. Luís Palenzuela Paéz (Havana, Cuba). "Considerations on Extraterritorial Adoption of Cuban Children," Commission 1, paper, XII International Congress of Family Law, Havana, Cuba, *Memorias* (CD), Sept. 22–27, 2002. Translated by Mercedes Ayala (Grand Island, Neb.).

Hamilton, Douglas. "Whiter Cuban Socialism? The Changing Political Economy of the Cuban Revolution," Issue 124, *Latin American Perspectives* 29, No. 3 (May 2002): 18–39.

Hernández, Lic. Zoraida Puentes, Lic. Ana Margarita Hoyo Pérez, and Lic. Issel María Veitia Cabezas (lawyers, Villa Clara, Cuba). "Finding Options for Legal Considerations on the Biological Expert Testing for Determination of Paternity and Maternity," Commission 4, paper, XII International Congress of Family Law, Havana, Cuba, *Memorias* (CD), Sept. 22–27, 2002. Translated by Mercedes Ayala (Grand Island, Neb.).

Hofferth, Sandra L. "Receipt of Public Assistance by Mexican American and Cuban American Children in Native and Immigrant Families," in Donald J. Hernandez (ed.), *Children of Immigrants: Health, Adjustment, and Public Assistance*, Washington, D.C.: National Academy Press, 1999, 576–578.

Howell, Ron (reporter, *Newsday*). Email interview by the author, Nov. 16, 2002.

Jones, Dr. Alberto N. (Caribbean American Children Foundation). "A Cuba in Diaz-Balart's Image or That of Today's Miami," *La Alborada*, Summer 1998, 10–11.

Juarez Fontanet, Dr. Ruth, Dr. Lazara Valdes Career, and Dr. Sigrid Isabel Pou Salvi (Institute of Medical Sciences of Havana, faculty, "General Calixto

Garcia" Institute of Legal Medicine). "Biological Forensic Investigation Report in the Processes of Filiation: Juridical Signification," Commission 4, paper, XII International Congress of Family Law, Havana, Cuba, *Memorias* (CD), Sept. 22–27, 2002. Translated by Marco Poblete (Spanish teaching assistant, Dept. of Modern Languages, Univ. of Northern Iowa, Cedar Falls).

Julian, Teresa W., Patrick C. McKenry, and Mary W. McKelvey. "Cultural Variations in Parenting: Perceptions of Caucasian, African-American, Hispanic, and Asian-American Parents," *Family Relations* 43: 1 (Jan. 1994), 30–37.

Kelliher, Brett. Religion, "Santeria." May 16, 2002 http://www.intl.pdx.edu/latin/religion/santeria2.html.

Koppel, Naomi. "U.S. Sanctions May Be Robbing Cuban Women of Rights, U.N. Expert Says," Geneva, NandoMedia/Associated Press, March 24, 2000. July 4, 2002 http://www.globalpolicy.org/security/sanction/cuba/cuba18.htm.

Lamb, Michael E. "Parental Behavior, Family Processes, and Child Development in Nontraditional and Traditionally Understudied Families," in Michael E. Lamb (ed.), *Parenting and Child Development in 'Nontraditional' Families.* Mahwah, N.J.: Lawrence Erlbaum Associates, Publishers, 1999, 1–14.

Landau, Saul. "The Day the Counterrevolutionaries Had Waited for Arrived, y en eso Ilgó Fidel," Issue 125, *Latin American Perspectives* 29, No. 4 (July 2002): 77–79.

Left, Sarah, and Agencies. "Bush Sets Tough Conditions for Easing Cuban Embargo," *Guardian Unlimited*, May 20, 2002. Dec. 18, 2002 http://www.guardian.co.uk/cuba/story/0,11983,719086,00.html.

Leyendecker, Birgit, and Michael E. Lamb. "Latino Families," in Michael E. Lamb (ed.), *Parenting and Child Development in 'Nontraditional' Families.* Mahwah, N.J.: Lawrence Erlbaum Associates, Publishers, 1999, 247–262.

Lichter, Daniel T., and Nancy S. Landale. "Parental Work, Family Structure, and Poverty Among Latino Children," *Journal of Marriage and the Family* 57 (May 1995): 346–353.

de Llano Cuesta, Katia. "Women in Cuba: Background," St. Paul, Minn., November 2000. May 16, 2002 http://www.canadacuba.ca/05aboutcuba/articleWomen.html.

Lorenzo, Orestes. "In Cuba, Family Isn't Everything," *New York Times*, Feb. 5, 2000, p. A27(N) p. A15(L). Dec. 28, 2002 http://www.nocastro.com/archives/elian36.htm.

Lutjens, Sheryl L. "Schooling and 'Clean Streets' in Socialist Cuba: Children and the Special Period," in Roslyn Arlin Mickelson, *Children on the Streets of the Americas: Homelessness, Education, and Globalization in the United States, Brazil, and Cuba.* London, New York: Routledge, 2000, 55–65.

Luxner, Larry. "Street Markets Offer Alternative Work Options for Cubans," *Cuba News*, 9, Issue 7 (July 2001): 10.

Mariátegui, Aldo. "The Revolution Comes Full Circle: Commerce's Fallen Idol Restored," *El Comercio* (centrist), Lima, Peru, Jan. 31, 2001, in *World Press Review*, April 2001, 23.

Marmol, Asley L. (Miami, Fla.). Interview by the author, Oct. 17, 2002.

Marmol, Leonardo M. (Ph.D.; ABPP; professor and chair, Dept. of Graduate Psychology, Seattle Pacific University). Interview by the author July 30, 2002.

Marquetti Pérez, Lic. Rosario and Lic. Lidice Crespo Sosa. "The Legal Protection of Minors Without Family Shelter in Cuba," Commission 1, paper, XII International Congress of Family Law, Havana, Cuba, *Memorias* (CD), Sept. 22–27, 2002. Translated by James C. Skaine and assisted by SYSTRAN Premium 4.0 translation program, Jan. 5, 2003.

Martinez-Alier, Verena. *Marriage, Class and Colour in Nineteenth-Century Cuba: A Study of Racial Attitudes and Sexual Values in a Slave Society.* New York, N.Y.: Cambridge University Press, 1974.

Martín Fernández, Dra. Consuelo (Training Center of International Migrations, University of Havana). "Communication: Duties and Law Assigned to the Emigrated Cuban Family in the Thought," Commission 1, paper, XII International Congress of Family Law, Havana, Cuba, *Memorias* (CD), Sept. 22–27, 2002. Translated by James C. Skaine and assisted by SYSTRAN Premium 4.0 translation program, Dec. 14, 2002.

Masland, Tom, and Brook Larmer. "Cuba's Real Religion," *Newsweek*, Jan. 19, 1998, p. 42.

MATP. "Iran Top of Terror List — War on Terror: Target — New York," *The Daily Telegraph* (Sydney), May 23, 2002, 33, Sec. World.

McGovern, George. *The Third Freedom: Ending Hunger in Our Time.* Lanham, Maryland: Rowman and Littlefield Publishers, Inc., 2001.

McLoyd, Vonnie C., Ana Mari Cauce, David Takeuchi, and Leon Wilson. "Marital Process and Parental Socialization in Families of Color: A Decade Review of Research," in Robert M. Milardo (ed.), *Understanding Families into the New Millennium: A Decade in Review.* Minneapolis, Minn.: National Council on Family Relations, 2001, 289–312.

McManus, Doyle. "Christopher Indicates U.S. May Strike Deal on Cuba," *Los Angeles Times* (Washington), August 29, 1994, 2. Jan. 31, 2003 http://www-tech.mit.edu/V114/N34/cuba.34w.html.

Mechanic, David, and David A. Rochefort. "Comparative Medical Systems," *Annual Review of Sociology* 22 (1996): 239–270.

Mickelson, Roslyn Arlin. *Children on the Streets of the Americas: Homelessness, Education, and Globalization in the United States, Brazil, and Cuba.* London, New York: Routledge, 2000.

Miller, Harris N. "16. U.S. Immigration Policy and Caribbean Economic Development," in Robert A. Pastor (ed.), *Migration and Development in the Caribbean: The Unexplored Connection*, Boulder, Colo.: Westview Press, 1985, 348–368.

Moses, Catherine. *Real Life in Castro's Cuba.* Wilmington, Del.: Scholarly Resources, Inc., 2000.

National Center for Health Statistics. *Health, United States, 2001 With Urban and Rural Health Chartbook.* Hyattsville, Maryland: 2001.

Net for Cuba. "Communist Party" and "Political Organizations." Jan. 29, 2003 http://www.netforcuba.org/index.htm.

_____. "Government, Electoral System." May 18, 2002 http://www.netforcuba.org/electoralsystem.htm.

_____. "Government, Justice System." May 18, 2002 http://www.netforcuba.org/justicesystem.htm.

_____. "Government — Political Organizations." May 18, 2002 http://www.netfor
    cuba.org/politicalorganizations.htm.
Nugman, Gulnar. "World Divorce Rates," Heritage Foundation, 2002. Dec. 2,
    2002 http://www.divorcereform.org/gul.html.
Operation Pedro Pan Group, "History," 2001. December 8, 2002 http://www
    .pedropan.org/html/history.html.
Panadero de la Cruz, Dra. Ediltrudis (faculty of law, University of Oriente, San-
    tiago, Cuba). "The Succession and the Protection to the Surviving Spouse of
    the Family House and Furniture: Tendencies in Comparative Law," Com-
    mission 2, paper, XII International Congress of Family Law, Havana, Cuba,
    Memorias (CD), Sept. 22–27, 2002. Translated by James C. Skaine and assisted
    by SYSTRAN Premium 4.0 translation program, Jan. 7, 2003.
Pastor, Robert A. "Introduction: The Policy Challenge," in Robert A. Pastor (ed.),
    Migration and Development in the Caribbean: The Unexplored Connection,
    Boulder, Colo.: Westview Press, 1985, 1–39.
_____. "Relating Migration and Development Policies: Summary and Conclu-
    sions," in Robert A. Pastor (ed.), *Migration and Development in the Carib-
    bean: The Unexplored Connection*, Boulder, Colo.: Westview Press, 1985, 409–
    429.
_____. (Vice president of International Affairs and Professor of International
    Relations, American University, Washington, D.C.). Interview by the author,
    June 28, 2002.
Pearson, Ruth. "The Political Economy of Social Reproduction: the Case of Cuba
    in the 1990s," in Joanne Cook, Jenifer Roberts and Georgina Waylen (eds.),
    Towards a Gendered Political Economy. New York: St. Martin's Press, Inc.,
    2000, 226–247.
Peltier, Michael. "Brother's Keeper," CNN.com/Inside Politics, June 10, 2002. Dec.
    19, 2002 http://www.cnn.com/2002/ALLPOLITICS/06/10/time.keeper/index.html.
Pérez, Lisandro. "Cuban American Families," in Ronald L. Taylor (ed.), *Minor-
    ity Families in the United States: A Multicultural Perspective*, 2nd ed. Upper
    Saddle River, N.J.: Prentice Hall, 1998, 108–123.
_____. "Immigrant Economic Adjustment and Family Organization: The Cuban
    Success Story Reexamined," *International Migration Review* 20, 1 (Spring
    1986), 4–20.
PRODOS Institute and PRODOS.com. "The Cuba Campaign." July 24, 2002 http:
    //www.cubacampaign.org/.
Randal, Judith. "Does the U.S. Embargo Affect Cuban Health Care?" 92 *Journal
    of the National Cancer Institute* 963 (June 21, 2000).
Reeker, Phillip T., acting spokesman, and Edmund J. Hull, acting coordinator for
    counterterrorism. Briefing Upon the Release of the U.S. Department of State
    Report, "Patterns of Global Terrorism 2000," Washington, D.C., April 30,
    2001. July 23, 2002 http://www.state.gov/s/ct/rls/rm/2001/2571.htm.
Reporter's Report of Commission 1B: "Family Law and Fundamental Rights: Insti-
    tutions a Means of Protection." Closing Ceremony, XII International Con-
    gress on Family Law: Family Law in Front of the Challenges of the New
    Millennium, International Conference Center, Havana, Cuba, Sept. 27, 2002.
    Broadcast translation by the Congress and transcribed by James C. Skaine.

Reuters (Havana, Cuba). "'Critical Mass' Favors Normalizing Relations with Cuba," Dec. 14, 2002. Dec. 19, 2002 http://www.cnn.com/2002/WORLD/americas/12/14/cuba.usa.reut/index.html.

Ritter, Archibald R.M. "Cuba in the 1990s: Economic Reorientation and International Reintegration," in Sandor Halebsky and John M. Kirk with Carollee Bengelsdorf, Richard L. Harris, Jean Stubbs and Andrew Zimbalist (eds.), *Cuba in Transition: Crisis and Transformation.* Boulder, Colo.: Westview Press, 1992, 128–135.

Rosenthal, Marguerite G. "Problems of Single Motherhood," in Sandor Halebsky and John M. Kirk with Carollee Bengelsdorf, Richard L. Harris, Jean Stubbs and Andrew Zimbalist (eds.), *Cuba in Transition: Crisis and Transformation.* Boulder, Colo.: Westview Press, 1992, 161–175.

Ruiz, Albor. "2 Cuban Kids Immigrating, Thanks to Elian," *Daily News* (New York), Sports Final Ed., July 2, 2001, Suburban, p. 2.

Safa, Helen I. *The Myth of the Male Breadwinner: Women and Industrialization in the Caribbean.* Boulder, Colo.: Westview Press, 1995.

SFBG News. "World View: Inside Cuba's Legal System," Nov. 3, 1999. May 18, 2002 http://www.sfbg.com/News/34/05/5world.html.

Shaikh, Nazia. "Cuban Women: Before and After the Revolution," May 19, 2000. May 16, 2002 http://www.saxakali.com/caribbean/nshaikh.htm.

Skop, Emily H. "Race and Place in the Adaptation of Mariel Exiles," *International Migration Review* 35, Issue 2 (Summer 2001), 449.

Smith, Lois M. "Sexuality and Socialism," in Sandor Halebsky and John M. Kirk with Carollee Bengelsdorf, Richard L. Harris, Jean Stubbs and Andrew Zimbalist (eds.), *Cuba in Transition: Crisis and Transformation.* Boulder, Colo.: Westview Press, 1992, 177–191.

Strug, David, Ph.D., and Walter Teague, Master of Social Work. "New Directions in Cuban Social Work Education: What Can We Learn?" Sept. 2, 2002. Jan. 12, 2003 http://users.erols.com/wteague/Cuba/Cuban_Social_Work_Education.htm. (Article also appears in *Social Work Today*, Sept. 2, 2002.)

Suárez, Zulema E. "Cuban Americans in Exile: Myths and Reality," in Harriette Pipes McAdoo (ed.), *Family Ethnicity: Strength in Diversity,* 2d ed. Thousand Oaks, Calif.: Sage Publications, 1999.

Sullivan, Mark P. (specialist in Latin American Affairs, Foreign Affairs, Defense, and Trade Division; and Maureen Taft-Morales, analyst in Latin American Affairs, Foreign Affairs, Defense, and Trade Division). "Cuba: Background and Current Issues for Congress," Congressional Research Service, RL30806, Jan. 17, 2001. May 16, 2002 http://usinfo.state.gov/regional/ar/us-cuba/crscub1.htm.

_____, and Maureen Taft-Morales. "Cuba: Issues for Congress," *Report for Congress,* Congressional Research Service (CRS) RL30806, the Library of Congress, Nov. 29, 2002. Dec. 20, 2002 http://fpc.state.gov/c4763.htm.

Suro, Roberto. "Counting the 'Other Hispanics': How Many Colombians, Dominicans, Ecuadorians, Guatemalans and Salvadorans Are There in the United States?" Washington, D.C.: Pew Hispanic Center, May 9, 2002, 33.

_____. "Explaining Cuban Americans' Success," in Nijole V. Benokraitis, *Contemporary Ethnic Families in the United States: Characteristics, Variations, and Dynamics.* Upper Saddle River, N.J.: Prentice Hall, 2002, 226–231.

Tamayo, Juan O. "Cuba Toughens Policy on Refugees: Illegal Emigrants Barred from Return," *Miami Herald*," Sept. 1, 1999. Jan. 31, 2003 http://www.fiu.edu/~fcf/cubtoughens.html.

Taslitz, Andrew E. "Article: Stories of Fourth Amendment Disrespect: From Elian to the Internment," 70 *Fordham Law Review* 2257 (2002).

Taylor, Ronald L. "Minority Families in America: An Introduction," in Ronald L. Taylor (ed.), *Minority Families in the United States: A Multicultural Perspective*, 2nd ed., Upper Saddle River, N.J.: Prentice Hall, 1998, 1–16.

Therrien, Melisa, and Roberto R. Ramirez. *The Hispanic Population in the United States: March 2000*, Current Population Reports, P20-535, Washington, D.C.: U.S. Census Bureau, 1–8.

"Transportation — Culture." 1998. November 24, 2002 http://library.thinkquest.org/18355/transportation_-_culture.html.

Triay, Victor Andres. *Fleeing Castro: Operation Pedro Pan and the Cuban Children's Program*, Gainesville, Fla.: University Press of Florida, 1998.

U.S. Census Bureau. Census 2000 Summary File 1 (SF 1) 100-Percent Data, "Percent of Persons Who Are Cuban," American Factfinder, 2000. Dec. 15, 2002 http://factfinder.census.gov/servlet/Thematic.

_____. Profile of General Demographic Characteristics: 2000, "Geographic Area: United States," Table DP-1.

U.S. Department of State. Bureau of Democracy, Human Rights and Labor, "Country Reports on Human Rights Practices— 2001: Cuba," March 4, 2002. May 16, 2002 http://www.state.gov/g/drl/rls/hrrpt/2001/wha/8333.htm.

_____. "Cuba, Country Reports on Human Rights Practices— 2001," released by the Bureau of Democracy, Human Rights, and Labor, March 4, 2002. May 16, 2002 http://www.state.gov/g/drl/rls/hrrpt/2001/wha/8333.htm.

U.S. Immigration and Naturalization Service. *Immigrants, Fiscal Year 2000*, A Report to appear as a chapter in forthcoming *Statistical Yearbook of the Immigration and Naturalization Service*, 2000, 1–67. July 7, 2002 http://www.ins.usdoj.gov/graphics/aboutins/statistics/IMM00yrbk/IMM2000list.htm.

Universalist Service Committee. "Votes in House of Representatives Send Strong Signal on Need for Cuba Policy Change," July 23, 2002. Dec. 18, 2002 http://www.uusc.org/index.html.

Uriarte, Miren, Ph.D. "Cuba Social Policy at the Crossroads: Maintaining Priorities, Transforming Practice," Boston, Mass.: Oxfam America Report, 2002. Jan. 12, 2003 http://www.oxfamamerica.org/pdfs/social_policy.pdf.

Valencia, Marelys. "Dollar Is a Tool, Not the Rule," *Granma Internacional*, Havana, Cuba, Jan. 26, 2001, in *World Press Review*, April 2001, 23.

Valle, Lic. Consuelo León, and Lic. Samuel Morales Castro (Pinar del Rio). "The One-parent Family: Legal Protection," Commission 2, paper, XII International Congress of Family Law, Havana, Cuba, *Memorias* (CD), Sept. 22–27, 2002. Translated by Mercedes Ayala (Grand Island, Neb.).

Vera Estrada, Dra. Ana. Coordinator, Panel: "Civil Society and Family Diversity," XII International Congress on Family Law: Family Law in Front of the Challenges of the New Millennium, International Conference Center, Havana, Cuba, Sept. 23, 2002. Translation broadcast by the Congress, recorded by the author and transcribed by Sue Ravn (Cedar Falls, Ia.).

Vidal Palmer, Dr. Luis Enrique (Degree Specialist First Class in Psychiatry, Professor and Vicedirector for the Psychiatry, Forensic and Legal Medicine, Psychiatric Hospital of Havana-Cuba). Email interview, Dec. 17, 200. Translated by Mercedes Ayala (Grand Island, Neb.), Dec. 18, 2002.

Waitzkin, Dr. Howard, Karen Wald, Dr. Romina Kee, Dr. Ross Danielson, and Lisa Robinson. "Primary Care in Cuba: Family Medicine Paper, Low- and High-technology Developments Pertinent to Family Medicine," April 1997. Dec. 28, 2002 http://www.cubasolidarity.net/waitzkin.html.

Wasem, Ruth Ellen. *Cuban Migration Policy and Issues*, CRS Report RS20468, Feb. 14, 2000.

XII International Congress on Family Law: Family Law in Front of the Challenges of the New Millennium, International Conference Center. Havana, Cuba, Sept. 22–27, 2002.

_____. Havana, Cuba and New York City Bar Association, Hospital Psiquiátrico de la Habana-Cuba Tour, September 24, 2002.

Yurkovsky, Andrew. "Cuba Goes Its Own Way: Looking Beyond Elian," *World Press Review*, April 2001, 19.

Index

politics 75, 83–84, 127, 130, 160, 163
polygamy 7
poor 22, 38, 46, 141, 160
Pope John Paul II 4, 37–38, 160
popular 20, 45; class 45
Popular Council Free Cuba 24, 66, 67
population 10, 12, 22, 25, 27, 29, 30–31, 34, 38, 41, 44, 48, 64, 89, 93–95, 97, 107, 119–122, 124, 126, 128, 133–134, 161, 163, 165; explosion 12
populist campaign 86
pork 36, 126; *see also* pig
Portland, Ore. 105
ports of entry 79, 81–82
posades 13
positions 18, 22, 65; prestigious 22
possessions 106
poverty 2, 21, 25, 27, 46, 57, 122–124, 127, 140; grinding 21
power 14, 16, 20, 61, 76, 98, 151; absolute 14; personal 20; political 16
power (electrical) 36; cuts 36; outages 110
preamble 57
preference 107
pregnancy 24, 64–65; pregnant 91, 92–93, 154
prejudice(s) 14, 22
premarital sex 133
pre-revolution 3, 4, 50, 142
Presbyterian 152; Church 152
prescholastic farms 67
preschool 27
presentation 60; of merits 60
presidents 16, 37, 41, 87, 156, 162
press 18, 43
pressure 76
pre-university schools 28
prevent 77
priests 38, 103
principle 60
priority 57, 69
prisoners 18, 21; political 18, 40, 80, 109, 110
prisons 18, 81, 87, 102, 109, 115, 121, 149, 150, 162
privacy 17, 18, 23, 28, 39, 47, 51, 55, 62, 80, 99; need(s) 47
privilege 77
probability 105
problem(s) 14, 18, 21, 41, 47, 69, 90, 120–121; social 69
pro–Castro 142
process 14, 57, 59–60, 69, 75, 76, 90, 122, 135; judicial 69; legal 59; migratory 14
pro-choice 135
procreation 68
production 21–22, 35–36, 44, 95, 161; coop-erative 52, 56; industrial 21; level(s) 36; unit(s) of 22
products 25–26, 41, 46; capital 41; consumer 41; medical 46
professionals 2, 24, 27, 29, 31, 45, 100–113, 118, 121–122, 128, 133, 142, 152, 165; highly trained 122; school(s) 27
professions 10, 50, 104
proficient 105
pro-government 17
programs 23, 89; social 23; U.S. 89
progress 142
prohibit 60, 69; prohibition 78, 88
project(s) 47, 57
Promised Land 75, 143
proof 59
propaganda 70
property 7, 10, 13, 21, 23, 47, 50, 72, 82, 88, 162; disputes 162; personal 13; private 23
proportion 123
proposals 18
prosecution 77, 94; legal 77
prosperity 142
prostitution 24, 28, 46, 51, 73, 142
protection 3, 11, 15, 60, 69, 77, 88; of minors 3, 11, 15; to children and young people 67–68, 73
Protestant religion 31, 37, 38, 151–152
protests 16, 150–151
Province Ciudad Habana 32
provinces 1, 32, 48, 54, 144
Provincial Prison of Pinar del Río 18
provisions 16, 21–22, 58
Psychiatric Hospital, Havana, Cuba 31–33, 52, 166
psychiatric services, Cuba 32–34
psychologist 159, 166
public assistance: Cuba 34; U.S. 124, 127
public charge 78
public health 29, 31
public service 22
public transportation 21
Puerto Rican 120, 124, 135
punishable 60
punitive 92
purchase 23
purchasing power 61
purpose 17
putative married union 72

quota system 109

rabies, human 31
race 2, 10, 50, 60, 85, 109, 120, 133–134, 166
racial 7, 13, 14, 27, 105, 109, 120, 135; category 120; discrimination 7
radio 76, 162

www.ingramcontent.com/pod-product-compliance
Lightning Source LLC
Chambersburg PA
CBHW031129270326
41929CB00011B/1562